Hear My Voice

Preaching The Lectionary Psalms

Cycles A, B, C

James Evans
Stan Purdum
Carlos Wilton

edited by Carlos Wilton

CSS Publishing Company, Inc., Lima, Ohio

HEAR MY VOICE

Copyright © 2006 by
CSS Publishing Company, Inc.
Lima, Ohio

All rights reserved. No part of this publication may be reproduced in any manner whatsoever without the prior permission of the publisher, except in the case of brief quotations embodied in critical articles and reviews. Inquiries should be addressed to: Permissions, CSS Publishing Company, Inc., 517 South Main Street, Lima, Ohio 45804.

Scripture quotations are from the *New Revised Standard Version of the Bible*, copyright 1989 by the Division of Christian Education of the National Council of the Churches of Christ in the USA. Used by permission.

Some scripture quotations marked (RSV) are from the Revised Standard Version of the Bible, copyrighted 1946, 1952 ©, 1971, 1973, by the Division of Christian Education of the National Council of the Churches of Christ in the USA. Used by permission.

Some scripture quotations marked (NIV) are from the Holy Bible, New International Version. Copyright © 1973, 1978, 1984 International Bible Society. Used by permission of Zondervan Bible Publishers. All rights reserved.

Some scripture quotations marked (NEB) are from The New English Bible. Copyright © the Delegates of the Oxford University Press and the Syndics of the Cambridge University Press, 1961, 1970. Reprinted by permission.

Some scripture quotations are from The Jerusalem Bible, copyright © 1966 by Darton, Longman & Todd, Ltd. and Doubleday, a division of Bantam Doubleday Dell Publishing Group, Inc. Reprinted by permission.

Some scripture quotations marked (KJV) are from the King James Version of the Bible, in the public domain.

Some scripture quotations marked (TEV) are from the Good News Bible, in Today's English Version. Copyright © American Bible Society, 1966, 1971, 1976. Used by permission.

Library of Congress Cataloging-in-Publication Data

Evans, James L., 1952-
   Hear my voice : preaching the Lectionary Psalms : cycles A, B, C / James Evans, Stan Purdum, Carlos Wilton ; edited by Carlos Wilton.
   p. cm.
   Includes indexes
   ISBN 0-7880-2400-0 (perfect bound : alk. paper)
   1. Bible, O.T. Psalms—Sermons. 2. Church year sermons. I. Purdum, Stan, 1945- II. Wilton, Carlos, 1956- III. Title.

BS1430.54.E93 2006
251'.6—dc22

2006011186

For more information about CSS Publishing Company resources, visit our website at www.csspub.com or email us at custserv@csspub.com or call (800) 241-4056.

Cover design by Barbara Spencer
ISBN 0-7880-2400-0   PRINTED IN U.S.A.

*For Shirley MacKenzie Wilton,
Professor Emerita:
with affection and respect
from her very first pupil*

Table Of Contents

Introduction   11

Preaching The Psalms   17

Cycle A

Advent 1	Psalm 122	23
Advent 2	Psalm 72:1-7, 18-19	24
Advent 3	Psalm 146:5-10 or Luke 1:47-55	25
Advent 4	Psalm 80:1-7, 17-19	28
Christmas Eve	Psalm 96	30
Christmas Day	Psalm 97 or Psalm 98	32
Christmas 1	Psalm 148	34
Christmas 2	Psalm 147:12-20	36
The Epiphany Of Our Lord	Psalm 72:1-7, 10-14	37
The Baptism Of Our Lord/ Epiphany 1/OT 1	Psalm 29	38
Epiphany 2/OT 2	Psalm 40:1-11	40
Epiphany 3/OT 3	Psalm 27:1, 4-9	41
Epiphany 4/OT 4	Psalm 15	42
Epiphany 5/OT 5	Psalm 112:1-9 (10)	44
Epiphany 6/OT 6	Psalm 119:1-8	45
Epiphany 7/OT 7	Psalm 119:33-40	47
Epiphany 8/OT 8	Psalm 131	48
Epiphany 9/OT 9	Psalm 31:1-5, 19-24	49
The Transfiguration Of Our Lord/ Last Sunday After The Epiphany	Psalm 2 or Psalm 99	51
Ash Wednesday	Psalm 51:1-17	53
Lent 1	Psalm 32	55
Lent 2	Psalm 121	57
Lent 3	Psalm 95	58
Lent 4	Psalm 23	59
Lent 5	Psalm 130	62
Palm Sunday/ Sunday Of The Passion	Psalm 118:1-2, 19-29; Psalm 31:9-16	63 65
Maundy Thursday	Psalm 116:1-2, 12-19	66
Good Friday	Psalm 22	68
The Resurrection Of Our Lord/ Easter Day	Psalm 118:1-2, 14-24	70
Easter 2	Psalm 16	71
Easter 3	Psalm 116:1-4, 12-19	73
Easter 4	Psalm 23	74
Easter 5	Psalm 31:1-5, 15-16	75
Easter 6	Psalm 66:8-20	76

The Ascension Of Our Lord	Psalm 47 or Psalm 93	77
Easter 7	Psalm 68:1-10, 32-35	79
The Day Of Pentecost	Psalm 104:24-34, 35b	80
The Holy Trinity	Psalm 8	82
Proper 4/Pentecost 2/OT 9	Psalm 46	83
Proper 5/Pentecost 3/OT 10	Psalm 33:1-12	85
Proper 6/Pentecost 4/OT 11	Psalm 116:1-2, 12-19	86
Proper 7/Pentecost 5/OT 12	Psalm 86:1-10, 16-17	86
Proper 8/Pentecost 6/OT 13	Psalm 13	87
Proper 9/Pentecost 7/OT 14	Psalm 45:10-17 or	88
	Song Of Solomon 2:8-13	90
Proper 10/Pentecost 8/OT 15	Psalm 119:105-112	92
Proper 11/Pentecost 9/OT 16	Psalm 139:1-12, 23-24	94
Proper 12/Pentecost 10/OT 17	Psalm 105:1-11, 45b or Psalm 128	95
Proper 13/Pentecost 11/OT 18	Psalm 17:1-7, 15	97
Proper 14/Pentecost 12/OT 19	Psalm 105:1-6, 16-22, 45b	99
Proper 15/Pentecost 13/OT 20	Psalm 133	101
Proper 16/Pentecost 14/OT 21	Psalm 124	103
Proper 17/Pentecost 15/OT 22	Psalm 105:1-6, 23-26, 45c	104
Proper 18/Pentecost 16/OT 23	Psalm 149	106
Proper 19/Pentecost 17/OT 24	Psalm 114 or	107
	Exodus 15:1b-11, 20-21	109
Proper 20/Pentecost 18/OT 25	Psalm 105:1-6, 37-45	111
Proper 21/Pentecost 19/OT 26	Psalm 78:1-4, 12-16	113
Proper 22/Pentecost 20/OT 27	Psalm 19	114
Proper 23/Pentecost 21/OT 28	Psalm 106:1-6, 19-23	115
Proper 24/Pentecost 22/OT 29	Psalm 99	116
Proper 25/Pentecost 23/OT 30	Psalm 90:1-6, 13-17	117
Proper 26/Pentecost 24/OT 31	Psalm 107:1-7, 33-37	118
All Saints	Psalm 34:1-10, 22	120
Proper 27/Pentecost 25/OT 32	Psalm 78:1-7	120
Proper 28/Pentecost 26/OT 33	Psalm 123	122
Christ The King/Proper 29	Psalm 100	123
Thanksgiving Day	Psalm 65	125

Cycle B

Advent 1	Psalm 80:1-7, 17-19	129
Advent 2	Psalm 85:1-2, 8-13	130
Advent 3	Psalm 126 or Luke 1:47-55	131
Advent 4	Luke 1:47-55 or Psalm 89:1-4, 19-26	133
Christmas Eve	Psalm 96	134
Christmas Day	Psalm 97 or Psalm 98	135
Christmas 1	Psalm 148	137
Christmas 2	Psalm 147:12-20	138
The Epiphany Of Our Lord	Psalm 72:1-7, 10-14	139

The Baptism Of Our Lord/ Epiphany 1/OT 1	Psalm 29	140
Epiphany 2/OT 2	Psalm 139:1-6, 13-18	142
Epiphany 3/OT 3	Psalm 62:5-12	143
Epiphany 4/OT 4	Psalm 111	145
Epiphany 5/OT 5	Psalm 147:1-11, 20c	146
Epiphany 6/OT 6	Psalm 30	147
Epiphany 7/OT 7	Psalm 41	148
Epiphany 8/OT 8	Psalm 103:1-13, 22	150
Epiphany 9/OT 9	Psalm 81:1-10	151
The Transfiguration Of Our Lord/ Last Sunday After The Epiphany	Psalm 50:1-6	152
Ash Wednesday	Psalm 51:1-17	154
Lent 1	Psalm 25:1-10	154
Lent 2	Psalm 22:23-31	155
Lent 3	Psalm 19	156
Lent 4	Psalm 107:1-3, 17-22	157
Lent 5	Psalm 51:1-12 or Psalm 119:9-16	158
Palm Sunday/ Sunday Of The Passion	Psalm 118:1-2, 19-29; Psalm 31:9-16	161 161
Maundy Thursday	Psalm 116:1-2, 12-19	163
Good Friday	Psalm 22	164
The Resurrection Of Our Lord/ Easter Day	Psalm 118:1-2, 14-24	165
Easter 2	Psalm 133	167
Easter 3	Psalm 4	167
Easter 4	Psalm 23	168
Easter 5	Psalm 22:25-31	169
Easter 6	Psalm 98	170
The Ascension Of Our Lord	Psalm 47 or Psalm 93	171
Easter 7	Psalm 1	173
The Day Of Pentecost	Psalm 104:24-34, 35b	173
The Holy Trinity	Psalm 29	175
Proper 4/Pentecost 2/OT 9	Psalm 139:1-6, 13-18	176
Proper 5/Pentecost 3/OT 10	Psalm 138	177
Proper 6/Pentecost 4/OT 11	Psalm 20	179
Proper 7/Pentecost 5/OT 12	Psalm 9:9-20 or Psalm 133	180
Proper 8/Pentecost 6/OT 13	Psalm 130	182
Proper 9/Pentecost 7/OT 14	Psalm 48	184
Proper 10/Pentecost 8/OT 15	Psalm 24	185
Proper 11/Pentecost 9/OT 16	Psalm 89:20-37	187
Proper 12/Pentecost 10/OT 17	Psalm 14	188
Proper 13/Pentecost 11/OT 18	Psalm 51:1-12	189
Proper 14/Pentecost 12/OT 19	Psalm 130	191
Proper 15/Pentecost 13/OT 20	Psalm 111	191
Proper 16/Pentecost 14/OT 21	Psalm 84	192

Proper 17/Pentecost 15/OT 22	Psalm 45:1-2, 6-9	193
Proper 18/Pentecost 16/OT 23	Psalm 125	195
Proper 19/Pentecost 17/OT 24	Psalm 19	196
Proper 20/Pentecost 18/OT 25	Psalm 1	196
Proper 21/Pentecost 19/OT 26	Psalm 124	198
Proper 22/Pentecost 20/OT 27	Psalm 26	199
Proper 23/Pentecost 21/OT 28	Psalm 22:1-15	201
Proper 24/Pentecost 22/OT 29	Psalm 104:1-9, 24, 35c	202
Proper 25/Pentecost 23/OT 30	Psalm 34:1-8 (19-22)	204
Proper 26/Pentecost 24/OT 31	Psalm 146	205
All Saints	Psalm 24	206
Proper 27/Pentecost 25/OT 32	Psalm 127	207
Proper 28/Pentecost 26/OT 33	1 Samuel 2:1-10	208
Christ The King/Proper 29	Psalm 132:1-12 (13-18)	210
Thanksgiving Day	Psalm 126	211

Cycle C

Advent 1	Psalm 25:1-10	215
Advent 2	Luke 1:68-79	216
Advent 3	Isaiah 12:2-6	218
Advent 4	Luke 1:47-55 or Psalm 80:1-7	219
Christmas Eve	Psalm 96	219
Christmas Day	Psalm 97 or Psalm 98	220
Christmas 1	Psalm 148	220
Christmas 2	Psalm 147:12-20	222
The Epiphany Of Our Lord	Psalm 72:1-7, 10-14	222
The Baptism Of Our Lord/ Epiphany 1/OT 1	Psalm 29	222
Epiphany 2/OT 2	Psalm 36:5-10	222
Epiphany 3/OT 3	Psalm 19	224
Epiphany 4/OT 4	Psalm 71:1-6	224
Epiphany 5/OT 5	Psalm 138	225
Epiphany 6/OT 6	Psalm 1	225
Epiphany 7/OT 7	Psalm 37:1-11, 39-40	227
Epiphany 8/OT 8	Psalm 92:1-4 (12-15)	228
Epiphany 9/OT 9	Psalm 96:1-9	229
The Transfiguration Of Our Lord/ Last Sunday After The Epiphany	Psalm 99	230
Ash Wednesday	Psalm 51:1-17	231
Lent 1	Psalm 91:1-2, 9-16	231
Lent 2	Psalm 27	233
Lent 3	Psalm 63:1-8	234
Lent 4	Psalm 32	236
Lent 5	Psalm 126	237
Palm Sunday/	Psalm 118:1-2, 19-29;	238
Sunday Of The Passion	Psalm 31:9-16	238

Maundy Thursday	Psalm 116:1-2, 12-19	240
Good Friday	Psalm 22	240
The Resurrection Of Our Lord/ Easter Day	Psalm 118:1-2, 14-24	240
Easter 2	Psalm 118:14-29 or Psalm 150	242
Easter 3	Psalm 30	243
Easter 4	Psalm 23	245
Easter 5	Psalm 148	247
Easter 6	Psalm 67	248
The Ascension Of Our Lord	Psalm 47 or Psalm 93	250
Easter 7	Psalm 97	250
The Day Of Pentecost	Psalm 104:24-34, 35b	251
The Holy Trinity	Psalm 8	252
Proper 4/Pentecost 2/OT 9	Psalm 96	253
Proper 5/Pentecost 3/OT 10	Psalm 146	253
Proper 6/Pentecost 4/OT 11	Psalm 5:1-8	254
Proper 7/Pentecost 5/OT 12	Psalm 42 and Psalm 43	255
Proper 8/Pentecost 6/OT 13	Psalm 77:1-2, 11-20	257
Proper 9/Pentecost 7/OT 14	Psalm 30	258
Proper 10/Pentecost 8/OT 15	Psalm 82	260
Proper 11/Pentecost 9/OT 16	Psalm 52	261
Proper 12/Pentecost 10/OT 17	Psalm 85	263
Proper 13/Pentecost 11/OT 18	Psalm 107:1-9, 43	264
Proper 14/Pentecost 12/OT 19	Psalm 50:1-8, 22-23	265
Proper 15/Pentecost 13/OT 20	Psalm 80:1-2, 8-19	266
Proper 16/Pentecost 14/OT 21	Psalm 71:1-6	268
Proper 17/Pentecost 15/OT 22	Psalm 81:1, 10-16	269
Proper 18/Pentecost 16/OT 23	Psalm 139:1-6, 13-18	271
Proper 19/Pentecost 17/OT 24	Psalm 14	271
Proper 20/Pentecost 18/OT 25	Psalm 79:1-9	273
Proper 21/Pentecost 19/OT 26	Psalm 91:1-6, 14-16	275
Proper 22/Pentecost 20/OT 27	Lamentations 3:19-26 or Psalm 137	276
Proper 23/Pentecost 21/OT 28	Psalm 66:1-12	279
Proper 24/Pentecost 22/OT 29	Psalm 119:97-104	281
Proper 25/Pentecost 23/OT 30	Psalm 65	282
Proper 26/Pentecost 24/OT 31	Psalm 119:137-144	284
All Saints	Psalm 149	285
Proper 27/Pentecost 25/OT 32	Psalm 145:1-5, 17-21 or Psalm 98	287
Proper 28/Pentecost 26/OT 33	Isaiah 12	288
Christ The King/Proper 29	Luke 1:68-79	290
Thanksgiving Day	Psalm 100	291

Scriptural Index 293

U.S./Canadian Lectionary Comparison 301

Introduction

O Lord, open my lips, and my mouth will declare your praise. — Psalm 51:15

One of the most significant gifts to the church in the latter half of the twentieth century has been the Revised Common Lectionary (RCL) of 1992. This was based on the older, Common Lectionary of 1983 (which was based, in turn, on the Roman Catholic *Ordo Lectionum Missae* of 1969). In just a few decades, the use of the lectionary as the basis for Sunday preaching and worship planning has gained remarkably wide acceptance in English-speaking Protestant churches. Liturgical scholar Horace T. Allen, Jr., writing in the mid-1990s, sums up the rapid acceptance of the RCL:

> *As reported at the meeting of the English Language Liturgical Consultation (ELLC) in Ireland (August 1995), RCL is now in official or alternate use in North America by Episcopal/Anglican, Presbyterian, Reformed, Lutheran, United Methodist, and Disciples denominations as well as countless local churches such as Baptist, Mennonite, and Unitarian. In Great Britain, it is used not only by "established" churches, the Church of England and the Church of Scotland, but also by a number of other denominations, as in North America. The same is true in Australia, New Zealand, and South Africa. There is also growing use of RCL by Presbyterian churches in Korea. Except for the latter instance, all of this is occurring in the English-speaking world. However, at a meeting of the scholarly body* Societas Liturgica *in Ireland in August 1995, no less than sixty people attended a seminar on the subject (fully one quarter of the total attendance at* Societas), *many of whom were from non-English-speaking countries.* (From the *Introduction to the Handbook for the Revised Common Lectionary*, by Peter Bower [Westminster John Knox Press, 1996], pp. 7-8.)

In the decade since then, use of the RCL has only increased. There are some very good reasons for the growing acceptance of lectionary preaching:

1. *It enhances Christian unity* — When parishioners travel, they are often pleasantly surprised to learn that the congregation of their own denomination they are visiting in a distant city is gathering around the same scriptural texts as their church at home. When they speak with neighbors in their own community who attend churches of different denominations, they are sometimes even more surprised to learn that the same is true even across town.

2. *It helps preachers avoid becoming trapped in a personal, homiletical canon* — It is only human for a preacher to have favorite biblical texts. Without a regular text selection discipline like the lectionary, it is all too easy to return to favorite texts again and again, neglecting the rich diversity of scripture. This is especially true of difficult texts. Often, the lectionary nudges preachers into the rewarding experience of wrestling through challenging passages they would never otherwise consider.

3. *It helps preachers begin with the text* — There is much to be said in favor of topical preaching, by which preachers address topics that are of significant interest or concern to their people. Yet these topics often have a way of finding their way into lectionary-based preaching anyway (if not on a given Sunday, then at the next opportunity afforded by the lectionary, which is generally not long in coming). The lectionary forces the preacher to begin with the text, rather than with a search through the Bible to find a passage to match the desired topic. This keeps preaching more biblically faithful in the long run.

4. *It enriches the congregation's observance of the liturgical year* — There used to be many congregations whose idea

of the liturgical year began with Christmas and ended with Easter. Now, a great many of those congregations have been tremendously enriched by their pastor's explorations from the pulpit of lesser-known days and seasons of the Christian year.

5. *It opens up a rich variety of musical resources and liturgical texts* — For the first time, many Protestant churches now have a common *corpus* of scripture texts corresponding to the liturgical year. This greatly simplifies the selection of hymns, choir anthems, congregational responses, organ pieces and praise songs that interact with the sermon in serendipitous ways.

6. *It opens up new avenues of collaboration in sermon preparation* — Sermon preparation used to be a solitary task, for the most part. Now, with colleagues across town working on the same texts for Sunday preaching, a profusion of informal lectionary study groups have sprung up, many of them crossing denominational lines. Some preachers have discovered the rich possibilities of involving church members in their sermon preparation as well, through local church lectionary study groups.

Of the four lessons the lectionary recommends for each Sunday, the one that is used least frequently as a basis for preaching is the Psalm. Numerous studies have indicated that the Gospel Lesson is by far the most commonly chosen by preachers, with the Epistle and the First Lessons taking second and third place, respectively. Running a distant fourth is the Psalm — which was originally conceived by the lectionary's designers as more of a liturgical aid than a homiletical one. The Psalm selections are intended to be sung in worship, and are designed to follow and amplify the message of the First Lesson.

The lectionary originated, of course, in the Roman Catholic church, a tradition that already had a rich tradition of psalm singing. In many less highly liturgical Protestant churches, the Psalm has languished in a kind of liturgical limbo. Lacking a rich library of psalm-based musical resources for worship, these churches have often had little alternative but to abandon the weekly Psalm texts — resulting in what is essentially a three-text, rather than a four-text, lectionary (some lectionary-using churches still read just two texts in Sunday worship, choosing a single New Testament Lesson from either the Epistle or the Gospel Reading for the day). That situation is changing, but slowly, as psalms-based musical resources are gradually being introduced in Protestant churches.

Yet, perhaps, introducing (or re-introducing) psalm-singing is not the most natural way for Protestant churches to benefit from the Psalms in worship. With their historic emphasis on proclamation of the Word, it makes more sense in many Protestant congregations for the pastor to simply choose to preach on the Psalm from time to time.

Preachers who resolve to do so are immediately struck by the lack of homiletical resources out there, to help them understand and address the Psalm texts. A rich profusion of lectionary-based preaching resources has arisen in recent decades, both in print and on the internet. Many of these are excellent — but even the high-quality resources often inexplicably ignore the Psalm for the day.

Recognizing this theological and liturgical deficit, the editors of the journal, *Emphasis* — a print- and internet-based resource for lectionary preaching published by CSS Publishing Company, Inc., of Lima, Ohio — began several years ago to include a weekly Psalm commentary along with their columns on the other three texts. These columns have been well-received. Now, the best of them are collected here in this volume.

Included in this book is a brief, homiletical commentary on every one of the Psalms recommended for Sunday worship in the three-year RCL cycle. Several special days other than Sundays are also included: The Epiphany Of Our Lord, Ash Wednesday, Maundy Thursday, and Good Friday — as well as the less-liturgically but pastorally important, Thanksgiving Day (placed in the calendar on the fourth Thursday in November according to United States usage, but useful also for Canadians on their earlier date). In cases where individual psalm selections (or slight variations of them) occur more than once in the three-year cycle, there are cross-references pointing to commentaries for other days that may be useful. In a great many cases of double or triple occurrences of the same psalm selection, more than one commentary is offered; readers are advised to follow the "alternative approaches" cross-references to find them.

My two fellow authors (James Evans and Stan Purdum) and I have written these weekly columns to help our colleagues in ministry across North America and beyond to explore the Psalms more deeply. We have found it a blessing in our own ministries to do so, and have discovered that the benefits of regular study of the Psalms overflow into our preaching on other texts as well. It is our hope and prayer that those who dip into this volume will discover the same to be true in their own preaching ministries.

Carlos Wilton

Preaching The Psalms

It has often been said that the Bible is not a single book, but a library. If that is true, then the book of Psalms is a library-within-a-library. Unique among biblical books, the book of Psalms' every chapter is a literary work unto itself. These individual songs were written over many centuries by a variety of authors, most of them anonymous. A great many psalms, of course, are attributed to David — although it is now clear that not all the "Psalms of David" were actually written by him.

Attributions such as "A Psalm of David" have little, in fact, to do with our modern understanding of authorship. In the case of songs like these — many of which likely circulated in oral form for centuries before being written down — the words "of David" really mean something more like "in the tradition of David." A rough analogy is the way some folk-music historians today speak of a "Stephen Foster song," or a "Leadbelly song" or a "Scott Joplin" song — including under that label songs that may or may not have been written by that individual. The label has become bigger than the person, bespeaking a whole genre of music. Much the same is true of the "David songs" of the psalter.

Even so, the imprint of David — more than that of any other author — is very evident in the psalter. Although the authorship of many individual psalms may be in doubt, he certainly had a tremendous influence on the family of psalms that forms the heart of the collection. Evidence elsewhere in the Bible confirms David's skill as a musician (1 Samuel 16:14-23; Amos 6:5), how David established worship in Jerusalem by bringing the Ark into the city (2 Samuel 6), and how he dreamed of building a temple there (2 Samuel 7) — even though the Lord ultimately decreed that task would belong not to him, but to his son, Solomon. David established the first guild of temple musicians (1 Chronicles 15:16). This greatest of Israel's kings casts a large shadow over the psalter, indeed.

Complicating matters further is the fact that the music for the psalms has been lost for millennia. All that remains is the text. When I was a postgraduate student in Scotland, attending Church of Scotland worship services, I soon discovered that the hymnals in the pews were different from those I had become used to in the United States. They were tiny volumes, easily held in one hand. This was because they were words-only hymnals. Paging ahead to see which hymns were coming up in the service, I would often recognize a hymn I thought I knew — only to discover that this congregation knew and loved it with an entirely different melody. Those who were truly serious about hymn-singing brought their own hymnals with them from home — editions with full musical notation they had purchased themselves. I soon joined their company.

A words-and-music edition of the psalter no longer exists — if, indeed, it ever did. A few of the psalms display superscripts containing tune names (Psalms 8, 9, 12, 22), or instrumental instructions (Psalms 5, 54), or both (Psalm 6), but even these tell little about how they were used in Israel's worship. A few of them — particularly those attributed to David — identify the psalm with an episode in the great king's life (Psalms 3, 18, 34, and 51). Such superscripts are often worth mentioning in sermons — although we can never be entirely certain whether they are accurate historically, or whether they reflect a later association.

With all this uncertainty, much preaching from the psalms must be intuitive. In approaching these ancient texts, particularly those lacking reliable attribution of context or authorship, preachers must scrutinize the words carefully, attempting to discern not so much the specific historical circumstance as the general emotional state of the author. A lament such as Psalm 42, for example, provides no hint of authorship, and only the broadest outlines of the situation that has led to such woe. We can tell this much about his situation: the author is depressed; he has been oppressed and taunted by others for being a person of faith; at one time he regularly and enthusiastically worshiped in the temple, and remembers those days with wistful longing; and at times he feels abandoned by God — but not all the time, evidently, because he is still able to pen this song of deep faith. The lack of background information actually gives the psalm more universality. Knowing few historical particulars, but having read a startling revelation of the author's inner life, we come to see him not so much as "Anonymous" as "Everyman."

As Bernhard Word Anderson reminds us in a classic book on the Psalms, it is also important to try to envision what each psalm meant to the worshiping community that preserved it:

> *The main question to ask about any psalm is not the situation in the life of David or in the life of some unknown individual which occasioned the composition. Nor is it essential to try to discover the historical situation in the life of the people Israel in which the psalm was composed, for with the exception of Psalm 137, which clearly presupposes life in Babylonian exile, there are very few historical hints for dating individual psalms. Rather the important question is the purpose of the psalm, and usually this question leads to an inquiry into the psalm's situation in worship.... Therefore the psalms in which Israel speaks to God are also intended for us who find ourselves caught up in the dramatic story of God's people. (Out of the Depths: The Psalms Speak For Us Today* [Philadelphia: Westminster, 1974], p. 18.)

So, then, we have at least two levels of tradition to consider in studying the psalms: that of the author, and that of the worshiping community. There is yet a third level to consider: that of the editors.

It is well to remember that, while individual psalms have their own historical provenance, the book as a whole belongs to the period following the Babylonian exile. As with large parts of the Hebrew Scriptures, the exile was a brutally formative experience for Israel's faith. It was a crisis that led the people to consider which portions of their religious tradition needed to be committed to writing, to be preserved for future generations. The silent contribution of the editors who put the collection of 150 psalms together is of far-reaching significance. Without those people's faithful labors, the faith of both Judaism and Christianity would be very different today.

In some Roman Catholic churches of Europe, there are bronze statues of saints whose feet are bright and shiny, while the rest of the statue is a dull, brown color. This is the result of generations of kneeling pilgrims who have planted kisses on the feet of those statues, and touched them with their hands as acts of prayer. While those of us who are heirs of the Protestant Reformation may not fully understand that style of devotion, we can still observe such statues and see the visible evidence of centuries of worship. Something similar is true of the psalms. While the distinguishing details are often worn away, still we can sense the accumulated smoothness of devotion — and we can seek to emulate it, in our own study and preaching.

Carlos Wilton

Abbreviations
Authorship of individual commentaries is indicated by the following abbreviations:

J. E. = James Evans
S. P. = Stan Purdum
C. W. = Carlos Wilton

Cycle A

Advent 1

Psalm 122

"Pray for the peace of Jerusalem" (v. 6). What better way could there be for us to begin the Advent season than by focusing our prayers on peace? The word, *shalom*, translated "peace," means much more than the mere absence of conflict. And of course, it is not only Jerusalem that is in need of peace; the whole world needs the *shalom* that the psalmist dreams about. So perhaps we should expand the breadth of this prayer, and deepen it with our awareness of the various meanings of the Hebrew idea of peace.

Pray for healing in our world. *Shalom* includes the idea of wholeness, or what we might describe as "healing." Africa is wracked by a devastating AIDS epidemic. Hundreds of thousands of people die weekly of this horrible disease. Our prayer for peace on earth cannot overlook the healing of the sick.

Healing is also needed in our political affairs. Our own country is frequently and angrily divided along partisan lines. Building a sense of national unity after a campaign is difficult because the rhetoric is so heated and so divisive. Pray for the healing of our land, that we may see ourselves as neighbors once again.

Pray for the feeding of the world. The Hebrew idea of *shalom* includes the notion of prosperity. In our culture, prosperity is the measure of everything; in the rest of the world, the lack of prosperity is the measure of misery. It is hard not to imagine that the two things are connected. Our great wealth is out of proportion to our size. America is only six percent of the world's population, yet we control most of the world's resources. Our prosperity contributes to the poverty of others. Perhaps if we prayed for the feeding of the world, our obsession with material gain could begin to give way to a more balanced view of the meaning of life.

Pray for the end of war. *Shalom* does include in its various meanings the cessation of conflict. As we begin our journey toward our celebration of the birth of the Savior, let us pray that we can find a way out of the warfare and bloodshed that marks so much of our world. Let us pray that we will find a way to use our great gifts of mind, heart, and faith to solve the problems we now

fight about. For the sake of the presence of God in our midst, let us pray that we will seek only the good for everyone.
Pray for the peace of our Jerusalem.

— J. E.

Advent 2

Psalm 72:1-7, 18-19
(See The Epiphany Of Our Lord, Cycle A, and The Epiphany Of Our Lord, Cycle B, for alternative approaches.)
    This psalm is a prayer for the king, and it asks God to extend divine rule over earth through the anointed one who sits on the throne. Although the inscription says the psalm is about Solomon, that is a scribal addition. More likely, this was a general prayer used for more than one of the Davidic kings, and it shows the common belief that the monarch would be the instrument through which God acted.
    The primary request of the psalm is that the king's rule be marked by godly characteristics — justice and prosperity for all within the kingdom, righteousness in all dealings, dominion over enemies, and submission from other kings. In all of this, the psalm is an appropriate one for this Advent Sunday as we consider the coming of the King of kings.
    The lectionary skips the middle verses of this psalm, but there is no special reason to do so. Most of the psalm, at least through verse 17, is a cohesive unit and does not deviate from the theme. Verses 18-19 are a doxological conclusion for the entire Book II of the Psalms (Psalms 42-72) and verse 20 is possibly a leftover marker from an earlier collection of psalms, whose purpose is to distinguish those attributed to David from those authored by others.
    For preaching purposes:

1. Note the similarity of theme between this psalm and the First Lesson for today. It may be enough simply to use the

psalm as a further example of the messianic hope Judah places in its kings.

2. Verse 11 can be interpreted symbolically to refer to the visit of the Magi.

3. Christianity has long seen the hope of this psalm as fulfilled in Jesus Christ. Consider focusing on verses 2-4 to discuss the ministry of Jesus.

4. Verse 3 refers to the yield of the mountains and hills. Though not an Advent theme, this verse could provide the basis for a sermon on how the wise use of the planet's physical resources could, under the rule of a just and righteous government, contribute to universal justice and prosperity.

— S. P.

Advent 3

Psalm 146:5-10
(See Proper 26/Pentecost 24/Ordinary Time 31, Cycle B, for an alternative approach.)
    It is the words, "whose hope is in the Lord their God" (v. 5), that draws this psalm into use during Advent. The theme of hope permeates not only the Advent season, but also the entirety of the gospel message. In Paul's famous trilogy of what is greatest, hope is mentioned alongside faith and love. And while love is the most important in the apostle's mind, hope may be the most difficult to achieve.
    Part of the reason for hope's difficulty is the ever-present danger of confusing hoping with wishing. Hope that is genuine can never be fully invested in a particular outcome. Standing by the bedside of a sick child, we can only wish the child well and whole. But if our hope depends on that outcome, it may not hold. Or, facing the uncertainty of a personal illness, our wish is that we

will survive and avoid the pain of radical treatments. But if our hope depends on this outcome, we may find ourselves with no hope.

Hope undergirds the big picture. Hope is that experience of grace — informed by faith, and enacted by commitment — that believes in a good overall outcome regardless of our particular circumstances. It is this general hope that allows us to face our losses, and to confront our pain without sinking into despair.

And when the pain is great, hope is difficult to maintain.

That's why the psalmist correctly celebrates the origin and direction of our hope. "Happy are those ... whose hope is in the Lord their God." Hope is not in our schemes and cures. Hope is not in our technology or our ingenuity. Hope is not in some amorphous future. Our hope, if it is real hope, is in the Lord.

The psalmist is right again when he recognizes that those who are able to place hope in the Lord are "happy." This is one of those difficult words, in Hebrew and in English, that forces us to think past our own cultural meanings. The word "happiness" in our culture often means having everything just as we want it to be. But our discussion of hope dictates that this "happiness," whatever it is, is present regardless of our circumstances.

The synonyms "fortunate" and "blessed" may offer some insight into the psalmist's meaning. Those people whose hope is in God, who are not knocked out by the ups and downs of life, are the ones who are truly blessed. They are fortunate in having a hope that holds against the storm, and does not crumble when life gets hard.

How fortunate indeed! No wonder they are so happy.

—J. E.

Luke 1:47-55

One day, back in the early years of computers, an engineer was asked to demonstrate to a group of reporters what his then "state-of-the-art" machine could do. His computer was one of those huge, room-sized machines — complete with whirring reels of tape, flashing lights, and a great, clattering punch-card machine. It probably accomplished about as much work as the typical personal computer today — and a lot more slowly, at that. Yet back then, its power seemed truly extraordinary.

The reporters were suitably impressed. As the engineer went on to boast of the amount of memory his machine had, one of the reporters in the back row was heard to mutter, in a loud stage whisper, "Yes — but will it remember me?"

It was just a wisecrack — but it carried within it a chilling question, one that's just as distressing today as it was back then. The more our culture becomes dependent on these remarkable machines — the more high-tech seems to crowd out high-touch in our lives — what is to become of us, who are made not of silicon chips but of living, breathing flesh?

One of the deepest longings of our race is to be assured that we will somehow be "remembered" — that to someone out there, we are more than one in a few billion humanoid life forms, on the third planet of a medium-sized star, off to the edge of the Milky Way galaxy. Is there something, someone, at the heart of the universe — someone who remembers?

Nearly 2,000 years ago, in an insignificant village in a far-off corner of the Roman Empire, a peasant girl was asking herself the very same question. It was the sort of question young people of any time or place can be counted upon to ask: Why am I here? What am I to do? Will my life make a difference?

The singular distinction of this young girl is that she got an answer. Whatever it was that Mary of Nazareth heard and saw that day — that portentous day, known forever after as "the annunciation" — it forever changed the course of human history.

Scripture tells of an angel named Gabriel who appears in Mary's presence, delivering to her the unexpected news that she will bear a son. This child "will be great," the angel announces, "and will be called Son of the Most High. Of his kingdom there will be no end."

And then, in the twinkling of an eye, Mary knows. She knows — in a flash of insight so dazzling she could never forget it. Mary knows that someone remembers.

And what does she do, in response? She sings. Mary's response to this glorious news is to throw back her head and let loose a rousing song of God's love and power.

This song of Mary's is known as the "Magnificat" — after the first word of her song in Latin: "My soul magnifies the Lord." And "magnify the Lord" Mary does — recounting not only the marvelous deeds God has done for Israel, but the astounding things the Lord has yet to do, through this babe who has not even yet begun to stir in her womb. "The Mighty One has done great things for me," she sings; "holy is his name."

Mary sings not only of the love of God; she sings also of God's justice. The Magnificat is no syrupy ballad of private inspiration, no ode to personal religious experience. The God of Mary's praises is one who "has scattered the proud ... brought down the powerful ... and lifted up the lowly." As for the rich, Mary's God has sent them away empty.

What could Mary possibly have seen, that heaven-touched day long ago, of things that were to come? What could she have known of all the mighty works her baby boy would accomplish? Surely she could not have foreseen the cross he would bear, or the cold, dark tomb from which he would rise. But she saw enough to be able to sing — and so can we, in these Advent days.

— C. W.

Advent 4

Psalm 80:1-7, 17-19
(See Advent 1, Cycle B, and Proper 15/Pentecost 13/Ordinary Time 20, Cycle C, for alternative approaches.)

The recurring phrase, "let your face shine" (vv. 3, 7, 19), offers an interesting opportunity to reflect on the meaning of God's presence in our world. This reflection takes on a particular significance during the Advent season.

The images of light and "shining," are associated with God throughout the Bible. From the moment God said, "Let there be light," light has been the defining characteristic of God's presence. God appears as light to Moses in the bush that seems to burn. God burns like a pillar of fire, leading Israel out of Egypt. The light is even infectious. After Moses spends time with God on the mountain, Moses himself begins to glow.

The light is symbolic of God's power and purity. Light is the opposite of darkness, which is often associated with evil. Light is good, life-giving.

But, the light associated with God is otherworldly. It does not have its origin in this world. The shining character of God's presence overwhelms us, drives us to our knees, and humbles us. We become like Isaiah in the temple, cowed by God's glorious appearance and by the rush of awareness of our sin that becomes evident in God's light.

That's one reason the imagery of light is so prevalent during the Advent season. The "light of the world" has come. We celebrate this glorious coming with candles and bright lights — all dim reminders of the hope and life that are found in God's presence. We sing with the psalmist "let your face shine," and pray for the salvation we need.

God does just that. Ironically, the shining of God's face is displayed in a human face. The ultimate appearing of God in our world is not as a supernatural shaft of light, but rather as a humble human being. The fullness of God's glory is revealed in a human face.

This, of course, changes everything. It changes the way we think about God and God's glory. God is with us, like us. It changes how we think about power and influence. God doesn't overpower us or force us or blind us. Rather, God walks with us, embraces us, becomes one of us.

Of course it changes everything we think about ourselves. Whatever view we once held of our human existence, and the value of being a human, is transformed forever in the belief that God became human with us. It changes how we think about one another. How can we ever call another person our enemy when that person reflects in his or her face the divine glory? How can we neglect the needs of a single hurting person when we realize that by neglecting them we neglect God?

We prayed with the psalmist, "let your face shine." And it has. God's face has illuminated the world for all time. The brightness of God's glory has sent its beams into every dark crevice and hole. The light of the world has come; God's face is shining. We have seen him, beheld his glory, and touched his flesh and heard his voice and felt his tears and watched him die.

Shine, O Lord, shine. Let your face shine in the life of your Son in our presence.

—J. E.

Christmas Eve

Psalm 96

(Occurs in all three cycles of the lectionary; see Christmas Eve, Cycle B, for an alternative approach.)

Psalm 96 is an enthronement psalm. This type of psalm was employed in worship to celebrate the unique presence of God with Israel in the temple and also to celebrate God's kingship over all creation. The presence of God was most likely symbolized by means of the Ark of the Covenant. The Ark was carried into the temple in a processional and placed in the holy of holies. Bringing the Ark into the worship place was the signal to celebrate the reality of God's presence in the world. That recognition was heralded with the words "the Lord reigns" (v. 10).

The psalm can be divided into two sections: verses 1-6 and verses 7-13. Each section follows the same scheme. Verses 1-6 are a call for worshipers in community to praise God. Verses 1-3 encourage worshipers to "sing a new song." In singing a new song, worshipers bless God's name and tell of God's salvation. Verses 4-6 explain why we should praise God in this way. God is great, God is to be feared, God is creator, and so on. Verses 7-13 are a call for all people to praise God. Verses 7-9 encourage "the families of the people" to worship God. Verses 10-13 describe how God rules over creation and judges all people.

Psalm 96 celebrates God's presence in the world and because of this we are encouraged to sing a new song. The old songs, while certainly filled with praise and thanksgiving, apparently are not able to capture the significance of the new reality created by God's presence. Once God enters the world, everything is different. All of our former ideas and notions have to be revisited and revised. God's arrival sparks a new beginning that must be celebrated with new praise. This psalm, of course, is intended to be such a new song. It has been made possible because God has used God's power to create security for us and provide salvation.

These themes are useful anytime in worship, of course, but they take on special significance in the celebration of Christmas. Jesus' entry into the world certainly marks the beginning of a new way of conceiving God's presence in the world. Through Jesus, God provides security and salvation. And what season of the year is filled with more music than the Christmas season?

We should heed the call of the psalmist to sing a new song. Not that the old hymns and carols are not meaningful; they certainly are. However, confessing that God has entered our world though the miracle of incarnation must remain before us a startling assertion. We cannot afford to let the wonder of this idea, the mystery of it, become mundane. We should be filled with awe and wonder every time the topic comes up.

If we are able to sustain our wonder, then as God is carried into the world — not symbolized by the Ark of the Covenant, but born incarnate as the babe of Bethlehem — it will surely be possible for there to slip from our lips a song of praise and thanksgiving that is fresh and new.

— J. E.

Christmas Day

Psalm 97

(Occurs in all three cycles of the lectionary; see also Easter 7, Cycle C, for an alternative approach.)

The lectionary includes two sets of readings for Christmas Day: those appointed for dawn services, and those appointed for services that take place later in the day. Psalm 97 is designated as one of these early-morning readings.

There are two possible reasons why this psalm has been included in the lectionary for Christmas Day. The first is its opening line: "The Lord is king! Let the earth rejoice; let the many coastlands be glad!" (v. 1). The second is this line from later in the psalm: "Light dawns for the righteous, and joy for the upright in heart" (v. 11).

Otherwise, Psalm 97 is a peculiar choice, for it presents God as an austere and fearsome figure, enthroned above the heavens, casting down thunderbolts upon the earth. This is not the sort of imagery most preachers would like to haul out of the ecclesiastical attic, to display alongside the shepherds, angels, and Wise Men.

For those who are determined to use this psalm as the basis for a Christmas sermon, the two verses identified above could serve very well. Verse 1 celebrates divine kingship — certainly an appropriate message at the birth of Jesus as king. Kingship, however, is not a theme that resonates strongly with most Americans. It is hard for most of our people to imagine the joy with which citizens of a monarchy could await the news of the birth of a new heir to the throne.

Verse 11 picks up the favorite Advent/Christmas theme of light. Advent and Christmas hymns are replete with images of inbreaking light and the dawning of a new day. The star of Betheleem from Matthew's Gospel is also a potent image of light. Malcolm Muggeridge's meditation on the meaning of light is appropriate on this or any occasion:

> *It is precisely when every earthly hope has been explored and found wanting, when every possibility of*

> *help from earthly sources has been sought and is not forthcoming, when every recourse this world offers, moral as well as material, has been drawn on and expended with no effect, when in the shivering cold every log has been thrown on the fire, and in the gathering darkness every glimmer of light has finally flickered out — it is then that Christ's hand reaches out, sure and firm, that Christ's words bring their inexpressible comfort, that his light shines brightest, abolishing the darkness for ever."* (From *A Twentieth-Century Pilgrimage* by Malcom Muggeridge)

— C. W.

Psalm 98

(Occurs in all three cycles of the lectionary; see also Christmas, Cycle B, and Easter 6, Cycle B, for alternative approaches.)

This psalm gives us the proper theme for a Christmas Day celebration: "Make a joyful noise to the Lord, all the earth; break forth into joyous song and sing praises" (v. 4).

There comes a time in our observance of Advent when we move purposefully from waiting and anticipation to embrace the fulfillment. We listen with longing and hope as the story builds in intensity and expectation. We listen with desperate need, hungering for the satisfaction that will come with the arrival of God's promised salvation. We let it build to a bursting point, to the place where we don't think we can wait another moment. And then we praise.

There comes a time when prose runs out. We hear the stories, and tell the stories, and recite the stories in liturgies. We do pageants with the stories and musicals with the stories, a myriad of dramatic readings. But there comes a point when the prose runs out. We reach the place where we have talked enough about the story. It's time to enter the story and as we do, we discover there are no words. We can only praise.

There comes a time when the visual symbols have done all they can do. The candles, the wreaths, the plastic stars, the ceramic angels, the wooden mangers. They have carried us as far as they can. They have helped us: without a doubt they have helped us. But the time comes when the props are inadequate. We are challenged to embrace the full reality of what God has done. We need the real star, the real angel, and we must find our way to the real manger. When we can, and do, we praise.

There must come a time in our celebration of the birth of Jesus when we really get it. It's not enough that we acknowledge it, or give lip service to it, or teach our children about it, or sweat blood trying to keep it. We must really get it. The full import of God entering the world as one of us must seize us and hold us and change us. And when it does, we will praise.

There comes a time when the only proper thing to do is sing. This is a moment for poetry and melody. The watershed moment of the universe has come, and we must sing. There comes a time when — from the heart and not from the head, from a real encounter and not just from hearsay, from the darkness of despair to the blazing light of hope — our only proper response is to sing "Joy To The World."

That time has come.

— J. E.

Christmas 1

Psalm 148
(Occurs in all three cycles of the lectionary; see Christmas 1, Cycle B; Christmas 1, Cycle C; and Easter 5, Cycle C, for alternative approaches.)

In his breathtaking "Hymn Of The Universe," Pierre Teilhard de Chardin uses the Roman Catholic mass as a metaphor for the majesty and the complexity of creation. As both priest and scientist, de Chardin was in a unique position to see the order and beauty of creation existing not only as a testament to God's creative power, but also as a response to that creative power. The stars and seas and plants and animals all follow their courses and play their roles.

In doing so, they comprise a powerful hymn that celebrates God's amazing accomplishment.

The person who wrote Psalm 148 has employed a similar pattern. Beginning with the highest heavens and working his way down through creation, the psalm writer calls upon every living creature, every created thing, to praise God.

Unlike Teilhard, however, this hymn of praise and the cause for praise is not creation itself. Creation is called to worship. It is called to bear witness, not to itself, but to another creative act accomplished by God. The full range of the universe is called to sing a hymn to "a horn."

In the final stanza the psalmist writes, "He has raised up a horn for his people, praise for all his faithful, for the people of Israel who are close to him" (v. 14).

The "horn" refers to a ruler or a king. The immediate context for the psalmist was probably a newly installed king of Israel. But for us, the context takes on genuine universal significance. The "horn" that has been raised for us, the ruler whose life and work we celebrate, is none other than the King of all kings.

In other words, we are invited to give voice to a new hymn: not to the universe, but to God's universal act of redemption. The whole created order, while certainly in awe of the Creator's boundless power and might, has its attention drawn to another creative act. God has poured the fullness of divine power and love into a singular life. That life stands as the hope for all people, for creation itself.

So we voice a song of praise. We fill our sanctuary with our praises. We listen for praise shouted from the heavens. We expect the animals to respond. The sea life, the birds of the air — all life is called to praise. Kings, rulers, presidents — the powerful and the powerless alike — are called to praise. The universe is brought together to make a choral offering to the one life that makes all other life possible and meaningful.

— J. E.

Christmas 2

Psalm 147:12-20
(Occurs in all three cycles of the lectionary; for an alternative approach to vv. 1-11 and 20, see Epiphany 5/Ordinary Time 5, Cycle B.)

This psalm was likely written for the people of Jerusalem after their return from exile (see vv. 2-3) and was intended to remind the hearers that the same God who runs the cosmos also cares for Israel.

In the verses designated by the lectionary for today, this theme shows up in reference to God's sending of snow and hail (v. 16) and winds and flowing waters (v. 18) upon the earth. We should be careful not to connect those verses directly to verse 20 — "He has not dealt thus with any other nation" — for the psalmist is not saying God's actions through nature are unique gifts to Israel. That would be the opposite of Jesus' assertion that God "makes his sun rise on the evil and on the good, and sends rain on the righteous and on the unrighteous" (Matthew 5:45).

Rather, the psalmist wants his audience to take heart that the God who has power over the functions of nature guards Israel. This mighty God is the one who is now the security of Jerusalem, who "strengthens the bars of your gates" and "blesses your children within you" (v. 13). Comfort may also be taken from the inverse of that point as well: the God who is the Savior and Security of Israel is the one who controls the cosmos.

A preaching theme arising from all of this is "From where does our security come?" — a subject especially critical in our post-9/11 world. There can be no easy answers, but we can talk about the ultimate security of living our lives in God's world — yes, this *is* God's world, as this psalm proclaims; it is not the terror-makers' world. And we can talk about the rituals of protection, including prayers for safety and the placing of our loved ones and ourselves in God's hands.

Vanessa Ochs, author of *Safe and Sound: Protecting Your Child in an Unpredictable World* (Viking Penguin, 1995), tells of certain rituals parents through the ages have undertaken to guard their children — everything from amulets and talismans to incantations, confessions of sins, and pictures of saints. Then, speaking of her own children and her feelings of fear for their safety, she concludes, "Only when I began to focus on the daily ceremonies of protection — the prayers, blessings, goodnights, and goodbyes that are part of our ritual regimen — was I able to relinquish the extreme overprotection and protect, as I had hoped, adequately."

An aside: The Roman Catholic lectionary uses these verses as the "Psalm for the Year: A Reading" for the Solemnity of the Most Holy Body and Blood of Christ (formerly called the Feast of Corpus Christi), celebrated on the second Sunday after Pentecost. The observance honors the real presence of Christ in the Eucharist, and the psalm connection is in verse 14b, "he fills you with the finest of wheat."

— S. P.

The Epiphany Of Our Lord

Psalm 72:1-7, 10-14
(Occurs in all three cycles of the lectionary; see also Epiphany, Cycle B, for an alternative approach; see also Advent 2, Cycle A, for vv. 1-7.)

Using the psalm during Epiphany provides an opportunity to create a message that moves from the lesser to the greater. The lesser, of course, is the king of Israel. The functions and expectations of the Davidic king are recited and celebrated in the context of worship. The people are able to hear, with the king listening in, exactly what is his responsibility to God and to them.

For instance, the psalm opens with a prayer that the king may be given justice and righteousness so his rule will establish a just, social order. The king is here presented as the one who is responsible for the maintenance of the social order.

The psalm also prays for the long life of the king (v. 5). This indicates the belief that the nation's longevity, prosperity, and well-being are all tied to the fate of the king. If the king does well, the nation will also do well.

This psalm is expansive in scope. The psalmist celebrates the reign of the king "from sea to sea," and mentions "the kings of Tarshish and of the isles." This language allows him to project the reach of Israel's king to the very limits of "the whole world" (vv. 8-11). The prayer is that the king will have far-reaching dominion over nations that will submit to his rule and pay generous tribute.

Finally, the psalmist reminds the king of his responsibility to protect and defend the weak members of society (vv. 12-14). There were no laws in ancient Israel requiring kings to protect the rights of the powerless and the vulnerable. However, society placed the king under moral obligation to defend the weak, help the needy, and have compassion on those most likely to be victimized by others.

In our celebration of Epiphany, we are invited to expand these ideals the psalmist applies to earthly kings and celebrate their fulfillment in the appearance of the King of kings. Justice and righteousness are his mantle. Caring for "the least of these" is his daily bread. His kingdom reaches far beyond simple borders. For the King who has appeared to us as Jesus the Christ, his kingdom is the universe and his reign is forever.

—J. E.

The Baptism Of Our Lord/ Epiphany 1/Ordinary Time 1

Psalm 29
(Occurs in all three cycles of the lectionary; see The Baptism Of Our Lord, Cycle B, and Trinity Sunday, Cycle B, for alternative approaches.)

The references in this psalm to God's appearance in the storm are strongly reminiscent of the creation narrative. The idea of the "Lord enthroned over the flood" (v. 10), connects with the image of God's presence "brooding over the waters."

Raising these images in connection with the baptism of Jesus, however, provides an opportunity to not only expand our thinking about baptism, but about creation as well.

In the biblical narratives of creation, narratives that certainly rumble through this psalm, God unleashes his power against the great primeval deep. The chaos and nothingness of the mysterious "waters" come under the influence of God's creative powers. While the Bible does not support the later theological and philosophical concept of creation *ex nihilo* — creation out of nothing — it does affirm that great order and beauty emerged out of desperate chaos. God subdued the storm and harnessed the waters in order that life might be sustainable.

In the waters of baptism God engaged in another act of creative power. The storm of human violence and poverty and fear, stirred by corrupt politics and religion, cried out for redress. Into the swirling mix God sent Jesus. Into the waters of human misery God sent Jesus to offer order and beauty.

In the waters of Jesus' baptism, a mission and its method were made clear. Jesus heard the voice of the Lord as it thundered over the waters. Jesus heard the voice that called for order to emerge from chaos — a call to him to be a Son in whom God delights.

In the chaos of world events, Jesus heard God singing Psalm 2: a coronation psalm heralding the anointing of a new king. Jesus also heard God singing the song of the suffering servant, the one who would heal with his own stripes and wounds.

"You are my Son, in whom my soul delights!"

These are the new words of a new world. These are words spoken in and over the waters that create and re-create life. These are the words that marked the beginning of the end of the chaos of human misery. These are the words of the new creation, made in the image of the Son, offered through an act of sacrificial love, and aimed at restoring every broken soul.

Out of the storm the Lord speaks. Above the waters the Lord thunders. Out of the waters and into the storm goes the Son on whom all our hope now rests.

— J. E.

Epiphany 2/Ordinary Time 2

Psalm 40:1-11

Psalm 40 is possibly a combination of two psalms. Verses 1-11 are a song of thanksgiving while 12-17 (or possibly 13-17) are a lament. Our lection for today is the thanksgiving portion, and what the psalmist is grateful for is deliverance — though from what, specifically, we cannot know. Whatever it was, the deliverance so impressed the psalmist that he is not satisfied to express thanks with his words alone. He also intends to live thankfully, delighting to do God's will (v. 8).

Preaching possibilities:

1. It apparently took a long time for God to answer the psalmist's plea for help and draw him up from "the desolate pit." It took a while until God put his feet on solid ground once more. The psalmist says he "waited patiently," but we wonder. Can any of us do that? Don't we want our heavenly help right now? But often our answering God seems to demand patience. The psalmist does not indicate how he spent his time while waiting, but he may have wondered if he had placed his "one phone call" to the wrong party. Possibly he considered whether he should have called to one of the other gods. But he waited, and was delivered so dramatically that it placed a new song in his mouth. A helpful sermon could be composed on the theme, "What do we do while waiting for God's answer?"

2. Verse 9, "I have told the glad news of deliverance in the great congregation," is a powerful statement of the importance of testimony. What's the point of keeping one's thankfulness bottled up in one's own heart? Our love for God should motivate us to proclaim that he first loved us. The sermon idea is "News that shouldn't be kept quiet."

3. Verses 6-8, about the Lord's preference for an "open ear" over sacrifice and offering, is quoted by the author of

Hebrews (10:5-10) as evidence that Christ, the once-for-all sacrifice, replaces the old cultic sacrifices. In his day, of course, the psalmist was not repudiating the cultic practices, but was seeing the bigger picture: that only the offering of the self gave any meaning to burnt sacrifices. The "you have given me an open ear" is literally, "you have bored ears for me." Is the sacrifice God wants from us today a listening ear — inclined to both the people around us and to God?

— S. P.

Epiphany 3/Ordinary Time 3

Psalm 27:1, 4-9
(See Lent 2, Cycle C for an alternative approach.)
The theme of this psalm is trust in the Lord. Verses 1-6 and 13-14 are expressions of that trust, stated to others. Verses 7-12 are a prayer to the God in whom this psalmist trusts. The reading for today includes verses from both the statements and the prayer.
Preaching possibilities:

1. Expressions of trust and prayers for help belong together. Trust stated without an appeal to God sounds incomplete, like mere bravado. In our human condition, trust is not a static thing, announced once and for all. Prayer for God's ongoing help is the discipline by which trust is nurtured.

2. In times of trouble, the psalmist knows where to go: to the temple of the Lord (v. 4). For us, the equivalent is not a physical building, but the place within us where we "center down" on God.

How different we are when God is not in that center! When Ralph Waldo Emerson finished reading Gibbon's *Decline and Fall of the Roman Empire*, he observed, "That man has no shrine" —

no center. But we each need an inner sanctuary, or shrine, a place inside ourselves where we can bask in the light of God's love for renewal and guidance and growth and, as this psalmist tells us, safety.

This internal holy place is what Paul referred to when he prayed for the Ephesians that "Christ may dwell in your hearts through faith" (3:17).

This psalm reminds us that when we relate to the world around us through the central focusing commitment to God, we tap into a confidence that lifts our heads, enables us to make melody to the Lord (v. 6) and helps us to "see the goodness of the Lord in the land of the living" (v. 13, which surely should have been included in the psalm lection).

— S. P.

Epiphany 4/Ordinary Time 4

Psalm 15

"There's Jackson, standing like a stone wall." Those words, spoken at the First Battle of Bull Run (Manassas), secured the reputation of Confederate officer Thomas Jonathan Jackson. Forever after, he has been known as Stonewall Jackson — the courageous general who could not be moved, even as the bullets whistled by him.

Jackson, a Presbyterian elder, was a man of deep personal piety. While some today may fault him for his choice of sides in the Civil War, he saw himself as defending his Virginia homeland against invaders. In Ted Turner's epic film, *Gods and Generals*, a fellow officer asks Jackson, following a battle, how he can remain so "serene" in the midst of the fray. "My religious belief," Jackson replies, "teaches me to feel as safe in battle as in bed. God has fixed the time for my death; I do not concern myself with that. But to be always ready, whenever it may overtake me — that is the way all men should live. Then all men would be equally brave."

Psalm 15 concludes with these words: "Those who do these things shall never be moved." What things? We need to return to the early verses of the psalm to find out....

The question posed in verse 1 is: "O Lord, who may abide in your tent? Who may dwell on your holy hill?"

Those words refer to the tent of meeting, the temporary worship place of Israel — that later, during the reign of King Solomon, would gain a permanent location as the temple (see 1 Kings 8). Who is worthy to ascend the temple mount, to enter into the presence of the Most High? Only those who walk blamelessly, who do what is right, who speak truth and do not engage in slander. So disciplined are these holy ones that they will honor the terms of an oath "even to their hurt." They do not exploit the poor by lending money at interest.

What do such faithful ones fear? Only the Lord (v. 4). Truly, those who fear the Lord and seek to fulfill God's purposes cannot be moved.

The story is told of an Oxford student who was sitting for a difficult philosophy exam. Normally, an eight-page essay was expected. The exam that day had a single question: "What is courage?"

One minute into the exam, the student wrote three words in his examination book, presented it to the professor, and left the room. His answer gained a perfect score. What he had written was: "This is courage."

Courage may be discussed at great length in philosophy classes, but at the end of the day, it comes down to character. What the author of Psalm 15 is saying is that those who cultivate a deep and abiding personal faith in good times will be able to stand like a stone wall when bad times come.

— C. W.

Epiphany 5/Ordinary Time 5

Psalm 112:1-9 (10)
    This is a dangerous psalm — dangerous, because it is so open to misinterpretation.
    "Happy are those who fear the Lord...." Well, who could quarrel with that? Yet this psalm goes on to describe, in concrete terms, exactly what form that happiness takes: "Their descendants will be mighty in the land.... Wealth and riches are in their houses" (vv. 2a, 3a).
    Power? Wealth? Are these the fruits of a godly life? The psalmist seems to think so.
    At least it seems that way, at first glance. There are plenty of shallow preachers, these days, who would jump at the opportunity to skim these out-of-context verses off the top and use them as grist for the gospel-of-prosperity mill. (*"Turn to the Lord, and God will bless you in this life, beyond your wildest dreams: with health, wealth and recreational vehicles. Call our 800-number now to buy our new book. Only $29.95: MasterCard and Visa accepted."*)
    But read on. Psalm 112 is about a lot more than wealth and power. It lists other characteristics of godly people. Such individuals are "a light for the upright." They are gracious, merciful, generous, and fair. They are immovable in their ethical resolve. They are, in every respect, admirable and well-rounded individuals (vv. 4-8).
    This psalm is in some ways reminiscent of the description of "a capable wife" in Proverbs 31. That wise woman, with her daunting daily to-do list, seems to be doing an amazing job of being all things to all people — but it quickly becomes apparent that the only reason she is able to do so is because God is her all-in-all.
    Wisdom, in the Hebrew Scriptures, is not a matter of intellectual erudition. It is an eminently practical concept, closely linked to an idea that has fallen into disfavor in our cynical, modern age: the idea of virtue. The truly wise, according to the biblical model, are expert practitioners of common sense. They know how to live well — and that sort of "living well" has nothing to do with expensive luxuries. If wealth does accrue to them, it's because they are successful, holistic practitioners of the art of living.

Our second president, John Adams, wrote these words in a letter to his grandson, John, then in his twenties:

> *Oh, that I may always be able to say to my grandsons, "You have earned much and behave well, my lads. Go on and improve in everything worthy." Have you considered the meaning of the word 'worthy'? Weigh it well.... I had rather you should be worthy possessors of one thousand pounds honestly acquired by your own labor and industry, than of ten millions by banks and tricks. I should rather you be worthy shoemakers than secretaries of states or treasury acquired by libels in newspapers. I had rather you should be worthy makers of brooms and baskets than unworthy presidents of the United States procured by intrigue, factious slander and corruption.* (From a letter quoted by David McCullough in *John Adams* [New York: Simon & Schuster, 2001], pp. 608-609.)

Adams — who was also a deeply religious man — would have intuitively understood the message of Psalm 112.

— C. W.

Epiphany 6/Ordinary Time 6

Psalm 119:1-8

There was a school crossing guard in Florida who had grown very frustrated with the many drivers who would race through his school zone at full speed. He thought he had tried everything to get them to slow down, until he finally happened upon a solution that worked. The crossing guard took a blow dryer and wrapped it in electrical tape, making it look like a radar gun. He discovered that all he had to do was point it at approaching car, and the drivers slowed down instantly.

"It's almost comical," he told a newspaper reporter. "It's amazing how well it works."

Such is the power of the law to restrain human behavior. While the drivers' response may demonstrate a grudging respect for legal consequences, the author of the lengthy Psalm 119 is speaking, in its opening verses, about a sort of respect for the law that goes far beyond mere compliance. "Happy are those," he testifies, "whose way is blameless, who walk in the law of the Lord" (v. 1).

"Walking in the law of the Lord" goes far beyond simply fearing the cost of a speeding ticket. The verb "walking" implies that the law accompanies the faithful through every moment of life. We could just as well say, "living, eating, and breathing God's Law" — for such is the whole-life outlook of this and many other psalms that celebrate the advantages of taking the Torah deeply to heart. The Torah, indicated here by a great many synonyms — among them "decrees," "precepts," "statutes," "commandments," and "ordinances" — is the Lord's greatest gift to the human race. Following God's Law brings numerous benefits.

There is an old Jewish story about a child who rebelled against studying the Talmud. His parents tried everything, and finally brought him to the rabbi in despair. The child feared the rabbi, who had been described by his parents as something of an ogre.

As the child and his parents stood before him, the rabbi did his best to live up to that reputation. "What is the trouble?" he roared.

"Our son doesn't like to study the Talmud," the parents replied, in fear.

"What?" screamed the rabbi, turning his wrath on the young boy. "You don't like to study the Talmud?" The rabbi ordered the parents to leave their son with him.

Then he turned toward the trembling child, picked him up, sat down in an overstuffed chair, and simply held the boy in his arms. For the longest time, the rabbi cuddled the boy. In time, the child's racing heartbeat calmed, and after a while he became aware that his own heart and the rabbi's were beating in sync with each other. They stayed that way for about an hour, until the parents hesitantly knocked at the door. The rabbi carefully set the child down, smiled, and winked at him, then stomped over to the door in a most fearsome way. Violently, he pulled the door open and announced gruffly, "*Now* the child will study the Talmud!"

It turned out he was right. The child grew up to become one of the most renowned Talmudic scholars in all the land. When someone asked him, late in life, where he had first learned to love the law, he replied, "It was when the rabbi held me next to his heart."

— C. W.

Epiphany 7/Ordinary Time 7

Psalm 119:33-40

Like last week's selection from the opening portion of this same psalm, today's selection celebrates the joy that comes of following God's Law, the Torah. As is usually the case with psalm selections in the lectionary, it amplifies the First Lesson from the Hebrew Scriptures — which this week happens to be Leviticus 19:1-2, 9-18.

Reading through verses 9-18 of the Leviticus passage, we quickly discover that following God's Law transcends mere legalism: at the root of each of these commandments is a deep and abiding ethical concern for the well-being of others. The command to leave something in the field for the gleaners (Leviticus 19:9-10) honors the needs of the poor. The prohibition against stealing has a human face: "You shall not defraud your neighbor" (v. 13a). "You shall not keep the wages of a laborer until morning" (v. 13b) is among the earliest examples of fair-labor legislation — the workers, after all, need their salaries if they are to feed their families. There is concern for the disabled (v. 14), and an admonition to treat everyone equally: "You shall not be partial to the poor or defer to the great" (v. 15). Ultimately, there comes a prohibition against hate itself (v. 17), followed by the greatest commandment of all: "you shall love your neighbor as yourself" (v. 18).

"Give me understanding," pleads the psalmist, "that I may keep your law and observe it with my whole heart" (Psalm 119:34). Perhaps the most important aspect of this understanding is the discovery that God's Law is about much more than statutes and regulations and ordinances and codicils. With love at its very heart, it is the concrete manifestation of the Lord's desire that we live in harmony with others, and even with ourselves. The law the psalmist begs to understand has, in the very deepest sense, a human face. "Turn my eyes from looking at vanities," he pleads; "give me life in your ways" (v. 37). Far from being a dead letter, the law is life-giving.

Such a view is expressed by hymn-writer Thomas Troeger, in the following stanza:

> *We are not free when we're confined*
> *To every wish that sweeps the mind*
> *But free when freely we accept*
> *The sacred bounds that must be kept.*
> ("God Marked a Line and Told the Sea," Oxford University Press, 1989)

— C. W.

Epiphany 8/Ordinary Time 8

Psalm 131

From the early sixteenth- to the mid-nineteenth centuries, one of the most popular forms of painting was the "miniature." Deriving its name from the Latin *minium* — which refers to the red lead-based paint used to emphasize letters in medieval manuscripts — the miniature was also physically tiny. A miniature painting could be held in the palm of the hand, or worn as a piece of jewelry. Many of them were portraits of the well-to-do — for only the wealthy could afford such trinkets. It took the greatest of artistic skill to shrink the image of human face down until it could fit within that minuscule frame and still be recognizable. Miniatures flourished as an art form until the advent of photography, which made it possible to produce tiny, detailed images much more quickly and without the same level of artistic skill.

Psalm 131 is a miniature. Just three verses long, the NRSV refers to it as "a song of quiet trust."

Think "lullaby." A lullaby is a brief little song that soothes a troubled child, causing the tears to stop flowing. It is not exalted in style, nor pretentious in any way. A lullaby is a small and simple melody that accomplishes its purpose admirably.

Such is the case with Psalm 131. It is a confession of humble trust in the Lord: "I do not occupy myself with things too great and too marvelous for me. But I have calmed and quieted my soul, like a weaned child with its mother" (vv. 1b-2a).

A weaned child, by definition, is one who has stopped nursing. Yet even the weaned child sometimes yearns to crawl up into its mother's lap and take to the breast. In this humble, maternal image, the psalmist witnesses to God's tender love.

— C. W.

Epiphany 9/Ordinary 9

Psalm 31:1-5, 19-24
(See Easter 5, Cycle A, for an alternative approach to vv. 1-5. See also Sunday Of The Passion, Cycles A, B, and C, for vv. 9-16.)

The dominant theme in the verses selected for this week's reading is that of refuge. Various other psalms make use of this word, which serves as a metaphor for the believer's ultimate trust in the Lord. The ordinary sense of the Hebrew was a shelter such as a rock or cave, in which a traveler could hide in the face of a fierce storm, or escape the onslaught of bandits or other enemies.

The lectionary's cut of this psalm is a bit awkward, because it interrupts verses 1-8, which are usually considered a distinct unit. Verse 5, of course, is well-known to Christians as Jesus' final statement from the cross ("into your hand I commit my spirit"); yet the theme of refuge continues for three more verses beyond this one, ending with the confident statement of deliverance in verse 8, "you have set my feet in a broad place." The once-frightened sojourner who ducked into a cave is now able to emerge into full sunlight, confident that his foes have been vanquished and that he enjoys the protection of the Lord.

The missing middle section, verses 9-18, provides some detail about the psalmist's particular situation. The author evidently has some dread disease, that makes his life a misery and that brings on the scorn and revulsion of his neighbors.

The concluding section (vv. 19-24) is a confident ascription of praise to the Lord who does provide refuge. When the psalmist was "beset as a city under siege," the Lord held off the invading hordes.

Although we cannot be sure that this was the psalmist's particular complaint, a story that could be told in connection with this psalm is the well-known tale of Father Damien and the lepers of Molokai, in the Hawaiian Islands. Nineteenth-century Hawaiians who contracted leprosy (Hansen's Disease) were treated unusually harshly by that taboo-based society. They were banished to the Makanalua Peninsula on the island of Molokai: a rocky, inhospitable spit of ground that offered only a hardscrabble existence. Woefully short of supplies, these poor unfortunates had to make do with driftwood huts and whatever food they could fish out of the sea.

Joseph de Veuster, a Belgian seminarian, arrived in the Hawaiian Islands in 1873. Upon his ordination as a priest, he took the name of Father Damien and began a ministry among the lepers of Molokai. He cajoled the government into providing decent supplies for the colony, and ran a pipeline to supply the lepers with clean water. Eventually, Father Damien contracted leprosy himself, continuing his ministry among the people whom he now addressed in his homilies as "We lepers...." He died of the disease in 1889, at the age of 49.

Father Damien transformed the Makanalua Peninsula from a place of exile into a place of refuge.

— C. W.

The Transfiguration Of Our Lord/ Last Sunday After The Epiphany

Psalm 2

Undoubtedly, the reason why Psalm 2 occupies its place in the lectionary is because it amplifies the divine theophany of the Transfiguration episode in the Gospel Lesson. When the voice of the Lord in Psalm 2:7b says, "You are my son; today I have begotten you," clearly it is prefiguring, in the lectionary committee members' minds, the heavenly voice in Matthew 17:5: "This is my Son, the Beloved; with him I am well pleased; listen to him!"

Yet there is a lot more at work in Psalm 2 than this prophetic link to the New Testament. The psalm stands alone, quite apart from the church's tendency to read between its lines and see Jesus.

Mitchell Dahood identifies Psalm 2 as a coronation psalm (*Psalms 1:1-50*, in *The Anchor Bible*; Doubleday, 1965, p. 7). Or, more accurately, it is an anointing-psalm — since the ancient Israelites set their kings apart not by placing a golden circlet upon their heads, but rather by anointing them with oil (see 1 Samuel 16:13). The word "Christ" literally means "anointed one" — another reminder of the Christian community's conviction that Jesus is the true spiritual heir of the Davidic dynasty.

The Lord's beloved son who is heralded in Psalm 2 — one of the royal psalms — is a warlord. At the ceremonial commencement of the king's reign, the Lord is presenting the nations of the earth to him as his heritage, and the very ends of the earth as his possession (v. 8). For his part, this warrior-king is fierce and fearsome. He "will break them with a rod of iron, and dash them in pieces like a potter's vessel" (v. 9). Against this mighty ruler, the nations may "conspire" and the kings of the earth may "plot" — but always "in vain" (v. 1). There is no defeating this king, who has at his disposal the mightiest weapon of all: the Lord's favor.

James Luther Mays identifies this psalm as "the only text in the Old Testament that speaks of God's king, messiah, and son in one place" (*Psalms*, in the *Interpretation* series [Louisville: John

Knox Press, 1994], p. 44). For that reason, it has a particular importance to the Christian community, despite the logical disjunction between the humble Jesus of the gospel narratives and the fearsome warrior-king of the psalm. (Of course, the book of Revelation presents a very different portrait of Christ, one that is perhaps more in keeping with the psalm.) The church has traditionally looked upon this psalm, and discovered in its ancient imagery a prefiguring of the cosmic Christ *Pantocrator* of eastern orthodox religious art: the exalted Lord, raised to rule over all. The Transfiguration episode itself is a brief revelatory moment, in which Jesus' most trusted friends are allowed to glimpse this aspect of his true nature. But first, there is a long journey ahead: to Jerusalem and the pain and disgrace of the cross. God's people must wait a while longer to see the vision of Psalm 2 — and of the Mount of Transfiguration — truly made manifest.

— C. W.

Psalm 99

(See The Transfiguration Of Our Lord/Last Sunday After The Epiphany, Cycle C, for an alternative approach.)

This psalm celebrates the kingship of God, and proclaims that divine kingship is related to holiness. Structurally, the psalm may be divided into three parts. Verses 1-3 proclaim the kingship of God over all the earth. Verses 4-5 announce God's justice and righteousness specifically for Israel. Verses 6-9 praise God as the one who answers those who call on God's name. Together, these three sections define a God who is holy: holy in majesty, holy in justice, holy in responsiveness.

This being Transfiguration Sunday, it is fruitful to consider why this psalm is used on this day. Surely the Transfiguration is an experience of God's holiness, and Moses, named in verse 6 as one of God's priests, performs along with Elijah a priestly function for Jesus. Also, the God who previously spoke from "the pillar of the cloud" (v. 7) also speaks in the dazzling white of the Transfiguration.

In preaching from this psalm, consider verse 8, speaking of the God who answers the people and forgives them. In the psalmist's day, it was a mark of a good king that he would respond to the petitions of those in need. Even greater is the king who graciously forgives. Our God, however, does both. Consider that many who sit in the pews today may be suffering from guilt, due to some real or imagined offense. In his book, *Whatever Became of Sin?*, Karl Menninger tells of a man standing on a Chicago street corner pointing to passersby and stating loudly, "GUILTY!" People hurried away from him, but one man — turning to another — asked, "But how did he know?"

We worship a God who stands ready to forgive the penitent. For those suffering guilt, divine forgiveness is at least a transforming experience.

— S. P.

Ash Wednesday

Psalm 51:1-17
(See Lent 5, Cycle B, and Proper 13/Pentecost 11/Ordinary Time 18, Cycle B, for alternative approaches.)

The superscription to this psalm identifies its origins with David's prayer after the prophet Nathan confronts him with his sin. Whether or not it was actually composed by David is impossible to say; yet the tradition of Davidic authorship is certainly strong, and very ancient.

Can our people identify with the sins of David? That is the pastoral question, in linking the psalm with David in our proclamation. Do the adulterous sins of an ancient oriental potentate, who misused his royal authority to commit what was effectively rape and murder, resonate with the people in our pews?

As is tragically often the case with successful political leaders, David has the proverbial "feet of clay." David sins — and when this larger-than-life figure sins, he predictably does so in a big way.

There are some who say David falls in love — but, in truth, it's more like falling in lust. David becomes obsessed with the beautiful Bathsheba, wife of one of his generals, Uriah. While the faithful Uriah is off fighting David's wars, David sends for the man's wife, and — exercising all his kingly authority in a way Bathsheba could not refuse — treats her as though she were his own. When Bathsheba tells David she is expecting his child, the king scrambles to cover up the scandal. First, David tries to convince Uriah he's the father — but when this doesn't work, he sends this brave and innocent soldier off on what amounts to a suicide mission, one that has no military significance. Uriah dies, his body pierced by enemy arrows — and, after only the briefest season of mourning for his widow, David takes Bathsheba to be his wife.

David has come a tragically long way from his days as a brave and naive young patriot. The years have taken the sparkle of innocent mischief out of the shepherd-boy's eye, and replaced it with the jaded leer of a middle-aged monarch who has for many years sought little more than to pleasure his own senses, and build his reputation as a ruler to be reckoned with.

All this intrigue has been going on secretly, with no one but David and Bathsheba the wiser — no one, that is, but God, who reads what is written on every human heart. God sends word to Nathan of what David has been doing. If anyone can convince this absolute monarch he's taken the wrong path, it's the wise and aged Nathan — for Nathan was the one who chose the young shepherd-boy David years ago, anointing him king over Israel.

Nathan tells the king a simple and homely story: of a poor man, whose beloved pet lamb is stolen by a heartless yet powerful landowner who lives nearby. The king quickly sees the injustice of this situation. He demands to know where this miserable offender can be found, so he can render justice. It is only at this point that Nathan looks the king in the eye and dramatically declares, "You are the man!"

It is as though, in that instant, the prophet holds a mirror up to his king. David looks back at him, enraged for the briefest of moments — then he sees his own image, and the magnitude of his unfaithfulness dawns on him.

What happens next demonstrates why David — despite his tragic flaws and his terrible sins — is renowned as the greatest of rulers. David repents. Then he goes out and writes a song. Tradition has it that song is Psalm 51: "Have mercy on me, O God, according to your steadfast love; according to your abundant mercy blot out my transgressions. Wash me thoroughly from my iniquity, and cleanse me from my sin" (vv. 1-2).

There is no denial here; no kingly cover-up; no closed-door conclave of spin doctors to discuss, in anxious whispers, how to manage damage-control in the media. Instead, David writes a song — a hymn for the public worship of his people. This hymn makes it clear how dark is his sin and how desperate he is to receive God's forgiveness: "Purge me with hyssop, and I shall be clean; wash me, and I shall be whiter than snow" (v. 7).

What a refreshing change this is from what we see so often in our national life! There is no attempt — as in Bill Clinton's sexual-ethics scandal — to redefine the meaning of the word "is." Nor, to be completely non-partisan, is there a Ronald Reagan-style attempt to exercise "plausible deniability," as in the Iran-Contra scandal. Once King David takes in the view in Nathan's mirror — once he realizes the fathomless depth of his sin — he casts all his fortunes on God's mercy, frankly and honestly admitting what he's done.

That is our task, as well, during the season of Lent.

— C. W.

Lent 1

Psalm 32
(See Lent 4, Cycle C, for an alternative approach.)

This psalm belongs to the group of psalms designated by the Christian church for confession and absolution. In the Hebrew calendar, a sequence of services provided for confession of guilt, and there was both a guilt offering (for personal sin against God) and a sin offering (for sin against the community). Thus, Psalm 32 reminds us that God forgives not only personal but also corporate sins. Obviously, this psalm is highly appropriate for the first Sunday in Lent.

Some preaching possibilities:

1. Some leaders of the Reformation wanted to have confession and absolution in a special sacrament, in addition to baptism and the Eucharist. They settled on the latter two only, but Martin Luther said, "Whenever private confession leaves the church, the church will die." So, although it was never made a sacrament, confession is just as important as those other means of grace. A sermon could focus on the painful manifestations of unconfessed sin — especially using verses 3 and 4, compared to the lightened heart of those who unburden themselves to God and receive forgiveness (vv. 1-2).

2. Note that this psalm begins with two beatitudes. Logically, they should come at the end of the psalm, after the acknowledgment of sin and God's granting of absolution (v. 5). But coming as they do at the beginning, together with additional expressions of joy in the final verse (v. 11), they serve to bracket the recognition of guilt and subsequent repentance with blessedness and joy. That can be a description of the Christian life — one lived in the joy and blessing of God, but in which, from time to time, the person becomes aware of a sin that has slipped in, and the means to deal with it that are readily available: confession and repentance. That done, the joy returns. This dealing with the sins of Christians is surely what the author of 1 John has in mind as he writes, "I am writing these things to you so that you may not sin. But if anyone does sin, we have an advocate with the Father, Jesus Christ the righteous; and he is the atoning sacrifice for our sins ..." (1 John 2:1-2).

3. Paul quotes verses 1 and 2 of this psalm in Romans 4:7-8, introducing the verses by saying, "So also David speaks of the blessedness of those to whom God reckons righteousness apart from works." Indeed, the psalm reminds us that it is repentance, confession, and forgiveness that put us in the right relationship with God. A sermon could discuss the common, if unspoken, reliance on works as a hoped-for way to please God, and why it alone is not enough.

— S. P.

Lent 2

Psalm 121

This is a hymn of praise. The psalm is easily understandable even without knowing the circumstances of ancient Israel. It straightforwardly says, "The Lord is my helper." Preaching possibilities include:

1. Knowing where our help comes from. A pastor had built a church with a freestanding altar placed so that he could look up through a translucent window, at mountains rising beyond. He said, "Isn't it wonderful to be able to say, 'I lift my eyes to the hills' when I preach and pray?" But he missed the question mark in the Hebrew construction of verse 1. Do I lift up my eyes to the hills that my help should come from there? No. My help comes from the Lord who has made the hills, not from nature itself. The majesty of the natural world can lift our sights, but only God can bring help.

2. Looking for the highest help. The great preacher of an earlier era, Phillips Brooks, preached a sermon on this psalm called "Help from the Hills" — which, despite its

misleading title, urged his hearers to seek their help from the highest place. While acknowledging other sources of help, Brooks said, "The real relief, the only final comfort, is God" and that we should "refuse to let ourselves be satisfied with any supply but him."

3. Being kept by God. In the NRSV, this psalm uses the word "keep" four times and "keeper" once. It is worthwhile to juxtapose this psalm with Cain's excuse in Genesis 4:9, "Am I my brother's keeper?" What does it show about the character of God, self-revealed as the keeper of Israel — and, by extension, our keeper as well? Another parallel could be drawn to Jesus' identification of himself as the gatekeeper of the sheepfold (John 10:3).

— S. P.

Lent 3

Psalm 95

This psalm has two distinct parts. Verses 1-7a serve as a call to worship, extolling the greatness of God. Verses 7b-11 comprise a stern warning about allowing one's spirituality to become stale and matter-of-fact — in the language of the psalm, "hardening of the heart." In an earlier version of the lectionary, this chapter was treated as though it were two separate psalms, with the first section used as the stand-alone response for Christ the King Sunday. The second portion, but with verses 6-7a added, was the psalter for one of the Sundays after Pentecost.

The Revised Common Lectionary, however, has brought the two parts back together, as the psalm always has: so it behooves the preacher to consider expounding the psalm in its entirety. For example, how can the call to worship be heard when the heart refuses to listen? In this regard, read the exposition on this psalm that the author of Hebrews gives (3:7—4:13), paying special attention to 4:2.

Another way to address the tension between the two parts is to remember the custom of Ash Wednesday, when the cross of ashes is inscribed on the forehead with the words, "Receive the token of the Holy Cross, the sign of his victory and of your defeat."

Still another way to treat the whole psalm is to view the first section as the joyful procession into the presence of God for worship, with the second section as the divine word addressed to the kneeling congregation. In other words, liturgy and sermon.

Other preaching possibilities include:

1. Verse 6 calls for kneeling before our Maker. A diplomat once said that a man kneels only before his God and the woman he loves. The first is an act of worship and the second may be, but in both cases, the posture evidences a trust that the one before whom we kneel will not misuse our position. Thus, a sermon on trust.

2. Verse 10, with its reference to the wilderness generation, which God "loathed" for forty years, provides an opportunity to address the topic of giving up on people too soon. What factors need to be present to enable us to stay in troubled relationships? When are we justified in excluding any members from the family circle? This would not be an easy sermon to write, but it could be a helpful one to many on a very personal level.

— S. P.

Lent 4

Psalm 23
(See Easter 4, Cycles A, B, and C, for alternative approaches.)

It is one of the best-known and best-loved passages of the Bible. Generations have memorized it, in Sunday school or at the knee of parents or grandparents. It is one of the first Bible passages we learn, and — as common as it is at funerals — it is among the last words said over us when we die. Psalm 23 has been a source of strength and comfort for many.

Its very familiarity makes it difficult to interpret, at least critically. Biblical scholars have always held that Psalm 23 presents problems of interpretation. It seems to be two psalms connected together, and the fit between them is not very good. There is a sudden and awkward transition between the first part (where the author seems to be envisioning himself as a sheep) to the second part (where he has become a hungry and thirsty traveler welcomed into a bedouin tent).

The images seem strained. What sheep have ever been concerned with "paths of righteousness," or contemplated their own end in "the valley of the shadow of death"? The words are beautiful, but the logic seems confused.

Scholars have spilled much ink over the years trying to explain Psalm 23. Some have speculated that an early editor combined two completely different psalms. Yet so lyrical is this religious poem, and so beautiful its language, that few readers have minded the abrupt change of scene, or the thought of sheep that display strangely human sensibilities.

Probably the most fruitful interpretation is one that has its roots in the original Hebrew. Not all biblical translations make this clear, but the New Revised Standard Version does. Unlike the more-familiar KJV, the NRSV does not say, "He leads me in paths of righteousness"; it says instead, "He leads me in right paths." It makes no mention of "the valley of the shadow of death"; instead, it speaks of "the darkest valley." The Bible translators chose these English words — risking the ire of those who are emotionally attached to the Elizabethan language — because they are truer to the original Hebrew. As we pay attention to the difference these changes make, the curtain of confused logic falls away, and a wholly new picture of this psalm emerges.

Imagine that the narrator is not picturing himself as a sheep at all, but as a lost and lonely traveler. The blazing noonday heat of the desert is long gone, and the bitter cold of desert night is coming fast. The road has disappeared into the twilight. Provisions of food and water ran out hours ago, and the traveler is parched and hungry. In the distance, a jackal howls. Fears of wild animals and bands of robbers cascade, unbidden, into his mind. He regrets having begun this journey, and wonders if it will be his last.

But then the traveler sees a figure on a hillside, outlined against the darkening sky. It is a shepherd — a common, ordinary man, but a man who knows these hillsides and ravines. The shepherd goes down to the weary traveler, and leads him up out of the shadowy valley to a place where the last beams of sun still light the way ahead. He leads the wayfarer to a grassy meadow, and invites him to lie down. The shepherd cups water from the oasis spring in his hands, and offers it. The traveler drinks and drinks.

He glances up to see the shepherd's rod, by which he guides the sheep, and also his staff, or walking-stick. It is comforting to see these symbols of a man who knows his way through the desert. When the traveler has rested a bit, the two walk on — following "the right paths" this time — to a black goatskin tent set amidst an encampment of other tents. These are bedouins, dwellers in dry and desolate places — determined people who know how to scratch a living from the desert. They are also outsiders to the rest of society, even outcasts. The bedouin have their own mysterious ways, unknown to our lost traveler (who would hardly have given them a thought, had he passed them in the town). It occurs to him that they may even be enemies, who wish to rob or kill him.

But this fear proves to be unfounded. The shepherd brings the man into his own tent. It is lit inside with oil lamps, and decorated with carpets that are as intricate and beautiful as the goatskin tent is plain. There is no fear now: the laws of Middle-Eastern hospitality are in effect. As long as the traveler is in the shepherd's tent, the shepherd is pledged to protect him from all enemies. The two sit cross-legged at a low table, and the shepherd spreads out a meal — a simple meal that somehow tastes better than any our traveler has ever had: steaming lamb stew, soft pita bread, succulent dates. In a timeless gesture of honor, the host pours a flask of fragrant oil over the guest's head, and pours wine into his cup until it overflows.

The fears of night have been transformed. Where once there was aching terror, now there is serenity and trust. Such is the power of desert hospitality. Perhaps it was this hospitality that David, or whoever wrote this psalm, once felt. So moving was this experience for the psalmist, so unforgettable his rescue from the very jaws of death, that he has come to see it as symbolic of God's love.

— C. W.

Lent 5

Psalm 130

(See Proper 8/Pentecost 6/Ordinary Time 13, Cycle B, for an alternative approach.)

An old *Peanuts* cartoon has Charlie Brown sitting at Lucy's psychiatric booth. After Lucy dispenses one of her typically twisted diagnoses, Charlie Brown is left sitting there, head in his hands. With a forlorn look on his face, he implores the cosmos: "Where do I go to give up?"

Perhaps that's a question some of us have asked, when we have found ourselves at the end of our ropes. It is much the same question the writer of Psalm 130 is asking: "Out of the depths I cry to you, O Lord. Lord, hear my voice!"

As with many of the psalms, we cannot know with certainty who wrote those plaintive words, or what the precise difficulty is: but we can empathize. We've been there. The only thing we can tell for sure about the psalmist's problem is this: it has something to do with guilt. "If you, O Lord, should mark iniquities, Lord, who could stand? But there is forgiveness with you, so that you may be revered."

The scholars call this a penitential psalm. Surely that is why it ends up at this place in the lectionary, deep in the season of Lent. Although this song may have been born "out of the depths," it does not dwell there. For not many verses after that despairing cry, there comes, abruptly, a confession of faith: "... my soul waits for the Lord, more than those who watch for the morning...."

In this age of technology — when streetlights cast broad circles across the pavement, and garish neon and subtle night-lights are both commonplace — not many people stand still anymore to "watch for the morning." Yet this was a common practice in biblical times. Each town had its night watchmen: public servants who would stay up all night on guard duty. Up and down the streets they would trudge, in the early-morning chill, making sure no enemies were lurking: making sure everything was all right.

Maybe only someone who has worked nights can fully discern what the psalmist is talking about. The sentry on the Army post knows all about it: how the hours drag on, how the senses get sharpened in the silence, how even the crunch of boot-heel on gravel sounds like it carries for miles. Anyone who has ever kept bedside vigil with someone who is dying knows it, too. Such a one knows how, in the wee hours, the mind plays tricks: how one hears imaginary, muffled conversations out in the hallway, how absurd images pass before the mind's eye.

Yet somehow, in the sepulchral blackness, the psalmist finds it within himself to calm his nerves and wait. He waits for the Lord, "more than those who watch for the morning." Who's to say how he makes it to that spiritual turning-point: how, precisely, he manages to transform his situation from despair into hope? But transform it he does.

It may sound pollyanna-ish to say to someone in the slough of despond, "Just wait, things will get better" — but the simple truth is, very often they do. They certainly do, if we boldly place ourselves in the caring hands of the God of love.

— C. W.

Palm Sunday/Sunday Of The Passion

Liturgy Of The Palms
Psalm 118:1-2, 19-29
(Occurs in all three cycles of the lectionary; see Easter, Cycle A, for an alternative approach to vv. 1-2, 14-24.)

This psalm, titled "A Song Of Victory," has rich associations in Christian liturgy. Portions of it occur in all three lectionary cycles for Palm Sunday (Liturgy Of The Palms), as well as in all three cycles for Easter Day.

The reason for the Palm Sunday connection is plain to see: "Open to me the gates of righteousness, that I may enter through them and give thanks to the Lord" (v. 19).

Are the "gates of righteousness" really synonymous with the gates of Jerusalem, through which Jesus enters? The answer is yes — for, by the time of Jesus, these words have become the liturgy for welcoming pilgrims to Jerusalem, particularly at Passover. They were sung responsively by pilgrims and Levites, as the pilgrims made their way up to the temple. Very likely, these are the very same words Jesus himself sang, as he and his entourage made their way into the city. To these words, the Levites habitually replied:

"This is the gate of the Lord; the righteous shall enter through it" (v. 20).

This psalm is the product of an institutionalized victory liturgy, through which the Jewish people recalled the military triumphs of their heroes of old. It is one of the *Hallel*, or "praise" psalms, traditionally sung at the most notable Jewish feasts, including Passover. Psalms 113-118 are known as "the Egyptian *Hallel*," because they recall the Lord's saving deeds of old, bringing the people safely through the Exodus.

The original situation of this individual song of thanksgiving is lost to history, but it possibly has royal associations. It is easy to see it as the song of a victorious king, entering the city in triumphal procession after defeating Israel's enemies. This king may be David himself.

"Open to me the gates of righteousness!" cries the king, in the victory liturgy.

"This is the gate of the Lord, the righteous shall enter through it" respond the sentries, atop the wall — as other soldiers, below, unbar the great doors and swing them wide, to welcome "the festal procession" on its way up to the high altar, where the king will make a public sacrifice of thanksgiving.

Only a truly righteous king can call upon the Lord's favor in such a way: and only a truly righteous king knows the importance of returning to the Lord after the victory, to give thanks. Whether or not this is the original situation of the psalm, it is impossible to say; but it surely would have created such associations in the minds of those who would later sing it liturgically.

"Save us, we beseech you!" cry the people, in verse 25 — the "save us" is the Hebrew *yesha*, etymological root of the names "Joshua" and "Jesus." The messianic associations are plain to see. Joshua bears the name given him by Moses in Numbers 13:16 — and Jesus, in turn, is named for Joshua. The New Testament cry, "Hosanna!" is a transliterated form of the Hebrew *yesha*, in a particularly emphatic form.

In preaching on this festival day, it is always important — whether choosing Palms or Passion texts — to avoid the pitfall of emphasizing the triumph and avoiding the tragedy. Even this Liturgy of the Palms reading contains, from the Christian perspective, a shadow of that which is to come: "The stone that the builders rejected has become the chief cornerstone" (v. 22).

In many churches, Palm Sunday is a day of festive celebration. Yet that celebration ought properly to be tempered by a reminder of the grim fate that awaited Jesus, on the other side of the city gates.

— C. W.

Liturgy Of The Passion
Psalm 31:9-16

(Occurs in all three cycles of the lectionary; see Liturgy Of The Passion, Cycle B and Cycle C, for alternative approaches; see also Easter 5, Cycle A, for an alternative approach to vv. 1-5, 15-16.)

On this day when preachers have to decide whether to pursue the palms or the Passion, it should be noted that Psalm 31:9-16 is part of the Liturgy Of The Passion, not the Liturgy Of The Palms, and it occupies that place for all three years of the Revised Common Lectionary. But even if one did not know that, the tone of these verses would surely push one away from any triumphalism. These words are the cry of a person in agony.

A couple of preaching possibilities:

1. Verse 9 and especially verse 10 can be taken literally, as references to serious illness. Many sufferers have found courage and hope in viewing the voluntary suffering of Jesus. One pastor mentioned visiting a Christian woman who was in the end stages of cancer, and was in terrible pain. Yet she said to the pastor, "If Jesus suffered for me, I can suffer for him." For his own part, the pastor thought the woman's comment was simplistic. How could her embracing her own suffering, which was caused not by sin but by rogue cells, be doing anything for God? But the fact was, that self-understanding was helping the woman handle her ordeal. Wisely, the pastor did nothing to challenge her view. Maybe the woman was right anyway. Here's a place to talk about redemptive suffering.

2. Verse 12, "I have passed out of mind like one who is dead," could easily be the lament of a person "downsized" out of a job and unable to find new employment. Those who have "been there" testify that it really does feel like being forgotten by one's former workmates, employers, and even the crowd one ran with while employed. What will it take to get a person in such straits to trust that "my times are in your hands" (v. 15)?

— S. P.

Maundy Thursday

Psalm 116:1-2, 12-19
(Occurs in all three cycles of the lectionary; see Maundy Thursday, Cycle B, for an alternative approach.)

The lectionary editors' decisions as to the carving of biblical texts are not always well advised. The decision to edit out the middle section of Psalm 116 disrupts the flow of its poetry. The editors' decision is possibly related to the fact that Greek and Latin Bibles typically divide the psalm into two separate psalms: verses 1-9 (Psalm 114) and 10-19 (Psalm 115). Modern scholars are agreed, however, that this is a single, unified work. The psalm is not that long, and could certainly be read in its entirety in a worship service.

As a whole, this individual song of thanksgiving bears witness to the joy and relief of a believer who has been healed from some dreaded illness. This was a potentially mortal sickness (v. 3). It led to incapacity for a time (v. 6). It caused emotional anguish, and possibly physical disability as well (v. 8). It was very much a serious affliction (v. 10).

And what is the psalmist's response to this good news? "I will lift up the cup of salvation and call on the name of the Lord, I will pay my vows to the Lord in the presence of all his people" (vv. 13-14).

The psalmist's deep intuition as to how best to respond to his experience of healing finds liturgical expression. His gratitude drives him to the temple. Meister Eckhart taught, "If the only prayer you ever say in your whole life is 'thank you,' that would suffice." Psalm 116 is surely a sufficient response, according to that way of thinking.

This ancient liturgical impulse found later expression in the way this Psalm came to be used as part of the Passover ritual. In the Passover liturgy it is typically read as one of the cups is raised in blessing. The salvation experience of the individual who wrote this song (the details of which are lost in the mists of time) thus becomes the prototype for any human experience of salvation. Passover worshipers, hearing this psalm, vicariously experience the psalmist's relief and gratitude, and claim those worshipful feelings for themselves. Christians, of course, will recognize these lines as frequently belonging to celebrations of the Lord's Supper.

Many people come to worship seeking to receive something from God. That is certainly a legitimate reason for coming, but perhaps a purer motivation is that expressed by the author of this poem. It is gratitude, pure gratitude that leads him to "lift up the cup of salvation and call on the name of the Lord." Would that we could remember to come to God more often, for just such a reason!

Addressing the subject of healing prayers, Frederick Buechner reflects on Mark 9:14-29, the story of the father of the sick boy, who exclaims, "Lord, I believe; help my unbelief!" Buechner writes:

> *What about the boy who isn't healed? When, listened to or not listened to, the prayer goes unanswered? Who knows? Just keep praying, Jesus says. Remember the sleepy friend, the crooked judge. Even if the boy dies, keep on beating a path to God's door, because the one thing you can be sure of is that down the path you beat with even your most half-cocked and halting prayer the God you call upon will finally come, and even if he does not bring you the answer you want, he will bring you himself. And maybe at the secret heart of all our prayers that is what we are really praying* for. (From *Wishful Thinking: A Theological ABC* [Harper & Row, 1973], p. 71.)

— C. W.

Good Friday

Psalm 22
(Occurs in all three cycles of the lectionary; see Good Friday, Cycle B; Lent 2, Cycle B; and Proper 23/Pentecost 21/Ordinary Time 28, Cycle C, for alternative approaches.)

Jesus spoke the opening words of Psalm 22 from the cross (Matthew 27:46), making it an obvious choice for the Good Friday responsorial psalm. But the larger psalm served the early Christian community as well, for it describes the suffering of a righteous one in terms that fit the crucifixion of Jesus, including verse 17, "they have pierced my hands and feet" (RSV) and verse 18, "for my clothing they cast lots." And beyond that, the psalm testifies to the vindication of those who suffer for righteousness (vv.

22-23). In all, five quotations from or allusions to Psalm 22 appear in the gospel passion narratives.

1. While the primary focus of this day is the suffering and death of Jesus, there is room to speak to all who suffer through no wrongdoing of their own. It will be the rare sufferer who cannot personally appropriate the words of verses 14 and 15. The preacher could delve into each of the metaphors of those two verses. What is the equivalent of being poured out like water? Of having one's heart melt like wax? Of having one's tongue stick to one's jaws? Those in the congregation who are suffering — physically, mentally, emotionally, socially, spiritually, or otherwise — can speak eloquently to their experience, informing the word of gospel that is spoken from the pulpit.

2. Take a look at the last phrase of verse 29. The NRSV translates it "and I shall live for him," but the footnote in that version gives it as "he who cannot keep himself alive," which is also how the RSV renders it. The difference between the two is important. The first assumes that the sufferer will survive long enough to serve God with his existence; the second alludes to faithful dying, which, of course, is exactly what Jesus was doing that dark Friday. For anyone to be able to praise God and pray while dying, as Jesus did, "My God," is to declare that even death is ultimately under the umbrella of the kingdom of God, and to give testimony that physical death, for the faithful, is a doorway to eternity. We need to remind people of that from time to time.

— S. P.

The Resurrection Of Our Lord/ Easter Day

Psalm 118:1-2, 14-24
(Occurs in all three cycles of the lectionary; see Easter, Years B and C, for alternative approaches; see also Palm Sunday, Liturgy Of The Palms, Cycle A, for an alternative approach to vv. 1-2, 19-29.)
With these same verses from Psalm 118 designated for Easter in all three cycles of the Revised Common Lectionary, it is clear that the lectionary committee considers this the preeminent resurrection psalm. Indeed, with the New Testament's repeated quoting of verse 22 (the rejected stone becoming the chief cornerstone, in Matthew 21:42; Mark 12:10; Luke 20:17; Acts 4:11; 1 Peter 2:4, 7 and alluded to in Ephesians 2:20), it's obvious that the first-century church also saw in it a reference to the resurrection of Christ.
Preaching possibilities:

1. In Jewish liturgical tradition, Psalms 113-118 are called "the Egyptian *Hallel*," meaning that they were intended for use during Passover, the festival that celebrated the liberation of Israel from Egyptian captivity. Thus, it is certainly possible, if not likely, that Jesus himself used this psalm in his own observance of Passover during his final week, perhaps even at the Last Supper. Did he see in it a promise of his resurrection? Here's the basis for a sermon on the promises that arm us as we face the dark valleys of life. How does that make us different from those who have no hope?

2. The fact that New Testament writers so often quoted this psalm reminds us of how the first-century Jews used their scriptures to interpret their present day. A sermon could explain how the Old Testament is not merely "pre-Christian" literature, but part and parcel of the scriptural foundation of the Christian life.

3. Verses 1 and 2 use the refrain, "His steadfast love endures forever!" "Steadfast love" is a translation of a Hebrew word, *hesed*, made popular by the prophets of the eighth century. It means the love of God that first comes to us, to be reflected by us into the world. Easter is powerful testimony to the steadfastness of God.

4. Verse 13, "I was pushed hard, so that I was falling," will resonate with many people today who are pushed by their schedules, job demands, family responsibilities, spousal expectations, unfulfilled dreams, and the like. What would resurrection look like for them?

5. Verse 17, "I shall not die, but I shall live" can be expounded in terms of resurrection, but could also be the testimony of a despairing person tempted to seek the dark peace of suicide, but who refuses to go there by sheer grit or conviction. What are the resources of faith that could support such a struggler?

— S. P.

Easter 2

Psalm 16

This psalm is a song of confidence and trust, and the first-century church found in it a prophecy of the Resurrection. Peter, in his Pentecost sermon, quotes verses 8-11 (Acts 2:25-28), applying them to the risen Lord. Thus, its designation as the responsorial psalm for Easter 2.

The psalm falls easily into three divisions: verses 1-4, there is no good apart from God; 5-8, the Lord is my portion and my counselor; and 9-11, there is joy and life with God.

Obviously, verse 10 could be of use to expound upon the Resurrection. Among the other preaching possibilities are these:

1. There is not much indication that the psalmist is in difficulties. With the possible exception of the opening line — "Protect me, O God, for in you I take refuge" — the singer says nothing that alludes to problems. And even that line can be read in the same general way as we might pray, "Be with me, O God," without having a specific trouble in mind. Why not talk about the importance of keeping one's relationship with God constant, and not just asking for help when hard times hit? This could be a springboard for a sermon on "Being a Christian When Everything's Coming Up Roses."

2. When the psalmist says, "I have no good apart from you" (v. 2), and expresses his delight in the "holy ones" (v. 3), he recognizes the truth of the "no man is an island" theme. He never talks as an individual separated from God, nor from the worshiping community. He is not the lonely self-seeking God, but the member of the fellowship who, carried by them, grows in his spirituality. A sermon could teach about the function of the church as not only a community that cares, but "a community that carries."

3. What is the meaning of verse 6: "The boundary lines have fallen for me in pleasant places"? It was probably a metaphor from the division of land by survey, but could it not be used to talk about the parameters of the righteous life? Yes, Christian living puts certain behaviors out of bounds, but only enriches life by doing so. It takes nothing away from the godly, but declares unloving actions off limits.

— S. P.

Easter 3

Psalm 116:1-4, 12-19
(See Maundy Thursday, Cycle A, and Maundy Thursday, Cycle B, for alternative approaches to vv. 1-2, 12-19.)

Classed as a song of thanksgiving, Psalm 116 both celebrates God's answer to the psalmist's prayers for help (vv. 1-2) and declares the psalmist's intention to now go to the temple and "return to the Lord" those things the psalmist had promised while praying the prayers (vv. 12-14). Admittedly that does give a bit of a *quid pro quo* feel to the psalm, but the psalmist can hardly be faulted for following through on what he had promised to do.

In the Greek and Latin Bibles, this psalm is divided into two, with verses 1-9 comprising Psalm 114 and 10-19 being Psalm 115, but the bargaining plot suggested above does give a unity to the whole passage. The Revised Common Lectionary cut of the psalm to verses 1-4 and 12-19 at least avoids the necessity of dealing with the difficult verse 11, "I said in my consternation, 'Everyone is a liar.' "

Some sermonic directions:

1. These same verses, minus 3 and 4, make up the responsorial psalm for Maundy Thursday. Although that is not our focus here, the psalmist's intention to "lift up the cup of salvation" is certainly an appropriate starting point for any communion sermon. It should be noted, of course, that as an Old Testament text, the cup here may have referred to one of those used in the Passover observance. Still, appropriated for the Eucharist, does not the cup become emblematic of our salvation, of the blood, "shed for you"?

2. Verse 15, "Precious in the sight of the Lord is the death of his faithful ones," deserves some attention. Some read the Hebrew word behind "precious" as "peculiar," as if the death of a faithful one were a unique event, something out of the ordinary. This suggests perhaps that long life was

the normal expectation for the righteous, which is a concept that does not wear well today. But others read the word as "costly," denoting that when a righteous person dies, God loses something. The deceased's praise is silenced and his or her witness to the living is no more. What indeed does it cost God when a faithful mortal passes from this world? Maybe it is a help for the grieving to know that their loved one's death grieves God, too.

3. Vows (vv. 14, 18) provide a good opportunity to preach about promise-keeping, but the idea needs to be larger than those promises literally called "vows," as in the marriage or baptismal promises. The righteous life simply cannot exist on any level without an intentional effort to live by promises made.

4. Verse 16, where the psalmist refers to himself as the child of "your serving girl," may have simply been a stock phrase meaning something like, "your trusted servant," but may also have reference to devoutness of the psalmist's mother. Here is a good chance to talk about the influence of upbringing on one's faith — although it should be pointed out that a simple claim to having a godly parent does not excuse one from the personal spiritual quest. God has children, it is said, but no grandchildren.

— S. P.

Easter 4

Psalm 23
(See Lent 4, Cycle A, and Easter 4, Cycles B and C, for alternative approaches.)

Easter 5

Psalm 31:1-5, 15-16
(See Liturgy Of The Passion, Cycle A, Cycle B, and Cycle C, for alternative approaches to vv. 9-16.)

We have already visited this psalm on Passion Sunday. Here it comes again, but with a different cut of verses, and we offer these additional preaching possibilities:

1. Verse 2 and 3 afford a good opportunity to talk about God's protection of the faithful. For the psalmist, God is a "rock of refuge," a "fortress." Note how different that is from those who merely pray, in the words of Charles Wesley's hymn, "Hide me, O my Savior, hide, till all the storms of life are past." Those people are asking to be excused from life's problems, and thus will also miss its joys. (What a shame that Wesley didn't find another line for this hymn!) In *Your God Is Too Small*, J. B. Phillips writes eloquently about an inadequate view of God he calls the "Heavenly Bosom," the "God" of psychological escapism. The psalmist is not asking to escape, however, but is calling for God to be the place of secure footing, a bulwark from which to battle the problems of life. That is a significant difference. That is trusting *Yahweh Sabaoth*, the Lord of Hosts, who protects us not by hiding us, but by equipping us to do battle.

2. Verse 5 was not included the way this psalm was cut for Passion Sunday, but it probably should have been. Clearly, the first phrase is the source of Jesus' cry from the cross, "Father, into your hands I commend my spirit" (Luke 23:46). Yet given that Jesus was quoting from this psalm, he would surely also have known the phrase that follows immediately after: "You have redeemed me, O Lord, faithful God." Here is the opening for speaking about the death of the righteous, and the hope in which they cross that

barrier into the next life. That, of course, is a theme that can be used anytime, but is especially appropriate during the Easter season.

— S. P.

Easter 6

Psalm 66:8-20
(See Proper 23/Pentecost 21/Ordinary Time 28, Cycle C, for an alternative approach to vv. 1-12.)

Psalm 66 is a song of communal thanksgiving, probably composed to celebrate some national deliverance. Because of the personal language of verses 13-20, there is some speculation that this psalm was originally two hymns, but as it stands, it contains a combination of corporate and personal prayers, both appropriate in worship.

Verses 8-12 talk about the troubles — some from other peoples (v. 12a) and some from unspecified sources — which have a refining effect (v. 10). The fire-and-water symbol of trouble in 12b is similar to that used by Isaiah in 43:2 and picked up by the hymn writer in "How Firm a Foundation." The notable thing here is the absence of any satanic force as the source of these problems. This is a good time to remind listeners that the Old Testament has no fully developed concept of the devil vs. God. As far as the singers of this psalm are concerned, although the trouble came through other peoples and situations, ultimately God is both the source of and the deliverance from (see v. 10: "For you, O God, have tested us"; v. 11: "You brought us into the net"; and v. 12: "you let people ride over our heads").

While we would not want to promote the idea that God capriciously does cruel things, the Old Testament's assertion that all things come from God does at least testify to God's full sovereignty over the creation. When a child dies tragically, we may be inclined to defend God by saying, "God didn't take your child," but that leaves open the frightening question, "Then who *did* take my child?" The people of Israel had no such concern. God was the source of all.

Of course, they saw that God does not abandon the faithful, and the third phrase of verse 12 provides interesting vocabulary to talk about the abundant life God gives: "you have brought us to a spacious place." According to the NRSV footnote, the Hebrew here can be read as "you have brought us to a saturation." This concept is also found in Job 36:16: "[God] also allured you out of distress into a broad place where there is no cramping, and what was set on your table was full of fatness" (RSV).

— S. P.

The Ascension Of Our Lord

Psalm 47
(Occurs in all three cycles of the lectionary; see The Ascension Of Our Lord, Cycle B, for an alternative approach.)

Both Psalms 47 and 93 (the alternative psalm for this day) are enthronement psalms, praise hymns celebrating God's rule over the nations. They were most likely used on festal occasions when Israel again declared that God was its king.

While Psalm 47 was for Israel's celebration, verses 1-2 call all the nations of earth to recognize God as their monarch as well. Verses 3-4, however, return to the specific relationship between God and Israel.

Verse 5 ("God has gone up with a shout") may be the reason the lectionary committee designated this psalm as an Ascension reading — although, to be true to the psalm, the ascension referred to here is that of God moving up to the heavenly throne. It is not a great stretch, of course, to see the similarity in Christ's movement "into heaven" (Acts 1:11).

Verses 6-9 repeat the call for all peoples to praise God as king of all nations.

There is an additional point of entry into this psalm in verse 2, which declares that God is "awesome." This may provide a way to speak to young people present in the worship service. Youth-speak changes fast, but it wasn't too long ago that "Awesome!" was the youth culture's exclamation of choice to express that the speaker was really impressed by something. The superlative was "Totally awesome!" Let's face it: "Awesome!" is at least an improvement on the earlier "Far out!" or the more recent "Sweet!"

It would be useful to explain that the word actually means "inspiring awe" or "worthy of awe." When the psalmist first used it of God, he knew no superlative could improve it, for God is all in all, and there is no word or words to convey that. So the sermon could proceed along the lines of how we picture God, and how none of the imagery we use to describe God is adequate. Perhaps this is a good time for a "Your God Is Too Small" discussion, following the still-timely J. B. Phillips book by that title.

— S. P.

Psalm 93

(Occurs in all three cycles of the lectionary. See The Ascension Of Our Lord, Cycle B, for an alternative approach.)

The brief Psalm 93 seems archaic, from the standpoint of our culture. The Lord is enthroned, here, as a cosmic king. The *accoutrements* of royalty are front and center: the robe of majesty, the girding-on of strength (suggesting a royal broadsword), the throne, the royal decree. Its message, loudly declared from the first verse onward, is simplicity itself: *the Lord reigns!*

Yet this one who reigns is like no ordinary king. The Lord rules over not only human affairs, but even the surging sea: the primeval waters, source of so many terrors for the Hebrew mind The turbulent waters of chaos bring no fear to the psalmist's heart, not this time. For God has tamed them, and God's providence continues to hold the floods at bay.

What does it mean to confess that the Lord reigns? Answering that question is hard, for in our secular democracy we have little experience of kings. They are an expensive luxury, long since discarded in favor of more utilitarian forms of government. (Some of us follow the latest tabloid scandals of the British royal family with salacious interest, but that's about as far as it goes.) We resist even using that word, "reign": our elected officials "serve" or "hold office."

Yet the Lord does reign, demanding our allegiance. Ancient Israel celebrated God's reign with an enthronement festival (which was in turn reminiscent of the vanquished gods of Mesopotamia, whom their worshipers ceremonially enthroned through cultic ritual). This psalm likely has its roots in such festivals, imported from foreign cultures.

Jerry Schmalenberger tells a story dating back to the time of the Nazi terror in Germany. In Wittenberg-Lutherstadt, a large statue of Christ stands in front of the Castle Church. Today, it is patched and repaired: for one Sunday afternoon long ago, a group of Nazi youth beat the statue to pieces with clubs. They painted the following words on a nearby fence: "The reign of Christ is over."

Later, a Christian youth group saw what had been done. They repaired the broken statue. Then, taking the same paintbrush and paint can the Hitler youth had used, they added three letters to the Nazi graffito: "a-l-l." It now read, "The reign of Christ is over all." (From Jerry Schmalenberger, *Lectionary Preaching Workbook, Series VII, Cycle C* [Lima, Ohio: CSS Publishing, 2003], p. 114.)

From time to time, the world may defiantly declare that the reign of God is ended. We know better.

— C. W.

Easter 7

Psalm 68:1-10, 32-35

At first reading, this psalm presents a scattering of themes. Some scholars think it was not a psalm at all, but a listing of headings to a number of liturgical pieces. Most, however, see in Psalm 68 the underlying theme of the victory and reign of God, the Divine Warrior — the God who was with the people of Israel in the wilderness (v. 7). Psalm 68 calls the kingdoms of the world to acknowledge that God is the warrior king who reigns over all. It presents God as the power and strength of the chosen people.

A preaching entry point may be found in verse 4, the God who "rides upon the clouds." This idea is repeated in verse 33, "O rider in the heavens, the ancient heavens," and together the two verses serve to bracket the content of this psalm. This title of cloud-rider represents a giant step away from idolatry for Israel — for, according to cuneiform tablets from the ancient Syrian city of Ugarit, that title usually belongs to Baal, the storm-god, who does battle with primal forces to restore fertility to the earth. But in this psalm, the people of Israel assert that Elohim is in control of even that function. From God, not Baal, comes "rain in abundance," which is "showered abroad" (vv. 8-9), but the rebellious live in a parched land (v. 6). Thus, as worshipers of Elohim, the people of Israel have no need for lesser gods to care for matters of fecundity. Regrettably, they did not always live up to the high concept of this psalm, but it shows us that some, at least, understood it.

This psalm could be the basis of a sermon on our image of God, and the lesser "gods" (fate, luck, deservedness) we sometimes credit with good outcomes in our lives. All good comes from the Lord God, this psalm insists — and nowhere else.

— S. P.

The Day Of Pentecost

Psalm 104:24-34, 35b
(Occurs in all three cycles of the lectionary; see The Day Of Pentecost, Cycle B, for an alternative approach.)

In his *Interpretation* series commentary on Psalms, James Luther Mays titles Psalm 104, "The Lord God Made Them All," a line from the well-known hymn. That is a good connection, for Psalm 104 is a hymn of praise for God's works in creation, one possibly sung during the annual springtime renewal.

The cut of the psalm designated for the lectionary reading includes three thought-blocks, each of which suggests a sermonic direction:

1. Verses 24-26 are an expression of amazement at the variety of species God has made, including even the creatures mysterious or frightening to the Hebrew mind. Leviathan, possibly the whale or a large breed of shark, might frighten humans, but the psalmist is able to conceive of this sea creature as something God made to "sport" (NRSV) or "frolic" (NIV) in the sea. An alternate reading, however, has it as "Leviathan whom you made to amuse you" (Jerusalem Bible) or "whom those hast made thy plaything" (NEB). Either interpretation — but especially the latter — provides grounds upon which to discuss God's lordship over the creation, and the idea that God created the world as much for God's own enjoyment as for ours. This can lead to a discussion of our stewardship of the planet.

2. Verses 27-30 acknowledge the absolute dependence of all creatures on God for food and even for breath itself (see Genesis 2:7). Here is an opportunity to discuss providence and God's ongoing care of the created ones (including us). Animals perhaps accept that better than we do — for it has been pointed out that no bird, freezing to death on a winter branch, has even one moment of self-pity or of feeling sorry for itself.

3. Verses 31-35 are a series of wishes and vows: appropriate doxological phrases to end this hymn of praise. The lectionary, however, conspicuously skips 35a, "Let sinners be consumed...." While we can understand the inclination to delete these words because of their jarring incongruity with all that has gone before them in this beautiful psalm, to do so misses some thought of the psalmist

— who apparently, even while praising God's work in nature, sees the fly in the ointment: sin. The lectionary's skipping of 35a is perhaps typical of our desire to sweep under the rug all that does not fit our ideal image of life. Thus, there could be a sermon on the marring effect of sin in our lives, and the need for God's gracious renewal, like God gives the earth at springtime.

— S. P.

The Holy Trinity

Psalm 8

(See also The Holy Trinity, Cycle C, for an alternative approach.)

Psalm 8 is an exuberant hymn of praise to God the Creator. It is, in fact, the only psalm written exclusively in the second person: its prayerful message is directed to the Lord from beginning to end.

There are some confusing textual problems in verses 1 and 2, which have led to a variety of interpretations. Who are the "babes and infants," out of whose mouths something significant flows: either praise, as some translations render it, or — rather strangely, as others have it — "a bulwark"? The Hebrew is, unfortunately, obscure, so there may never be a satisfying answer to this conundrum.

Recent advances in computer-enhanced satellite technology have spawned some amazing websites, through which it is possible to view highly detailed photos of the earth taken from space. On some of these sites, it is possible to start with a map of an entire continent, then to zoom in, by successive mouse clicks, to a view of one's own neighborhood. That is the sort of perspective envisioned by the psalmist, millennia before either satellites or computers had even been conceived in the human mind. From the perspective of the vast expanses of heaven, "What are human beings that you are mindful of them, mortals that you care for them?" (v. 4).

There is a spirit of humility woven deeply into the stanzas of this elegantly crafted poem. Viewed from a God's-eye perspective, the crises and troubles of this human life of ours — not to mention its joys — pale into insignificance. Under the shimmering stars, we see ourselves as we really are.

Yet, wondrously, we humans have been made "a little lower than God." We are "crowned with glory and honor" (v. 5). There is order to this God-created cosmos. Certain parts of the creation are subservient to other parts, and everything is subservient to the Creator. Just below God in the cosmic hierarchy are human beings, acting as God's plenipotentiaries. God has given humanity "dominion" over the other creatures. This whole concept of dominion — which harkens back to Genesis 1:26 — is fraught with difficulty, from the standpoint of modern ecological ideals. Indeed, the whole notion of ecology — which presupposes an interdependent, global system of which human beings are a part, rather than standing over and against it as managers — is foreign to passages like this one. Human dominion over creation, in the modern sense, means something very different than what it meant to the Hebrew mind.

Perhaps this could be a bridge, on this Trinity Sunday, to a doctrinal discussion of the Trinity. Some of the richest theological understandings of the Trinity have portrayed it as an interdependent system. Father, Son, and Holy Spirit are interrelated, and the positive force that binds each person of the Trinity to the others is love. Psalm 8 is overflowing with a joyous love that binds Creator and creation together.

— C. W.

Proper 4/Pentecost 2/Ordinary Time 9

Psalm 46

Categorized as both a "song of Zion" and "a psalm of confidence," Psalm 46 celebrates God's choice to be present in the midst of the people — specifically, in Jerusalem, "the city of God, the holy habitation of the Most High" (v. 4). It is not the city itself that breeds confidence, however. The city is secure only because God, the Lord of hosts, makes it so (v. 7). This theme sounds again in Martin Luther's great hymn, "A Mighty Fortress Is Our God," which is written from Psalm 46.

Here are some sermon possibilities:

1. The psalm expresses confidence especially in the presence of two fearsome things: the threatening seas (vv. 2 and 3) and the threatening nations (vv. 6 and 9). In the worldview of that time, the seas were especially terrifying. The earth, in the ancient Hebrew understanding, rested on mountains rooted deep in the oceans. If those mountains shook, the seas rose. (In Revelation 21:1, one of the blessings of the new age is that the "sea is no more.") But though the seas "roar and foam," the city of God "shall not be moved" (v. 5), for God is with her. Likewise, amidst the raging of the nations, God is the refuge of faithful people. What are the things we fear most? Cancer? Terrorism? Meaninglessness? Financial loss? How is God our refuge against those things?

2. For all its singing about Zion, note that the psalm never says the city is the people's refuge. Only God is. Jerusalem is a temporal expression of Zion, but the real City of God is wherever God chooses to dwell. In the Hebrew understanding, God chose for a time to dwell in Jerusalem and its temple, but some may have forgotten that the Lord's presence was focused in a moveable Ark. In the New Testament, that presence came into focus in Jesus Christ. A sermon could be written on the tendency to confuse the symbol with the reality to which it points. The events of September 11, 2001, reminded us of the frailty of physical locations as the source of confidence and security.

—S. P.

Proper 5/Pentecost 3/Ordinary Time 10

Psalm 33:1-12

Psalm 33 praises the God in whom the righteous trust. It was perhaps sung on the occasion of some national deliverance. Verses 1-3 are a call to praise and verses 4-5 provide the basis for the praise. The rest of the psalm details reasons for praising God and expresses confidence and trust in God.

The psalm contains the same number of poetic lines as there are letters in the Hebrew alphabet (22) probably signifying comprehensiveness of praise.

In preaching from this psalm, individual verses could be selected:

1. Verse 1 asserts that praise befits the upright. "Befits" is an acceptable word, but the KJV version of this verse could also be referenced: "Praise is comely for the upright." Though "comely" covers the meaning of "befits," it adds the sense of "beauty" and "attractiveness" that surely are qualities of praise. Is it not true that there is something beautiful about the personality that points away from itself to praise another? And by the way, praise is comely not only for the upright, but also for the reprobate and scoundrel, especially when it is part of an expression of repentance.

2. Verse 3 touts the value of singing a new song to God. Newness is not a virtue in and of itself, but old testimonies, repeated over and over, often lose their effectiveness as a witness to the goodness of God. Updated songs grow naturally out of thriving religious experiences.

3. Verses 7 and 9 both celebrate God as Creator. One of the first creative acts was bringing organization to the primeval sea, forcing it into boundaries (Genesis 1:6-7). Verse 9 says that God spoke the world into creation. Again and

again, Genesis 1 describes creation happening because "God said." This verse connects also with John 1:1. What new things do we need to allow God to say in our lives, to recreate us?

— S. P.

Proper 6/Pentecost 4/Ordinary Time 11

Psalm 116:1-2, 12-19
(See Maundy Thursday, Cycle A, and Maundy Thursday, Cycle B.)

Proper 7/Pentecost 5/Ordinary Time 12

Psalm 86:1-10, 16-17

Some psalms display a clear context, a human situation that has led to the writing of the hymn. Such is the case with Psalm 86. While we cannot discern the context in every detail, it is clear that this psalm arises from the lips of a person who is surrounded by fearsome enemies. These enemies are "insolent"; they rise up against the psalmist, threatening to take his life (v. 14). For his own part, he is "poor and needy," and has nowhere else to turn for protection but to the Lord (v. 1). While the superscription identifies David as the author of this psalm, this poverty and need could be seen as belonging to David's younger days. Or, perhaps it refers to a sense of spiritual poverty.

There is a real sense of confidence, here, that the psalmist's cry for help will not be in vain. While there is a certain tone of urgency, even desperation, there is never any doubt that the worshiper's cry will be heard and heeded. More than simply begging for a timely rescue, the author asks for more: he asks for a sign, so his enemies may be confounded (v. 17). "Show me a sign" is a common-enough prayer. So often we speak our prayers into the silence, and we wonder whether anything will come back to us. Some concrete sign of God's favor would powerfully encourage us. We, too, yearn for such a sign.

What is the purpose of a prayer of supplication? Is it to get something done? Or is it somehow to voice the deepest desires of our hearts, as we enter into personal dialogue with our Maker, seeking spiritual communion? Addressing this conundrum, Kathleen Norris observes, in *Amazing Grace: A Vocabulary of Faith* (Riverhead, 1998, pp. 60-61):

> Sometimes people will say things like, "Your prayers didn't work, but thanks," as if a person could be praying for only one thing. A miracle. A cure. But in the hardest situations, all one can do is to ask for God's mercy: "Let my friend die at home ... Let her go quickly, God, and with her loved ones present." ... I have learned that prayer is not asking for what you think you want but asking to be changed in ways you can't imagine. To be made more grateful, more able to see the good in what you have been given instead of always grieving for what might have been. People who are in the habit of praying — and they include the mystics of the Christian tradition — know that when a prayer is answered, it is never in a way that you expect.

— C. W.

Proper 8/Pentecost 6/Ordinary Time 13

Psalm 13

This psalm is an individual lament with which almost every Christian can identify, for almost all of us have known times when God seems far, and may perhaps even be "hidden" from us (v. 1). How many of us have begged God for a reply and heard none? Psalm 13 provides a text for talking about the silences of God.

Many will remember the day, back in 1999, when the beepers went silent. When a communications satellite died, the signals for about ninety percent of the United States' pagers suddenly went nowhere. Some of us feel like that sometimes, when we pray. As one unnamed writer put it, "Even after Christ's coming, God has painfully kept his distance that we are like spouses married to one who is frequently away on business." And W. H. Auden said, "Our dominant experience of today is of God's absence, of his distance."

We don't know why God sometimes keeps silent when we most desire to hear a divine word. Maybe the Lord's refusal to give us all the answers we want is an indication that God wants to relate to us not as a giver of answers but as a giver of strength. Perhaps God is silent to force us to learn hard lessons of life. We simply don't know.

But we do know that God is not always silent, and that when the Lord does speak to us — and most of us can recall at least one time when we were conscious of guidance or a calling outside of ourselves — it is an experience that is life-changing and unforgettable.

— S. P.

Proper 9/Pentecost 7/Ordinary Time 14

Psalm 45:10-17
(See Proper 17/Pentecost 15/Ordinary Time 22, Cycle B, for an alternative approach, emphasizing vv. 1-2 and 6-9.)

Perhaps some worshipers will remember the pomp and circumstance connected with the wedding of Charles, Prince of Wales, to Lady Diana Spencer on July 29, 1981. This event, televised around the world, attracted vast numbers of viewers. Golden vestments, an elegant, one-of-a-kind, designer wedding dress, swords and sashes, multiple choirs, the rumbling organ of Westminster Abbey — their wedding had it all. There were even choir anthems composed especially for the occasion.

Psalm 45 displays the superscript, "Ode To a Royal Wedding." It is an ancient version of the anthems composed for this singular sort of occasion — and, from its colorful description, it appears that ancient Israel's royal wedding festivities were every bit as elaborate as a royal wedding today. Verses 1-9 — not part of the lectionary reading — provide some of that colorful detail. This king is handsome and full of grace. His elegant sword and sharp arrows are a sign of his eagerness to fight for justice. His throne and his scepter, his rich garments fragrant with the aroma of anointing-oil, the soaring melodies of stringed instruments — these details bear witness to the joy and gravity of this solemn occasion.

Beside the king stands his queen, attired in garments of equal majesty. The portion of this psalm that is today's lectionary reading is addressed to her. Its goal is to encourage her to bow down and honor the king, showering him with praises and offering herself as the vessel by which he will have many sons. (Feminists will find no comfort here.)

The one who speaks is a royal scribe. Evidently more than a mere recorder of legal documents, this man is a court poet. This is a rare psalm, in that the identity of the author shows briefly through the veil that separates him from the subject-matter. We can sense the scribe's awe and excitement, as he finds himself close enough to the wedding pageantry to witness this notable event.

Where is the sermon in this passage? To those who live in secular democracies, it would appear that this psalm belongs to the "state" side of the famous church-and-state divide. Yet in ancient Israel, there was no such division. Israel was a theocracy, and the king was viewed as God's chief agent on earth. The celebration of a royal wedding was overflowing with theological as well as civic significance.

It would be fruitful to contrast the extravagantly positive language of this psalm with the reality of kingly rule. Even David — whom all regard as representing at the pinnacle of Israel's monarchy — acted cruelly at times and fell into very public sin. The advice of Psalm 118:9 is wise, reflecting a more realistic assessment: "It is better to take refuge in the Lord than to put confidence in princes."

There is something in us that urges us to seek salvation from rulers of government — but there is no ultimate salvation to be found there. Psalm 45 is a cautionary tale, for no human king could ever fulfill the hopes and dreams it expresses. Only a future king of Israel will be able to do that: and this king will wear a crown not of gold, but of thorns.

— C. W.

Song Of Solomon 2:8-13

Today the lectionary identifies a second, alternative psalm selection besides the Psalm 45:10-17 royal-wedding passage. Both have evidently been chosen to illuminate the First Lesson, which tells of the courtship and marriage of Isaac and Rebekah.

Due to our tradition's historic discomfort with matters of sexuality, the Song Of Solomon is one of the most neglected of biblical books. Today the lectionary offers a rare opportunity to preach on this beautiful but little-known love-poem.

The attribution of authorship by Solomon is undoubtedly spurious. Much of the wisdom literature of the Old Testament has been attributed to Solomon at one time or another, with little basis in fact. This is because Solomon is himself the prototypical biblical image of a wise king. At a certain time in Israel's history, to identify Solomon as the author of a text was a shorthand way of saying it was wisdom literature.

With the Song Of Solomon, however — unlike Proverbs and other wisdom books — the Solomonic attribution has stuck. That is surely because, once the Solomonic attribution is removed, the question remains of who did write it — which begs the further question of what sacred use is this lyrical love-poem, which glorifies the spiritual and physical attraction between men and women.

To generations of Christians, the Song Of Solomon has been a kind of embarrassment. It is one of only two books in the Bible that never mention God (the other one is Esther). Yet the real cause for embarrassment is the Song of Song's subject matter.

There is a story from the high school I attended that illustrates this. A few readers may remember the days of daily Bible reading in public schools. I don't, personally — I'm too young — but I do remember a story one of my teachers told me.

It was school tradition, in those days, to have a different student read each week from the Bible as part of the opening exercises. The chosen student was given free rein to pick any passage at all. Few students paid much attention to that disembodied voice, crackling out of the public address system.

It was already Wednesday or Thursday of that particular week, before some students began to sit up at their homeroom desks and take notice of the words they were hearing, in the venerable King James Version:

> *How beautiful are thy feet with shoes, O prince's daughter! The joints of thy thighs are like jewels ... Thy navel is like a round goblet, which wanteth not liquor; thy belly is like a heap of wheat set about with lilies. Thy two breasts are like two young roes that are twins. Thy neck is as a tower of ivory...*

The effect of those words, I'm told, on a schoolful of adolescents first thing in the morning, was — shall we say — *memorable*. Let's just say the reading did little to encourage concentration in geometry class.

There's more to the story. By order of the principal, the student reader was instantly sacked — despite his fervent protests that all he'd been doing was reading from the Bible. From that day forward, until the Supreme Court banned school Bible reading altogether, students at the Toms River High School of Toms River, New Jersey, read from assigned passages. Dangerous stuff, those Bible verses!

During the Middle Ages, biblical scholars went to elaborate lengths to interpret the Song Of Solomon as entirely symbolic. Some taught that it was really about the soul's relationship with God. Others claimed it was about God's love for the Virgin Mary. If, say these medieval scholars, we think we hear echoes in this poem of lovers sighing to each other in a moonlit glade, we ought to think again. When we hear the woman's voice crooning, "Let him kiss me with the kisses of his mouth! For your love is better than wine ..." all this is a kind of secret code for an earnest and devout — and thoroughly respectable — piety.

Such explanations are highly doubtful. What possible reason could the anonymous author have for hiding religious sentiment behind steamy love-poetry?

We need to take the Song Of Solomon at face value. This collection of poetry joyfully celebrates committed love — on every level, including the physical — as a wonderful and perfect gift of God. Such is a message we would all do well to rediscover, in this era when our society is veering erratically between the extremes of utter repression on the one hand and pornography on the other. There is a middle ground, and the Song Of Solomon can lead us there.

— C. W.

Proper 10/Pentecost 8/Ordinary Time 15

Psalm 119:105-112

Psalm 119 is a rich treasure trove of wisdom. The longest of the psalms, it follows an acrostic design, with 22 sections each beginning with a different letter of the Hebrew alphabet. This particular section is filled with various wisdom sayings, of which verse 105 is by far the most familiar: "Your word is a lamp to my feet and a light to my path."

That verse offers a familiar, yet important, theme for preaching: an opportunity to teach about the authority of scripture. What can we say about scripture, based on this verse? Several things:

1. Scripture provides *illumination* for our lives. Seduced by our society's technological might, we have come to believe that we provide our own illumination. This was not true for the ancients, who knew better. Marcus Borg has written:

    > *The symbolism of light and darkness is ancient, archetypal and cross-cultural. It has many rich resonances*

> *of meaning. Darkness is associated with blindness, night, sleep, cold, gloom, despair, lostness, chaos, death, danger and yearning for the dawn. It is a striking image of the human condition. Light is seen as the antidote to the above, and is thus an image of salvation. In the light, one is awake, able to see and find one's way; it is associated with relief and rejoicing that the night is over; in the light one is safe and warm. In the light there is life.* (From "The Meaning of Jesus: Two Visions," by Marcus J. Borg and N. T. Wright, in the *Christian Century*, December 16, 1998, pp. 1218-1221.)

2. The illumination that scripture provides is *indirect lighting*. Many of us have indirect lighting in our homes. It provides beauty as well as functionality. The lamp mentioned in the psalm shines downward, at the portion of the path immediately ahead. It does not project a spotlight's brilliant glare far down the road, as do many modern electric lights. The "lamp to my feet" is more modest than that. Scripture is more like a simple flashlight than a set of automobile high beams. Yet at the slow pace of foot travel, it is really all a traveler needs. In the words of Jewish biblical scholar Abraham Joseph Heschel in *Between God and Man*:

    > *The surest way of misunderstanding revelation is take it literally, to imagine that God spoke to the prophet on a long-distance telephone. The truth is that things and words stand for different meanings in different situations. Gold means wealth to the merchant, a means of adornment to the jeweler, and kindness to the rhetorician (a golden heart). Light is a form of energy to the physicist, a medium of loveliness to the artist, and an expression of grandeur in the first chapter of the Bible. Ruah, the Hebrew word for spirit, signifies also breath, wind, and direction. And he who thinks only of breath, forfeits the deeper meaning of the word....*

3. Scripture is meant to be a *constant companion*, a light we carry with us. In technically advanced societies such as our own, we have long since ceased to be familiar with true darkness. Our cities and towns are awash with light. Starlight is all but unknown. For biblical people, much of life after sundown was lived in darkness. The light a lamp provided was modest and limited. If you ventured out, most nights, a lamp was no luxury; it was a necessity. It could be the one thing that kept wild animals at bay, and that kept you from getting lost. Referring to the study of scripture, Harry Emerson Fosdick said, "Read until you stumble upon yourself on its pages." The light of scripture does so much more than illumine the road ahead. It illumines our lives as well.

— C. W.

Proper 11/Pentecost 9/Ordinary Time 16

Psalm 139:1-12, 23-24
(See Epiphany 2/Ordinary Time 2, Cycle B, and Proper 4/Pentecost 2/Ordinary Time 9, Cycle B, for alternative approaches to vv. 1-6 and 13-18.)

Psalm 139 begins with a strong statement that God knows us as we really are and concludes with a sincere prayer that God will further search our hearts and reveal to us our sinfulness. If that's not enough to throw a chill into us, then what is? Affirming both God's omniscience and omnipresence, this psalm reminds us that whether we are in the womb (v. 13) or the tomb (v. 8) or anywhere in between (v. 2), whether we be in this world (v. 2) or in another realm altogether (v. 8), God is there. Even darkness does not keep the Lord from seeing us (v. 12).

Yet the purpose of this psalm/prayer is surely not to frighten, but to help us pray those final lines: "See if there is any wicked way in me."

Do we believe it when we are shown a wicked way? How do we feel, singing hymns like: "Alas! And did my Savior bleed, and did my Sovereign die? Would he devote that sacred head for such a worm as I?"

On many days, we might object to being called a worm, but sometimes, when we have done something we consider downright selfish or wrong, our sense of ourselves as good people collapses and the word "worm" doesn't sound all that far-fetched. But even when we have not committed conspicuous wrong, our "goodness" pales next to God's holiness.

Then it is important not to forget to pray the very last line of the psalm: "Lead me into the way everlasting." The psalm reminds us that we can be forgiven, redeemed, and made whole.

— S. P.

Proper 12/Pentecost 10/Ordinary Time 17

Psalm 105:1-11, 45b

(See Proper 14/Pentecost 12/Ordinary Time 19, Cycle A, for an alternative approach to vv. 1-6, 16-22, 45b; and see Proper 20/Pentecost 18/Ordinary Time 25, Cycle A, for an alternative approach to vv. 1-6, 37-45.)

The portion of this psalm selected by the lectionary committee is in support of today's Old Testament Reading about the ongoing events in Jacob's life, the one who became the carrier of the covenant in his generation. Verses 1-8 and the verse 45b tag are all general expressions of praise about God, but verses 9-11 expressly praise God's "sworn promise" to Abraham, Isaac, and Jacob — and, from God, to all of Israel.

This psalm provides an opportunity to talk not only about God's promises to us, but also ours to the Lord and to each other. Promises, contracts, and pacts are necessary to make society work. Marriage vows, oaths of office, pledges of support, codes of ethics, parenting promises, product warranties — these things and many similar assurances are crucial fibers of communal life. Promises are also essential in the life of faith. Baptismal vows, ordination declarations, stewardship pledges, church covenants, our word as our bond — all these and more take their life from the promises God has made to the people.

In the movie and play, *A Man for All Seasons*, Thomas More, Lord Chancellor of England under King Henry VIII, fell out of favor with Henry when he refused to support Henry's divorce from Catherine of Aragon. The king dealt with More's resistance by having More beheaded. At one point during his final days, More could have saved his life by renouncing an oath he had made. His daughter, Meg, begged him to do so. But More refused, saying, "When a man takes an oath, Meg, he is holding his own self in his hand, like water. And if he opens his fingers, then he needn't hope to find himself again."

— S. P.

Psalm 128

This Psalm is difficult to preach in our modern culture, because of the central section (vv. 3-4) which addresses devout men exclusively, and which celebrates the gifts of a fertile wife and many children as a blessing from God. That portion of this psalm may preach in Amish country, but in any other part of the twenty-first-century Christian church, its message seems quaint at best and archaic at worst. In a world threatened by overpopulation, there are major ethical questions connected with the image of a large crop of children springing up "like olive shoots around your table."

There are two other portions of this brief psalm, however, that do offer preaching possibilities:

1. "Happy is everyone who fears the Lord" (v. 1). Fear of the Lord is likewise a hard sell in our self-centered, God-is-my-copilot religious culture, but one can at least address the experience of fear in a pastoral way. What is it that our people most fear? Would it not be better to seek to fear the Lord, rather than lesser things?

2. "You shall eat the fruit of the labor of your hands" (v. 2). Perhaps this text could be paired with the prophetic challenge of Isaiah 55:2: "Why do you spend your money for that which is not bread, and your labor for that which does not satisfy?" There was a time when a great many Christians could readily see the labor of their hands. In that simpler era, most people either worked the land, or worked in small cottage industries. Even assembly-line industries had some kind of visible output — however far that output may have been from an individual worker's position on the production line. In our present economy — dominated by service and information industries, and characterized by frequent employment disruptions and job changes — it is hard for many of our people to gain the satisfaction of knowing their work has accomplished something. It is truly a blessing to see the labor of our hands, to know we are exercising our God-given talents to make the world a better place. As one of the characters in Gail Godwin's novel, *Evensong*, says: "Your vocation is something that keeps making more of you." Frederick Buechner describes Christian vocation as "the place where your deep gladness and the world's deep hunger meet" (*Wishful Thinking: A Theological ABC* [New York: Harper & Row, 1973], p. 95). May more and more of our people come to discover that blessed place of meeting!

— C. W.

Proper 13/Pentecost 11/Ordinary Time 18

Psalm 17:1-7, 15

This psalm belongs in the category of "personal lament," which means it probably was not used for corporate worship, but by an individual pray-er. From the tone, the person is clearly in some unspecified distress, probably from persecutors of some sort. Protesting his innocence and his faithfulness to God, the psalmist asks for divine relief, and concludes with an expression of confidence that God will come to his aid (v. 18: "I shall awake satisfied").

Psalm 17 could easily be the prayer of a penitentiary inmate imprisoned for a crime he or she did not commit, a circumstance that unfortunately is not that rare in the penal system. With the number of DNA exonerations, revelations of lab errors, and manufactured evidence cases in the news these days, it would not be unreasonable to use this psalm as the basis of sermon leading to prayer for those wrongly accused. A summary of the 1999 Denzel Washington movie, *The Hurricane*, which tells the story of boxer Rubin "Hurricane" Carter's imprisonment for a triple murder he did not commit, would make a good opening hook for the sermon.

Then there is the case of Gerald Amirault, sixteen years in the Massachusetts penal system (at the time of this writing, in 2002). Accused of child abuse in a case that for most people has been convincingly debunked (including the editors of *The Wall Street Journal* who have advocated his immediate release), Amirault has been denied a parole hearing because he has refused participation in a treatment program for sex offenders. He says it is because the crime did not happen; the Massachusetts Department of Corrections maintains he is "in denial." If indeed he is innocent, as he says, then why should he "confess" to the crime to get a hearing? This psalm could be his prayer.

Talking about wrongly accused inmates may seem too far removed from many congregations, but there is always the possibility of using this psalm to talk about our individual sense of sinfulness. When is it appropriate and when is it a hypersensitive conscience that accuses, when even God does not?

— S. P.

Editor's Note: Gerald Amirault was released April 30, 2004.

Proper 14/Pentecost 12/Ordinary Time 19

Psalm 105:1-6, 16-22, 45b
(See Proper 12/Pentecost 10/Ordinary Time 17, Cycle A, for an alternative approach to 105:1-11, 45b; and see Proper 20/Pentecost 18/Ordinary Time 25, Cycle A, for an alternative approach to vv. 1-6, 37-45.)

These selections from the lengthy Psalm 105 are paired, this week, with the Genesis story of the betrayal of Joseph by his brothers. The Psalm provides a note of hope following the narration of that grim episode: for verses 16-22 remind us how the Lord "sent a man ahead of them" in a time of famine: "Joseph, who was sold as a slave" (v. 17). "His feet were hurt with fetters, his neck was put in a collar of iron" (v. 18) — until such time as Pharaoh released him, and set him up as lord over his entire house.

This psalm is not just about the sufferings of Joseph. Its author — or, at least, the editor of the book of Psalms, in the event that the original version of this psalm was written earlier — undoubtedly has in mind the sufferings of his own exiled people at the hands of the Babylonians. Memories of fetters on the feet and a collar around the neck would still have been painful. Hope that sustains people in exile can only happen through the providence of God, the one who sends the champion, Joseph, out ahead of the people.

The *Heidelberg Catechism* — one of the great Reformation-era confessions of faith — defines providence in this way. It is "the almighty and ever-present power of God whereby he still upholds, as it were by his own hand, heaven and earth together with all creatures, and rules in such a way that leaves and grass, rain and drought, fruitful and unfruitful years, food and drink, health and sickness, riches and poverty, and everything else, come to us not by chance but by his fatherly hand."

"What advantage," the *Catechism* then asks, "comes from acknowledging God's creation and providence?"

"We learn that we are to be patient in adversity, grateful in the midst of blessing, and to trust our faithful God and Father for the future, assured that no creature shall separate us from his love, since all creatures are so completely in his hand that without his will they cannot even move." (Questions 27 and 28.)

The opposite of providence is chance. That is the prevailing secular view, and there is little comfort in it. The secular view is that our lives are aimlessly adrift in a vast and turbulent sea of chance. The psalmist's view of the world — like that of the authors of the *Heidelberg Catechism* — is very different. God cares about us, the people of the covenant: watching over us, protecting us. God may not always give us everything we want, but God will get us through.

Many of our listeners will be familiar with the saga of Antarctic explorer, Ernest Shackleton, who led the crew of his ice-trapped ship, the *Endurance*, on a perilous journey to safety, by open boat and on foot across barren ice and snow. The final part of that journey was accomplished by a hiking party composed of Shackleton and the two strongest of his men, who made it back to civilization and summoned help to rescue the others. Reflecting on his survival experience, Shackleton later recalled:

> *When I look back on those days, I have no doubt that Providence guided us, not only across those snowfields, but across the storm-white sea that separated Elephant Island from our landing place in South Georgia. I know that during that long and racking march of thirty-six hours over the unnamed mountains and glaciers of South Georgia, it seemed to me often that we were four, not three. I said nothing to my companions on the point, but afterwards Worsely said to me: "Boss, I had the curious feeling on the march that there was another person with us."*

Maybe it's only in the crises of life, as unexpected trials come our way, that we sense another presence there beside us — one who is providentially guiding us. Psalms like this one remind us of the cyclical nature of the human life of faith. No generation has a monopoly on sinfulness, or suffering. Neither does any generation have a monopoly on God's goodness and grace. Time and again, God's people engage in the same dance steps — first away from the Lord in disobedience, then back again, as divine *hesed* pulls us closer.

— C. W.

Proper 15/Pentecost 13/Ordinary Time 20

Psalm 133

This little gem of a psalm celebrates the joy of unity among comrades in the faith. While unity is a theme anyone can appreciate, the cultural setting of the psalm sounds strange to modern ears. A good bit of cross-cultural translation is needed to enable modern listeners to enter into the experience.

The chief homiletical obstacle is the presence of fragrant anointing-oil — and lots of it. Apart from olive oil's culinary uses in salad dressings or to grease a frying pan, most of our people have scant familiarity with the many ways oil was used in ancient times, including anointing the human body. The psalm vividly portrays the greasy, pungent stream being poured profusely upon Aaron's head and over his ears, coursing down his beard to form a puddle near the collar of the robe. The sheer abundance of valuable oil demonstrates that this, truly, is an occasion of deep gladness. Money is no object. (Aaron, of course, is the prototypical priest of ancient Israel; the psalmist, here, is perhaps thinking of the anointing of a priest as Aaron's liturgical successor — see Exodus 29:7.) The oil functions, here, as a symbol of celebration — although, to most of our listeners, the whole scene sounds more like a laundry nightmare.

In ancient times, the anointing of a guest with oil was a cherished act of hospitality. We read of this practice in Psalm 23:5. Anointing with "the oil of gladness" is also mentioned in Psalm 45:7; Isaiah 61:3; and Hebrews 1:9. Because the man referred to as "Aaron" is anointed with such a profusion of oil, it is clear that there is an excess of joy in this place.

One of the most difficult circumstances some families experience is a public worship service at which not everyone is at peace with one another. Weddings and funerals, for example — milestone occasions that ought to be characterized by peace, beauty, and solemnity — can be marred by conflict, if two or more family members are feuding or estranged. How good and pleasant it is when family members can sit side-by-side in unity!

There are few more important tasks for Christians than seeking to become agents of reconciliation. C. S. Lewis, in *Mere Christianity*, wisely observes that this unity is not found in positive emotions, but rather in hard work:

> *Do not waste your time bothering whether you 'love' your neighbor — act as if you did. As soon as we do this, we find one of the great secrets. When you are behaving as if you loved someone, you will presently come to love him. If you injure someone you dislike, you will find yourself disliking him more. If you do him a good turn, you will find yourself disliking him less.*

If the church as a whole could manage to accomplish this hard work of reconciliation more often, this would — as *Christian Century* editor John Buchanan suggests — make a world of difference in our evangelism efforts:

> *Wouldn't it be something if we could show the world the transforming power of a gospel that turns ideological opponents into brothers and sisters who love one another, who can't stop enjoying ... praying ... caring for ... protecting one another? If we did that, the world might even find us interesting again.*

— C. W.

Proper 16/Pentecost 14/Ordinary Time 21

Psalm 124
(See Proper 21/Pentecost 19/Ordinary Time 26, Cycle B, for an alternative approach.)

"Kids," as old-time television host, Art Linkletter, used to observe, "say the darndest things." That's what one mother found out, when her son turned to her one morning at the breakfast table and asked, "Mom, is it true that God's not only up in heaven, but also here with us on earth?"

"Why, yes," replied his mom.

"Then, is it also true that God is right here in this town?"

"It certainly is," replied Mom (beginning to get his drift).

"Then, is God even right here in our house — I mean — right here in this very room?"

"Why, of course; God is right here in this room!"

"Mom, is God even here at this table, while we're having breakfast — is God in this food?"

"Of course," said Mom — beginning to get a little nervous about where this was leading.

"Mom — is God right here in this empty glass in front of me?"

"Yes," said Mom, cautiously, "God is right there in that glass!"

Quick as a flash, the boy placed his hand over the top of the glass. "Gotcha!" he exclaimed.

There are times in life when we wish we could capture God like that: to be sure, God is at our beck and call, under our command, like a genie in a bottle. There are times we wish we could be sure God is on our side.

The times when most of us wish most intently we could be certain of God's favor is the hour of greatest need: when we are suffering, when tragedy intrudes, when life tumbles in. In such an hour of need, we may find ourselves asking, "Whose side is God on?"

The author of Psalm 124 is asking that very same question. The heading of the psalm says it was written by David — and that would certainly make sense, since it clearly belongs to a time of war. Yet the attempt to place God on the side of any human enterprise is always a risky business.

This psalm displays a three-part logical structure: first there is remembrance of historical deliverance (vv. 1-5), then praise for deliverance in the recent past (vv. 6-7), and finally a liturgical declaration of trust (v. 8). This logical movement is one that can be replicated in our own experiences of trouble or difficulty. Truly it helps, in such times, to remember that God has been faithful in the past: both in the collective memory of our people, and in our own personal experiences of deliverance. The Lord whom we recall in such a way surely can be trusted to be faithful again, even though the signs of that faithful response may be invisible at the moment.

God is on our side — not because we are worthy, but because God is worthy.

— C. W.

Proper 17/Pentecost 15/Ordinary Time 22

Psalm 105:1-6, 23-26, 45c

This is a psalm of salvation-history. It relates, in narrative fashion, the principal high points of the Lord's covenant relationship with Israel. We have recently seen a slightly different cut of this psalm for Proper 14/Pentecost 12/Ordinary Time 19. The selection appointed for that day made special reference to the perseverance of Joseph, through his descent into slavery and his eventual rise to power in Egypt. Now, the inclusion of verses 23-26 focuses our attention on God's selection of Moses to lead the now-enslaved Israelites to freedom.

Verse 25 presents certain theological difficulties. The Lord turns the hearts of the Egyptians to hate the Israelite slaves. God is portrayed, here, as the master puppeteer of human history. It is hard to envision a place for human free will, when God is managing human actions so thoroughly.

Yet for Israel, envisioning such an all-powerful, interventionist God is not cause for existential despair. Rather, it is a tremendous source of hope. The Psalms — which were edited into their final edition around the time of the Babylonian exile — are calculated to speak to a people who are feeling both powerless and hopeless. If the Lord is managing even their sufferings for the sake of Israel's salvation, then the violence and struggles that have hitherto seemed terrifyingly random are now laden with meaning.

Pastorally speaking, does this line of reasoning work in the modern era? Does it comfort our parishioners suffering with chronic illness, unemployment, or family turmoil to believe that God is in control even of these painful events? It is a difficult line of reasoning to present.

One who tries to do precisely that is the Roman Catholic spiritual writer, Ron Rolheiser. In an internet column, he shares the story of a woman who found herself sitting in the back of a church one day, with a cast on her lower leg. She had been visiting her sister, who lived near a major ski resort. On Sunday, her sister invited her to go to church with her. The woman went skiing instead, and broke her leg on the slopes. On the following Sunday, when her sister asked her once again to go to church with her, she agreed. She had nowhere else to go, really.

As it so happened, the designated readings for the day were about Jesus, the Good Shepherd. It also happened that the regular priest was away, with the homily being delivered by a visiting priest from Israel. The priest could not possibly have seen this woman, nor could he have known she was sitting there in the back pew with a cast on her leg. He began his homily by telling of an ancient practice among shepherds in Israel, one still in use today — a practice that sheds light on the meaning of the phrase, "Good Shepherd." Sometimes, early in the life of a lamb, a shepherd may sense that this one particular animal is going to be a congenital stray — that will always be drifting away from the flock, where it could be injured or die. In such cases, the shepherd deliberately breaks the leg of the lamb, so he has to carry the animal until its leg is healed. By that time, the lamb has become so attached to the shepherd that it never strays again.

"I may be dense," said the woman — after hearing this sermon — "but, given my broken leg and all these coincidences, hearing those words woke something up inside me. I have prayed and gone to church regularly ever since!"

"In the conspiracy of accidents that make up the ordinary events of our everyday lives," reflects Rolheiser, "the finger of God is writing and writing large. We are children of Israel, children of Jesus, and children of our mothers and fathers in the faith. We need therefore, like them, to look at each and every event in our lives and ask ourselves the question: 'What is God saying to us in this?' The language of God is the experience that God writes inside our lives."

—C.W.

Proper 18/Pentecost 16/Ordinary Time 23

Psalm 149
(See All Saints, Cycle C, for an alternative approach.)

In the scheme devised by the Revised Common Lectionary committee, the weekly psalm is viewed less as a reading in its own right and more as a meditation in support of the First Lesson. But to consider Psalm 149 a meditation on the Passover story is a troubling thought. If verses 6-8 of the psalm, and especially verse 7, are to be taken as a comment on the meaning of the death of Egypt's firstborns, then those deaths have to be defined as Divinely approved "vengeance" and "punishment." Furthermore, the psalm appears to be hymn in support of holy war, and in this day with *jihad* having been forced into the national vocabulary, using Psalm 149 too enthusiastically seems objectionable.

But preachers who do choose to go with the psalm this week can profit by looking at its second sentence: "Sing to the Lord a new song." This is not the only psalm that calls for a new song, but here the summons is especially appropriate. The new song in this psalm seems to be a hymn to holy war, but in our day, holy war is now an old song, and one that does not serve us very well any more, if it ever did. So a sermon could be built on the question, "What new song should we sing to God today?"

Back in the 1970s, Barry Manilow had a hit with a song called "I Write The Songs." The opening line was, "I write the songs that make the whole world sing." It was a happy melody. The singer expressed the joy he felt from giving others the words to sing, to express their songs.

For David, the "sweet psalmist of Israel" (2 Samuel 23:1 RSV — or see TEV, "the composer of beautiful songs for Israel") there must have been a similar pleasure. Sure, as a successful ruler, he was sometimes the object of Israel's praise, but his songs expressed joy at being able to point to God as the only one really worthy of praise. As David puts it in 2 Samuel 23:2, "The spirit of the Lord speaks through me, his word is upon my tongue." There must have been a delight that came from composing the psalms that helped the people of Israel praise their Maker.

What we need to do is to be reporters of God's deeds, songsters singing of God's glory.

— S. P.

Proper 19/Pentecost 17/Ordinary Time 24

Psalm 114

This psalm falls into four cantos. Verses 1-2 refer to Israel's foundation story and most importantly, to how God selected that nation as a dwelling place. Verses 3-4 explain that God's presence with Israel had an effect on the actual workings of nature. Verses 5-6 revel in the wonder of how the earth responded obediently to God's presence in Israel. Verses 7-8 are a summons for the rest of creation and the other nations to feel the power of God's presence as well.

Obviously, then, the presence of God is a dominant theme in this psalm, and that presence is of first importance. A certain father went to visit his son's preschool on a day when dads were invited. He was surprised that only a handful of fathers had come. Later, all the children and those fathers who had come were sitting on the floor in a circle, and the teacher asked the children to tell the group something about their fathers, something that was special. One little boy said, "My daddy is a lawyer. He makes a lot of money and we live in a big house." Another child said, "My father is very smart. He teaches at the college and a lot of important people know him." When it was time for this father's son to say something, the little boy looked up at his father, and then he just smiled and proudly said, "My dad ... my dad is here!"

So what does it mean that our Heavenly Father is here with us? For one thing, it means that we cannot sin in peace. We can sometimes do things wrong and get away with them as far as other people are concerned. But the reality of God's presence means that our attitudes and deeds are open knowledge to God. In those circumstances, there may be times when we would just as soon not have God present. But think about the times when we have benefited from someone else's knowledge of God's presence. Perhaps they have been angry with us, and have been inclined to do something hateful against us, but their knowledge that God was present would not let them sin in peace.

Of course, it also means that God is with us through trouble. In the scriptures, deep water is often a metaphor for serious trouble and extreme danger. So this psalm celebrates the "turning back" of the Red Sea and of the Jordan as evidence of God's presence with Israel.

I talked once to a young woman who survived a terrible car crash — a "deep water" experience. She was alone in her car when a large truck went out of control and careened toward her. I asked her what she did. She said that, in the split second when it was clear that she was going to be hit, she threw herself down on the front seat. And she added, "I think I screamed, 'Oh, my God.'"

"Oh, my God." What is that? A throwaway phrase? Mild profanity? I don't think so. In its barest form, it's a prayer. And what is there within us that causes such words to leap to our lips in moments of pure terror? For many, it is the conviction deep down that God really is present and is the only one who can confront the terror with us.

— S. P.

Exodus 15:1b-11, 20-21

This alternate psalm follows immediately after this morning's Old Testament Lesson, the story of the parting of the Red Sea. It contains two ancient hymns — known, respectively, as the Song of Moses and the Song of Miriam.

Of the two, the Song of Miriam is unquestionably the oldest. It is composed of just two lines — lines which have been incorporated into the opening of the longer Song of Moses: "Sing to the Lord, for he has triumphed gloriously; horse and rider he has thrown into the sea" (v. 21).

Both these songs may sound troubling to modern ears, because of their bloodthirsty exultation in the death of Israel's enemies. The Song of Moses positively gloats over the grim fate of the Egyptian army: "Pharaoh's chariots and his army he cast into the sea; his picked officers were sunk in the Red Sea. The floods covered them; they went down to the depths like a stone" (vv. 4-5).

This is neither a pretty nor a pleasant song. Perhaps these lines will call to mind the terrifying underwater images from the film, *Saving Private Ryan*. Those images of American GIs of the Normandy invasion force — struggling to shed heavy backpacks that are dragging them to the bottom of the ocean while machine-gun bullets silently zip by, trailing tiny bubbles in their wake — is an unforgettable image of the horror of war, and of its dreadful impact on individuals. Somewhere in ancient Egypt, many mothers wailed and keened at the deaths of their sons, drowned beneath that tsunami-like wave. Did the Lord not care about Egypt's sons as well?

Yet as troubling as these martial images are, these are songs born out of a life-or-death situation, a dilemma of desperation and fear — fear which was suddenly and fortuitously lifted, in a way no one expected.

Some commentators have considered these songs as symbolic of greater issues, larger conflicts. In the words of Martin Luther King, Jr., "Egypt symbolized evil in the form of humiliating oppression, ungodly exploitation, and crushing domination" (*Strength to Love* [Philadelphia: Fortress, 1981], p. 73). Expanding on King's point, T. E. Fretheim observes:

> *Against such an enemy, traditional weapons will not do (cf. Isa. 59:17; Eph. 6:10-20). God fights the chaos monster with "weapons" appropriate to the enemy, as in the plague cycle, from within the sphere of nature. God's activity in creation overturns that which is chaos. God's control over the waters (see Job 41) is shown in the divine use of those very forces to undo the anticreation monster. The justice of God's created order exacts an appropriate judgment on the anticreational oppressors.* (*Exodus*, in the *Interpretation* series [Louisville: John Knox Press, 1991], p. 169.)

Some in the Jewish tradition have long felt uncomfortable with the brutality of these songs. Consequently, a midrash has grown up that portrays the God of the Exodus in a more compassionate light.

Some angels are standing off to one side, watching the action as the Egyptians advance toward the water. As the last former slave sets foot on the far shore, a great cheer erupts from this spectators' gallery. The angels look on with eagerness, as the waters rise up and drown the Egyptians.

"We got them! We got them!" cry the angels. They're dancing around, clapping one another on the back.

But then there sounds another voice, the voice of God: "What do you think you're doing?" asks the Lord, angrily. "You are dismissed from my service."

The angels answer back, in their defense, "But all we did was celebrate the vanquishing of the Egyptians."

"Do you not know," responds the Lord, "that the Egyptians are my children, too?"

There are two central and powerful truths arising out of the Exodus story. The first is that, for the Israelite people, it is a transforming experience. The Israelites fled Egypt as slaves on the run, carrying only the belongings they could sling over their backs. They arrived on the other side of the sea as a people who had felt the transforming power of God, and who were now bonded together as a people of faith. As 1 Peter says — speaking of the Christian church, but harking back to their spiritual ancestors in

Israel: "Once you were not a people, but now you are God's people; once you had not received mercy, but now you have received mercy."

The second great truth is related to this. The Israelites are saved through no merit of their own. They do not bring about their salvation: God is the only true actor on this stage.

The message of Exodus is that there is no such thing as "dumb luck" — or luck of any kind, for that matter. The Lord rules, sovereign over all, and our very lives are always in God's hands.

— C. W.

Proper 20/Pentecost 18/Ordinary Time 25

Psalm 105:1-6, 37-45
(See Proper 12/Pentecost 10/Ordinary Time 17, Cycle A, for an alternative approach to vv. 1-11, 45b; and see Proper 14/Pentecost 12/Ordinary Time 19, Cycle A, for an alternative approach to vv. 1-6, 16-22, 45b.)

This is our fourth encounter with Psalm 105 in this cycle of the lectionary. The new material this time is verses 37-45, which speaks of God's care of Israel in bringing her out of Egypt, feeding her in the wilderness and helping her take possession of the promised land. There is an obvious link between these verses and the First Lesson for today, as well as an obvious connection to the idea of "providence" — the matter of who's in control of our world. Christianity does not claim that God always manages the minutiae of our lives, but that at root, our lives are in God's hands. And the word for that is providence.

Providence comes from the same root word as "provide" and "provisions." And it means that, in an ultimate sense, nothing happens that cannot be subject to God's purposes. That is something quite different than saying God plans everything that happens to us. It does say that this is God's world, and that God — not luck, fate, superstition, astrology, or any other so-called force — determines the meaning of this life of ours. It also means that no matter how terrible are the things that may happen to us, none of them can separate us from the love of God. Providence means there is a creating, saving possibility in every situation that cannot be destroyed by evil or by anything else.

Back in the 1960s, the U.S. nuclear submarine, *Thresher*, while on military maneuvers, had something go fatally wrong. It sank with all hands. It was the first nuclear ship casualty and the worst submarine disaster up to that time. As it happened, one crew member, Lt. Commander Raymond A. McCoole, was not on board. Shortly before the *Thresher* was to sail, McCoole's wife had attempted to open a bottle of liniment. The stopper blew suddenly out of the bottle, spewing the liquid into her eyes and temporarily blinding her. Because of the accident, McCoole had been excused from the maneuver to care for his wife: so he was not on board when the sub went down for good. Some would call that fate: "His number just wasn't up," or "It wasn't meant to be."

Providence doesn't buy the idea of predetermined fates. It declares that neither McCoole nor his mates who died aboard the sub are separated from the love of God. Even if God intervened for some reason to keep McCoole off the boat, that doesn't lessen God's love for those who were on board.

Providence is sometimes used as another name for God: for when we declare our faith in providence over luck, fate, astrology, and superstition, we are expressing our conviction that the agent behind the events in our lives is not the devil, nor blind, uncaring fatalism, nor even something called "the odds."

Rather, we are declaring that we are in the hands of One who loves us, cares for us, guides us, provides for us, and never lets us go.

Providence. It's a great word. God is at work in his world, and will win.

— S. P.

Proper 21/Pentecost 19/Ordinary Time 26

Psalm 78:1-4, 12-16
(See Proper 27/Pentecost 25/Ordinary Time 32, Cycle A, or an alternative approach to vv. 1-7.)

This is one of the "Wisdom Psalms," and part of the wisdom it extols is the importance of telling our children about our faith (v. 4), including telling them of the glorious deeds of God in the past (as, for example, vv. 12-16) as evidence for what God continues to do in the present.

We hear a lot these days about how rebellious many teens are, and how many seem to abandon the values of their parents. But studies have shown that most teens, despite their rebelliousness and the agony they put their parents through, when grown up, eventually adopt the values of their parents.

What better reason is there than that for us to speak of the meaning and importance of faith in our homes — and to do so in front of the children growing up around us? If they are going to eventually embrace at least some of the things we hold important, then hadn't we better let them know how much our God means to us personally?

Speaking of our faith may seem more difficult and awkward with youth than with adults, but it's actually not that hard. At our church, during the confirmation classes, we assign each young person in the class an adult mentor. Week after week, I give the kids some questions to ask of their mentors. The kids phone the adults and then report back to the class the next Sunday the results of those conversations.

Those adults have no problem explaining their faith to young people. In each case, all that is required is for the kids to ask. In our homes, in our classes at church, at family gatherings and other places, what we need to do is talk freely about our faith without waiting for the questions to be asked. We may think the kids aren't listening, but we are often surprised by how much they have soaked up.

— S. P.

Proper 22/Pentecost 20/Ordinary Time 27

Psalm 19

Psalm 19 celebrates two different media through which God is revealed: nature and the law.

The first part of the psalm calls our attention to the presence of God in nature — "The heavens are telling the glory of God." The word "glory" is the Hebrew *kabod* and literally means weight or heaviness. The derived meaning is something akin to "reputation." God's reputation is evident in the heavens.

But reputation for what?

Herein lies the difficulty of relying only on nature for our understanding of God. The message of nature is not clear, and in fact may contradict what we believe about God from other sources of revelation. For instance, we can infer from the sheer magnitude of creation, especially as we now understand the universe, that God is magnificent, capable of enormous creative and life-giving power. From the great variety of life forms, not to mention their sheer numbers and the ingenious way in which our world supports this life, we realize that God is a great nurturing presence. All of this seems to point to a God who cares deeply for both creature and creation.

But there is a dark, violent underside to creation. In the billions of years since the formation of the universe, there has been tremendous violence in the heavens and on earth. In the course of the development of life on our planet there have been innumerable losses. Entire species have appeared and then disappeared forever. Even among the existing life forms there is a "dog-eat-dog" quality to life that seems to suggest something violent and dangerous. What does this reveal about God?

The psalmist helps us by pointing us to the law. The law provides the content of God's character. The law is the lens through which the psalmist sees the glory of God in the heavens. God's reputation for order, for mercy, for caring, is learned in the law and is only then discernible in the heavens.

The appearance of Jesus allows us to take this process one step further. As the fulfillment of the law, Jesus fills in the parts of

God's character that even the law was incapable of making known to us. For what the law could not do, and what nature cannot do, Jesus did fully. The appearance of Jesus makes clear the character and purpose of God not only in the heavens, but also in the law. In the incarnation, heaven and earth come together perfectly to proclaim the glory of God in the face of the Son.

—J. E.

Proper 23/Pentecost 21/Ordinary Time 28

Psalm 106:1-6, 19-23

Psalm 106 is recitation of the sins of Israel, an enumeration of the ways in which the nation failed to trust their well-being to the Lord. In verse 6, the psalmist confesses that his own generation has been as sinful as their ancestors, but the catalog of sins that follows sticks to those of the forebears.

In choosing verses 19-23 from this psalm as the reading, with its focus on the golden calf incident, the lectionary presents modern readers with a practice totally foreign to today's people. A cartoon some time ago illustrates this. It showed a man and wife sitting in church. Down in front, the pastor is vigorously preaching, and a sign on the wall behind him says, "Today's Sermon: The Ten Commandments."

The wife is glaring at her husband, and the husband, looking guilty, is saying to her, "Well, at least I haven't made any graven images."

Nor, I suspect, have any of us. If we were to ask for a showing of hands in our churches as to how many have ever worshiped an idol, not one hand would go up. In fact, when it comes to applying the second commandment to ourselves today, we have to take it metaphorically because we don't break it literally.

For example, we may talk about putting first priority on our own desires, rather than on God's will, as a kind of idolatry. There may not be an actual statue, but our own image reflected back in the mirror may serve about the same function. "There is no god but what I want." "The only authority I ultimately recognize is that which I can't get away with breaking." Or we may talk about those who worship God, but who hedge their bets by paying homage to some other "powers" as well. "I worship God but it can't hurt to stay home on Friday the 13th, or to make sure I don't walk under ladders."

But the real application from the idolatry stories today is to show how we treat God as less than God is, try to cut God down to a "manageable" size. We say such things as, "Surely God wouldn't condemn us for this," or "God wants me to be happy." When we define God to fit our desires, we are doing what the psalmist accused the Israelites of in verse 20, exchanging the glory of God for a less-adequate image.

By the way, since this is the only time in the three-year cycle that the Revised Common Lectionary uses anything from this psalm, it is a pity the editors omitted verse 15, which is the basis for an excellent sermon on the causes of spiritual poverty. God provided manna; the Israelites demanded meat. God gave them what they wanted, but, as the KJV puts it, God "sent leanness into their soul."

— S. P.

Proper 24/Pentecost 22/Ordinary Time 29

Psalm 99
(See The Transfiguration Of Our Lord/Last Sunday After The Epiphany, Cycles A and C.)

Proper 25/Pentecost 23/Ordinary Time 30

Psalm 90:1-6, 13-17

Psalm 90 is a prayer, expressing gratitude for God's abiding presence in the face of the transient and frail nature of human life. Any human life, no matter how noble or helpful or wise, is terminal. Time marches on, and generations come and go. Some people have more years than others but none have life unending — not in this existence, anyway. The psalmist does not bemoan that fact. Instead, he prays that in this lifetime, we will gain the wisdom to value the days we have and the fact that God is with us in them.

One stark difference between God and us is that the Lord is eternal and we are mortal. H. Richard Niebuhr once wrote that "we are in the grip of power that neither asks our consent before [he] brings us into existence nor asks our agreement to continue us in being beyond our physical death."

The wisdom the psalmist prayed for is the clarity to see ourselves rightly in relationship to the eternal Creator. It is to acknowledge joyously, not grudgingly, that we did not make ourselves, but are contingent on the one who grants us life. Then wisdom calls us to trust God, to praise God, to seek God's will.

It may seem obvious to say that God is eternal and we are not, but things are not quite that simple. Think how, in our sense of loneliness in the world, we have sought another human being whom we believe can free us from our loneliness. This is the way it often is when we fall in love. At that moment we may have the notion that this other person can meet our needs — for love, for romance, for companionship. "Now I'll never be lonely again," we may say to ourselves. "Never" is a very long time, and in placing another person in the position of banishing our aloneness forever, we act as though we are to live forever. Because we are mortal, we cannot escape loneliness forever. Only an immortal can do that. The psalmist was wise enough to know that the only permanent anchor for the solitary individual is in God, who is immortal. For, in attempting to defend ourselves against what is a part of every human existence — aloneness — without including God, is to act as if we were divine ourselves.

"Every time we build new defenses to protect our life as inalienable property, we find ourselves caught in the tenacious illusion of immortality," says the late priest/writer Henri Nouwen (*Reaching Out* [Doubleday, 1975], p. 116). Whenever we give eternal value to things — either things we are or the things we own — we have forgotten that we are only here temporarily.

Human togetherness, which does briefly allay some loneliness, is not an ultimate solution. The loneliness of existence is a seed God has planted within us to drive us to look beyond ourselves, to God.

The psalmist tells us that while our relatively short existence here on earth is extremely valuable to us, it is not everything. God is all in all. When we live as though our lives are even more important than God's existence, we behave as though we were designed to live forever right here.

— S. P.

Proper 26/Pentecost 24/Ordinary Time 31

Psalm 107:1-7, 33-37
(See Lent 4, Cycle B, for an alternative approach to vv. 1-3 and 17-22.)

Consider for a moment the word "remember." Normally, when we hear the word or are encouraged to "remember" something, we immediately begin trying to recall certain facts, names, numbers, dates, and so on. And that is exactly what is intended. But the word "remember" takes on an added dimension when used in the context of worship. When, for instance, Jesus instructs his disciples during the Last Supper to "do this in remembrance of me," he does not have in mind that they should merely recall the night and its events. The "doing of remembering" is an act of "re-membering" and "re-connecting" — becoming a part of something again.

That is one facet of the biblical meaning of the word "remember." By an act of the will and the imagination, we put ourselves back into events or moments and re-experience their significance. We re-enact in ourselves some biblical truth and thereby allow the importance and the meaning of that truth to change us or heal us.

The first several verses of Psalm 107 are designed to accomplish this act of faithful imagination. They are intended by the writer as a way of helping worshipers remember the mighty acts of God on behalf of God's people. That is the significance of the psalmist's opening statement, "let the redeemed of the Lord say so" (v. 2). Let those who "re-member" what God has done make their remembering known to others.

The allusions that follow almost certainly have reference to the great escape from Egypt. Led by Moses, the people of Israel traveled into the wilderness, met God, lost God, but finally allowed God to lead them into the promised land. Theirs was a story of faith and failure and redemption. "Do you re-member?" the psalmist asks.

But the worship leader may have another purpose in mind. It is not just to celebrate the past that we are called to "re-member." Sometimes we need to re-connect to some sacred moment in the past in order to have hope in a difficult moment in the present. The call to "re-member" achieves a certain pastoral function.

For the people of Israel, re-connecting to wilderness wanderings (v. 4) could have multiple applications. Any momentary distress can be a wilderness wandering. The psalmist could be addressing a tragedy shared by his congregation. And of course, wilderness wandering can be literally so. The psalmist may be addressing the experience of the exile — going in, coming out, or living through.

Regardless of the nature of the wandering, the hope we need is found in re-membering. God finds us in the wilderness and cares for us. "They cried to the Lord in their trouble, and he delivered them from their distress" (v. 6). If we can re-connect to that experience of being delivered back then, we can face the wilderness of the present with every hope that we will be delivered now.

The psalmist recites several examples which allow worshipers entry-points to dip into the memories. As we are able to re-connect with these memories, we find ourselves growing: emotionally, spiritually, and even intellectually. The psalmist acknowledges this outcome as he closes the psalm with these words: "Let those who are wise give heed to these things, and consider the steadfast love of the Lord" (v. 43). Or in other words, "re-member ... the last word is always God's love."

— J. E.

All Saints

Psalm 34:1-10, 22
(See Proper 25/Pentecost 23/Ordinary Time 30, Cycle B.)

Proper 27/Pentecost 25/Ordinary Time 32

Psalm 78:1-7
(See Proper 21/Pentecost 19/Ordinary Time 26, Cycle A, for an alternative approach to vv. 1-4 and 12-16.)

This is the second time in this lectionary cycle that Psalm 78 has made an appearance. Using verses 1-4 and 12-16, Psalm 78 was the psalter for Proper 21/Pentecost 19/Ordinary Time 26, and there we noted that this "Wisdom Psalm" touts the importance of telling our children about our faith.

That theme is no different when reading verses 1-7; if anything, the addition of verses 5-7 strengthens it. Those verses tell of God's decree that the ancestors of the psalmist's generation were to teach their children the deeds and Law of God (Deuteronomy 6:1-9, especially v. 7), "that the next generation might know them ... and rise up and tell them to their children, so that they should set their hope in God."

Someone has rightly pointed out that "Christianity is always only one generation away from extinction," and this psalm affords a good opportunity to remind our hearers of that stark reality. If our own children don't hear the testimony of faith, how will their children know to "set their hope in God"?

When I was a child growing up in the Salvation Army, which was my church then, we had an item in the Sunday evening services called "testimonies." That was a time when worshipers were invited to stand up and speak about what God had done in their lives. Some people never spoke, others spoke almost every week and still others only occasionally, but the point was, we were encouraged to talk about our experiences of God so that others present might be helped in their own faith journeys.

I remember one older man named Larry Waldron. He had little formal education and had worked most of his adult life in the rough and tumble world of a paper mill in upstate New York. Evidently it had been a tough place to work. At one point, Larry had seen a fellow employee thrown to his death into one of the chemical vats during a labor dispute.

Late in his life, Larry found God, and his life changed. During those Sunday evening testimony times, he would sometimes speak about the difference in his life since he had committed himself to Christ. I really don't remember his words, but I remember the sincerity and the conviction with which he spoke, and his witness had a bearing on my own Christian journey. In fact, one thing that helped me as a Christian was that I heard the adults around me, including my parents, talk about their faith.

In Scott Peck's introduction to his 1997 book, *The Road Less Traveled and Beyond*. There, Peck, though only sixty at the time, says he is not in the best of health and feels worn out. He confesses a need to set his affairs in order and to share what he has learned. In the body of the book, he explains what life and faith have taught him. Although he does not say so in so many words, his book is a witness to readers of his own generation and those following.

Most of us will not have the opportunity to leave behind a published *corpus* of Christian testimony for succeeding generations, but we can learn to talk comfortably about our faith at the dinner table, where younger people are listening. I would change one word in the old gospel song:

> *If you cannot preach like Peter,*
> *if you cannot pray like Paul,*
> *go home and tell your neighbor [children]*
> *that he died to save us all.*

— S. P.

Proper 28/Pentecost 26/Ordinary Time 33

Psalm 123

This short psalm is a communal lament, pleading as a nation for God's mercy, though in what particular circumstances we cannot tell. There are, however, two excellent images pertaining to the human/God relationship, both using the metaphor of "the eyes lifted up." The two are that of servants to a master and a maid to her mistress. The singers of this psalm view themselves as asking for God's mercy from a similar position of subservience.

Have you noticed how God's mercy is often mistaken as coincidence? God's mercy frequently takes the form of problem-resolution or pain-amelioration or intervention, but to those without faith, God's action is labeled (mis-labeled, really) as coincidence.

My favorite example of God's mercy is one I witnessed firsthand. One of my first funerals was for a young man I'll call Eddie, who had been shot to death as an innocent bystander in someone else's quarrel. He had grown up in our church, and was just 21 and newly married.

The midsummer day of the funeral dawned bright and sunny. We held the service in the funeral home and then traveled in procession to the cemetery. There, the casket bearing Eddie's body was placed on the lowering-rig that had been set up over the gaping grave. The group of us, perhaps sixty strong, gathered around it while I spoke the traditional words of committal.

Throughout the time at the cemetery, Randy, Eddie's younger brother, had been quietly weeping, but as I brought the graveside service to a close, his emotion overflowed, and he began sobbing loudly. Suddenly he jumped up and threw himself across his brother's coffin, clutching it tightly and crying, "No, no, no!"

For a moment we all stood there, not quite sure what to do. Then his mother and father came to him and tried to get him to leave the casket, but Randy was lost in his grief and held on fiercely. Others of us tried to comfort the young man, too, but none of us could break through.

Unnoticed, however, the sky had been changing. In a matter of moments it shifted from bright blue to dark gray, and without preamble, heavy rain suddenly began pelting us, a furious sudden summer storm. The drenching downpour accomplished what the rest of us could not. Randy, still shaking with emotion, finally loosened his grip on the casket and allowed himself to be led to a waiting car.

Some might say the sudden and unexpected rain was a fortunate coincidence. But given the circumstances, I suspect it was a gift of divine mercy for a family that had already lost too much.

— S. P.

Christ The King/Proper 29

Psalm 100

This brief psalm is among the most familiar in the psalter, but that is primarily because its verses have been excerpted in so many hymns and liturgical texts. There is something to be gained from looking at Psalm 100 in its entirety, and trying to recover its ancient liturgical context.

Psalm 100 is a hymn of approach. Very likely it was sung by pilgrims on their way to Jerusalem, both as they drew near to the holy city and as they actually entered the temple precincts. We can easily imagine those ancient worshipers coming into the Lord's presence "with singing," entering first the gates and then each of the temple courts in succession. As they do so, songs of praise and thanksgiving like this one tumble from their lips.

There is something about the act of worship that puts these pilgrims' lives in proper perspective. They know who God is: eternal and self-evident — "Know that the Lord is God." This is an exclusive claim: Yahweh is the one, true God. It is a very different sort of declaration than the one many Christians are inclined to make today. According to James Luther Mays:

> *In Israel's day the question was not, "Is there a god?" but "Who is god?" In a profound though culturally different way, that is still the real question. Human beings are intrinsically polytheistic.* (*Psalms*, in the *Interpretation* series [Louisville: John Knox Press, 1994], p. 319.)

Human beings today are polytheistic not in the traditional sense of worshiping a pantheon of deities, but rather in adoring all sorts of lesser idols: money, fame, power, and all the rest.

Psalm 100 overflows with exuberant joy. Perhaps more than any other of the 150 psalms, this one captures the joyous spirit of worship. Perhaps we can use it as a sort of standard, to see how our worship measures up.

Joy surprises. It's unexpected. Joy steals upon us when we are not seeking it, when we're going about other business. "Our brightest blazes of gladness," writes Samuel Johnson, "are sometimes kindled by unexpected sparks." Joy is also different from the pleasure that our culture seeks with such desperate, plodding intensity. In the words of C. S. Lewis, "Joy is never within our power, but pleasure often is." Art historian, Sister Wendy Becket, in one of her popular BBC television documentaries on great paintings, observed:

> *Joy is not a constant condition. Most people manage a settled cheerfulness, but this — no matter how admirable — has nothing to do with joy, which flashes suddenly on our darkness. Like the light in an El Greco painting, joy does not merely illuminate the landscape. It transforms it.*

The worshipers on their way to the temple in Jerusalem sing as though they were people being transformed — which, in a very real sense, they are.

— C. W.

Thanksgiving Day

Psalm 65
(See Proper 25/Pentecost 23/Ordinary Time 30, Cycle C, for an alternative approach.)

I've been unable to learn who first coined the phrase "the groaning board," with its implication of a table so loaded with food that it threatens to topple, but it comes to mind every time I read Psalm 65. This is especially so when I read it in the RSV. In that version, verse 11 speaks of the tracks of the Lord's chariot that "drip with fatness," and verse 12 says that the wilderness pastures also "drip." The NRSV renditions — that "your wagon tracks overflow with richness" and "the pastures of the wilderness also overflow" — just don't carry the same punch.

In any case, the imagery is one of bounty, of a planet upon which the Creator has lavished wonderful resources in great abundance. Thus, it is not difficult to see why the lectionary committee designated this psalm for Thanksgiving. If God's material abundance is to be the message, verses 9-13 are certainly a fine text.

The whole psalm, however, is the designated reading, and in its entirety it speaks of more than simply a profusion of provisions. Verses 1-4 remind us that praise is due to God, which calls into question whether one day a year is sufficient to render such "payment." (It's not, of course.) A life lived in gratitude to the God who "forgives our transgressions" and satisfies us "with the goodness of your house" is more like it.

Verses 5-9 praise God for the gift of life itself. God makes "the gateways of the morning and the evening shout for joy." These two times bracket the days of our lives, days that are God's gift to us.

In Yuma, Arizona, one of the hotels carries a sign over its veranda that reads, "Free board every day the sun doesn't shine." A new arrival, checking in during a downpour, often hopes to capitalize on that. But the proprietor doesn't worry. He has lived in Yuma many years, and always during some part of the day the sun appears, even if only for a few moments. So far, no one has been able to get a free day's board at the hotel. Life tends to be like that too. It never rains all the time, and when we think about our lives, we are likely to see some blessings there as well, even amidst pain.

As a preacher, though, I always find it hard to use verses referring to God's bounty. That's because I am haunted by pictures of starving children in other parts of the world, people who have none of that bounty. But in the end, of course, thanksgiving isn't about how many blessings we have received, but about who God is. This psalm, which refuses to look only at the bounty of the earth, reminds us that praise is indeed due for who God is, not for how much we have.

— S. P.

Cycle B

Advent 1

Psalm 80:1-7, 17-19
(See Advent 4, Cycle A, and Proper 15/Pentecost 13/Ordinary Time 20, Cycle C, for an alternative approach.)
This psalm with this exact selection of verses is used two different years during the Advent season: here in Cycle B for Advent 1, and in Cycle A for Advent 4. Obviously, the lectionary committee wants us to find an Advent theme in it.

Certainly, one may be found in verse 4. "O Lord of hosts, how long will you be angry with your people's prayers?" That "how long" is the cry of Advent. The Jews of the Old Testament and the inter-testamental period were living in that "how long" time, a prolonged wait for the promised Messiah. To paraphrase, the psalmist is saying, "We've been waiting long enough. Come down here and straighten out this mess, so we can gain control of our own lives."

That is the tone of Advent. Hymns like "O Come, O Come, Emmanuel" emphasize the sense of waiting for something that has not yet happened, something that will eventually bring so dramatic a change that people will gain mastery over their conditions and control of their own destinies — or, at least, so they hope.

The irony is that, although Advent points us backward to the time before Jesus came, and we live in the time after he came, we often still find ourselves swamped by Advent-like moods. We live after the event to which the people of the Old Testament looked forward, the coming of the Messiah. But we still don't have mastery of our conditions. So in many ways, the Advent mood still seems to fit even though the Christmas event has happened. The difference is now, instead of struggling to believe that a Messiah is really coming, we are working to keep faith alive that the final victory will be God's.

And so we may look at the hopefulness of Advent with jaded eyes and minimal expectations. Perhaps we come with a kind of resignation that leads us to just "go with the flow" and not really expect things to get much better.

Yet, waiting can release a kind of creative energy in us. Paul Tournier, a Christian author and psychiatrist, had a happy marriage to a woman he fully loved. When she died young, he was heartbroken and become painfully aware of what it meant not to have a companion to grow old with. He missed the rich conversations they'd had and the warmth of her presence. He did believe, however, that her absence was not forever, that there would be a reunion someday in God's kingdom. Nonetheless, in the meantime, he discovered that while waiting for that day, his energies could be redirected, and he found a rebirth of his creative urge. He went on to write some of his most helpful books after the death of his wife.

Waiting can be creative.

— S. P.

Advent 2

Psalm 85:1-2, 8-13
(See Proper 12/Pentecost 10/Ordinary Time 17, Cycle C, for an alternative approach.)

This psalm is a communal prayer for help. After acknowledging the great help of the Lord to their ancestors (v. 1), these psalmsingers plead with God to do the same again (v. 4). Though the circumstances are not named, many scholars believe this psalm refers to impending return from exile, looking forward to the intervention of God in history. The themes of the psalm are like those of Second Isaiah — "his salvation at hand," "that his glory may dwell in the land." Thus the themes are also those of Advent. In fact, though not quoted in the New Testament, verse 13 brings to mind John the Baptist, the herald of Christ. In this setting, however, righteousness is the herald of God.

Note especially verses 10-11, with the poetic naming of characteristics of the day when the Lord will return. The situation of Israel as this psalm was written was far from ideal, and it was not characterized by steadfast love, faithfulness, righteousness, and peace. Together those things are the ideal conditions for human life together, but they are never fully present this side of the Lord's coming. Perhaps, to speak of them poetically (and with hope) is the only viable option for those who do not wish to surrender to despair. So the psalmist waxes poetic: "Steadfast love and faithfulness will meet; righteousness and peace will kiss each other."

Two weeks after 9/11, Terri Gross of National Public Radio's *Fresh Air* interviewed the new U.S. poet laureate Billy Collins. She asked him if the terrorist attacks affected how he saw his role as poet laureate. Collins replied, in the days following the attack:

> *There was a kind of surge of poetry activity, and it seemed there was a kind of need for poetry — and people turning to me as the laureate for reactions to this ... I found it interesting that in a time of national crisis, that we don't turn to the novel. We don't say, well we should all go out and see a movie that would kind of make us feel better. We turn to poetry....*

He added that the attacks tore a hole in the nation and that normal language cannot fill it. But poetry is the best effort for this, he said, adding that one of poetry's "oldest functions is to give a place for grief to go, a place to ritualize grief and make it possible to express in some coherent way feelings that seem to resist expression" (from *Fresh Air*, broadcast September 26, 2001).

Maybe it will be useful to acknowledge the poetic nature of the psalms, and this psalm particularly — and then to ask, how can the poetry of the scripture fill the holes in our hearts?

— S. P.

Advent 3

Psalm 126

There is perhaps no greater challenge to the life of faith than suffering. There is an implicit expectation that God, who is strong and loving, will protect those who are weak. When tragedy befalls the innocent, it is hard not to wonder about God's strength or goodness, or both.

That experience was writ large for the people of Israel during the exile. For those Jews who believed God had called them and formed them into a covenant people, it was nearly impossible to understand how they could have been conquered by a foreign power. Instead of impugning God with charges of lack of love or lack of strength, however, the prophets interpreted the exile as punishment for sin.

The fact is, all pain feels like punishment. How many times have we heard someone in the midst of a struggle say — or have said ourselves — "What did I do to deserve this?"

Obviously the mystery of evil and suffering will not be solved in the course of one sermon (or even 1,000 sermons!). But it is interesting to observe what the psalmist does with the suffering of the people of Israel. Drawing on the power of memory, the psalmist evokes praise for the past deeds of God's goodness. In the narrative of Israel's history there are many examples of God's gracious intervention just in the nick of time. Out of this memory, the psalmist draws a prayer: "Restore our fortunes, O Lord" (v. 4).

But what to do with the suffering? What is the point of having a powerful God who refrains from protecting us?

The psalmist offers a beautiful image for dealing with suffering. He describes the tears we shed during times of difficulty as "seeds for joy."

Comparing our tears to seed is a powerful way of expressing hope at several different levels. For instance, thinking of our tears as a prelude to joy is intended to help us realize that though we suffer now, we will not always be in pain. After all, the courage to endure is directly related to our belief that our suffering will eventually end.

Another instance, the things we learn about ourselves during times of distress and difficulty, may contribute to the strengthening of our character and our resolve. There is wisdom gained from pain and loss that cannot be gained any other way. As the saying goes, you just have to be there.

And finally, experiencing the distress of privations and pitfalls can have an enormous impact on the way we view the world when we are not deprived. "Living without" for a while may help us, later, to express deep and sincere gratitude when we do have what we need.

In these ways, the seeds of our tears can produce joy. We rejoice when our sufferings end. We rejoice from the new perspectives we gain. We give thanks for the way God cares for us. And, as the psalmist begins his poem, we learn to remember the good things God has done for us in the past.

The folk who worship in our churches will know something of the doubt and fear that comes from loss. This psalm may be an effective medium for giving voice to those feelings, while at the same time engendering hope where hope is almost dead.

—J. E.

Luke 1:47-55
(See Advent 3, Cycle A.)

Advent 4

Luke 1:47-55
(See Advent 3, Cycle A.)

Psalm 89:1-4, 19-26
(See Proper 11/Pentecost 9/Ordinary Time 16, Cycle B, for an alternative approach to vv. 20-37.)

If you read only the verses from Psalm 89 designated by the lectionary for today, you may well see 89 as a royal psalm, perhaps even used as a hymn during a ritual of enthronement of a Davidic king. A reading of the whole psalm, especially verse 38ff, however, shows that it is more a communal lament, written at a time when the continuity of the royal line of David was in doubt. Still, the portion selected by the lectionary editors for today focuses on God's promise of the throne belonging continually to David's line (actually the reading should not stop at v. 26, but should go all the way to 37). Thus, the psalm can also be read as a messianic text, with the promised one coming from the house of Judah.

It is unlikely that most preachers will choose to preach from the psalter rather than the gospel or the epistle on this Sunday before Christmas Day — and not just because the latter are more directly applicable. The harder issue is that the psalm asks us to consider the bloodline of the Messiah — whereas, for most Americans, one's ancestral line has little meaning. We have, probably quite rightly, learned to evaluate people on their own performance and track record rather than how well or ill their great-grandparents did. Indeed, some of us have little knowledge about our own relatives that far back.

Those who are going to base a sermon on this psalm do well to admit up front that we aren't much moved by lineage. In fact, this psalm functions in Advent readings only to show that the Incarnation was the fulfillment of a divine promise made centuries earlier. So this psalm, read by us after the first coming of Jesus, invites us to understand Christmas as concrete evidence of God keeping promises. Clearly the New Testament writers understand Jesus as the fulfillment of God's promise and view Christians as the inheritors of that promise. When we are convinced of that, we can live our lives in a context of ultimate optimism and confidence.

— S. P.

Christmas Eve

Psalm 96

(Occurs in all three cycles of the lectionary; see Christmas Eve, Cycle A, for an alternative approach.)

This is a hymn of praise, calling all the earth to glorify God, who is the righteous judge. Most of Psalm 96 also appears in 1 Chronicles 16:23-33, where it is one of the hymns sung by Asaph and the official singers, once the Ark of the Covenant has been brought to Jerusalem. The Ark was understood as the "throne" of the invisible God, so bringing that visible symbol into the city was a way of recognizing the presence of God amidst the people. Likewise, the Christmas event was a visible manifestation of the presence of God to the people of the first century. That, at least, may be why the lectionary committee assigns this psalm for Christmas Eve for all three years of the lectionary.

This psalm calls the congregation of Israel to sing a "new song." The "old song" was the song of Moses and the people at the Red Sea (Exodus 15), a celebration of the mighty deeds of God in delivering the Israelites from the pursuing Egyptians. But, by the time of the psalmist, that was old news. The new song was needed to sing the praise of God's current mighty works among the people, symbolized perhaps by the arrival of the Ark in Jerusalem. But also in the case of this psalm, one of the new songs was that Yahweh was not merely God of Israel, but of "all the earth" (v. 1), and of all "families of the peoples" (v. 7). This understanding was a giant step forward for Israel, who once thought of Yahweh as their God alone.

In the book of Revelation, yet another new song is sung by those around the Lamb of God (Revelation 14:3). Thus, one connection to Christmas from this psalm is the new song instituted by Jesus' birth. Thus, "Joy to the world, the Lord is come!"

—S. P.

Christmas Day

Psalm 97
(Occurs in all three cycles of the lectionary; see Christmas Day, Cycle A; see also Easter 7, Cycle C, for an alternative approach.)

Psalm 98
(Occurs in all three cycles of the lectionary; see also Christmas, Cycle A, and Easter 6, Cycle B, for alternative approaches.)

Like Psalm 96 (see Christmas Eve), Psalm 98 is a psalm proclaiming the glory of Israel's God. Verses 7 and 8 speak of the whole orchestra of nature chiming in to praise God, including "the world and those who live in it."

Perhaps it is not too much of a stretch to go on from there to talk about the birth of Christ in a stable for animals, as an indication of his lordship over them as well. Actually, during Advent last year, a young man in my congregation asked me, "Do dogs go to heaven?"

We who have been around animals readily understand how attached we can become to them, and in the case of a faithful pet, we'd like to believe that there is some kind of happy afterlife for them. But since they are not reasoning creatures, and, as far as we know, can't make the kinds of decisions about right or wrong that humans can, we may conclude that, while for us there is a world to come, there is not one for animals.

Nonetheless, it seems that Christmas and animals go together. On the secular side, we have Dasher and Dancer and the rest of the reindeer cohorts. But, even the more serious side of Christmas has some critters. "Silent Night," for example, never would have been written, we're told, had mice not eaten the bellows of a church organ, forcing the composition of a simple carol that could be accompanied by guitar. Most of all, we've got Jesus born in a stable — presumably in the presence of animals — so we can assume that all of that means something.

Certainly, it can be a reminder that all life is interconnected. We get jolted by that sometimes when we change the balance of nature by eliminating all the natural predators in an area. Pretty soon, we find ourselves overrun by rabbits or other creatures that are normally part of the food chain for other animals.

Yet in other ways, animals are part of the richness of our lives. Several years ago, I took a church youth group to a nursing home at Christmas time. That year, in addition to singing Christmas carols and passing out little remembrances, we had the children bring their pets along. We had a dog, a couple of cats, and even a mouse. As we went from room to room, the residents wanted to pet and hold the animals. Even some of the people who were unable to talk and seemed deep in senility responded to the animals.

Maybe the animals were there that first Christmas to remind us that God's love doesn't come only in big dramatic gestures like unique stars in the sky. Maybe God's love comes, sometimes, through the faithful companionship of God's other creatures. There are many people whose lives would be sadder and darker without a pet for companionship, or whose lives would be less open without an animal to care for.

Animals also challenge us to be better than we are. How much we all would improve if we lived as the kind of people our dogs seem to think we are!

That the seas should roar, the floods clap their hands, and the hills sing is poetic imagery to be sure, but the words remind us that the whole world has a stake in the redemption of creation.

— S. P.

Christmas 1

Psalm 148
(Occurs in all three cycles of the lectionary; see Christmas 1, Cycle A; Christmas 1, Cycle C; and Easter 5, Cycle C, for alternative approaches.)

The last five songs in the book of Psalms are hallelujah psalms, bringing Israel's hymnbook to a close with a tremendous shout of praise. (Which, by the way, is also a good way to bring the year to a close.) Psalm 148 is the third of those five, and it calls for praise of the Lord from every creature and from every corner of the universe, as well as from the heavens themselves. (This psalm has echoes in Saint Francis' great hymn, "All Creatures Of Our God And King.")

The topic of praise reminds us that there is a significant difference between praising God and praising others. Much of the time, when we praise someone else, it is for one of two reasons. Either we are seeking to bolster the other person — a noble enough reason — or we are hoping to advance ourselves by appearing generous — not always noble and sometimes called "bootlicking."

Praising others to lift them is worthy. Each school year, a certain teacher makes a practice of finding the most unattractive child in her class and whispering to her, "You're getting prettier every day." The teacher says it almost always works. The child begins to blossom into something beautiful.

When we praise God, however, we have no expectation of either appearing generous ourselves or lifting God's spirits. Rather, praising God is good for us. Like many human activities aimed toward God — prayer, worship, devotional life, commitments, vow-making — praising bestows its benefits more on the "praiser" than the "praisee." Praising God is yet another way for the blessings of God to flow to us.

Another way to look at the matter of praising is to think of how a talented accompanist makes a lead performer look even better. My daughter — who as a pianist has accompanied singers, and as a singer has been accompanied by others — tells me that regardless of how well she is prepared to perform, the skill of the accompanist can make all the difference in how the presentation comes across. This psalm invites us to be talented accompanists for the Lord, to enhance the whole presentation of the divine message and the divine blessings by filling the background with our melody of praise.

— S. P.

Christmas 2

Psalm 147:12-20
(Occurs in all three cycles of the lectionary; see Christmas 2, Cycle A.)

The Epiphany Of Our Lord

Psalm 72:1-7, 10-14
(Occurs in all three cycles of the lectionary; see also The Epiphany Of Our Lord, Cycle A, for an alternative approach; see also Advent 2, Cycle A, for vv. 1-7.)
    Psalm 72 is the psalm selection for Epiphany during all three years of the lectionary cycle. Epiphany traditionally celebrates themes surrounding the visit of the Magi. There are several possible directions to go with these themes. The most common celebrates Jesus' first appearance to the non-Jewish world. This both provides a textual setting to discuss the inclusive nature of the gospel and sets the stage for the church's mission work in the wider world.
    Psalm 72 is an excellent vehicle for either of these themes. The psalm is structured as a prayer. It was probably used as part of the coronation ceremony of a new king. The prayer expresses the brightest possible hope for the new king. In fact, the description of what is hoped for runs past the bounds of what is humanly possible, even for a king.
    From the very start, the psalm has an eye toward the poor. The congregation prays for the king to rule with justice and righteousness (vv. 1-2). These words ring with prophetic significance, as well they should. Doing justice has the same force for the psalmist as it does for the prophets.
    The psalm also offers a prayer for "prosperity" (v. 3). It is hard for us to hear this word and not think of money. Prosperity for us is all about wealth, but the Hebrew word translated here as "prosperity" is *shalom*. The word, *shalom*, often translated as "peace," actually means well-being, wholeness, even healing. The psalmist's prayer for *shalom* reflects a desire that all God's people might prosper in all aspects of their existence — physical and spiritual.
    Amazingly, the psalmist tells us that the mountains will produce this *shalom*. Clearly, the reference here is partly economic. Prosperity from the mountain refers to harvest and crop yields, but it is also from the mountain that the Lord appears. It is upon the holy mountain that God's people gather for worship. In other words,

the psalmist's prayer is for the well-being that comes to a nation or even a world when all of its people are able to enjoy the bounty of the earth and the presence of God.

As the mountains yield *shalom*, the king should defend the cause of the poor (v. 4). There is a reciprocal relationship suggested by God who supplies the bounty of the earth and the king who defends the right of the poor to have access to it.

This need continues today. In our world, huge corporations are able to purchase for themselves favorable treatment in terms of tax breaks and land use. Meanwhile, the weak and the poor have no one to lobby for their cause.

But a new king has arrived. He has made himself known to the world. This new king champions the cause of the poor, and he calls to us to do the same.

—J. E.

The Baptism Of Our Lord/ Epiphany 1/Ordinary Time 1

Psalm 29
(Occurs in all three cycles of the lectionary; see The Baptism Of Our Lord/Epiphany 1/Ordinary Time 1, Cycle A, and The Holy Trinity, Cycle B, for alternative approaches.)

It seems likely that this psalm was inspired by a storm. The psalmist hears the voice of the Lord "over the waters; the God of glory thunders, the Lord, over mighty waters" (v. 3). The imagery of a great storm also calls to mind the vast primeval storm that preceded the creation (Genesis 1:2). It is more than likely that the psalmist wants us to make those connections.

The psalm opens with an imperative section calling on all "heavenly beings" to give glory to God (vv. 1-2). This call to praise is repeated three times, each call becoming progressively longer. The "heavenly beings" called to praise are those supernatural creatures (angels?) who surround the Lord's throne.

"Glory" is an important word in this psalm, occurring in verses 1, 2, and 9. The basic sense of the word is "abundance," or "heaviness." A cloud, for instance, may be described as being "heavy" with rain.

When used of the Lord, the derived meaning of "glory" (*kabod*) has reference to splendor, majesty, magnificence. If we wanted to find a rendering in the vernacular, the idea of "reputation" comes close to the meaning of glory.

After the introductory call to praise, the psalm continues by giving reasons for praise (vv. 3-9). This is where the imagery of the storm becomes important. The thunder heard in the approaching storm is like the voice of God. Additional divine power is revealed in the lightning flash and in the wind that brings down the mighty cedar (v. 9). God is the great power in the world that gives and sustains life. God is able to defeat the chaos with storm-like power. For those who live through occasional encounters with chaos, this is good news.

The open heavens, the voice of God, and the imagery of water are also features in the narrative of Jesus' baptism. This explains the selection of Psalm 29 for The Baptism Of Our Lord Sunday. However, it is not these images alone that allow us to draw parallels between this storm and Jesus' baptism.

The voice of God that Jesus hears establishes and affirms his messianic identity. The voice reveals the direction and character of Jesus' ministry. Jesus emerges from the storm of baptism committed to this identity and the path it demands.

In the psalm, the voice of God in the storm affirms the identity of the gathered congregation as God's people. The psalmist sees in the great power unleashed in the storm the power needed to protect and sustain God's people, assuring them of their ability to achieve what God has called them to do. The God who speaks through the storm will attend to God's people, giving them strength and providing for them peace (v. 11).

— J. E.

Epiphany 2/Ordinary Time 2

Psalm 139:1-6, 13-18
(See Proper 4/Pentecost 2/Ordinary Time 9, Cycle B for an alternative approach; see also Proper 11/Pentecost 9/Ordinary Time 16, Cycle A for an alternative approach to vv. 1-12, 23-24.)
 The psalmist raises an interesting question. He writes: "You hem me in, behind and before, and you lay your hand upon me" (v. 5). He also writes, "Where can I go from your spirit? Or where can I flee from your presence?" (v. 7).
 The latter questions are rhetorical, of course. They are questions that make an assertion: There is nowhere I can go where God's Spirit is not present.
 The problem this raises is the problem of free will. The psalmist's statement that God "hems me in" makes it sound as though human beings have no choice. Like a master chess player, God so maneuvers the field of choices and options that the only real option is for the writer to do what God wants.
 But if that is true, then are we correct in believing we are really free to choose at all? If we are left with only one choice, as the psalmist seems to be saying, does that mean that our lives are scripted? Are we merely puppets on strings, dancing and acting according to God's predetermined dictates?
 There are many who are ready to read the psalm that way, and in fact find a good bit of comfort in that sort of reading. The ambiguity and uncertainty of this world yields to the governing forces of God's infallible choices. We need only to "wait on the Lord," and enjoy the life God has crafted for us to live.
 But the absence of choice removes the demand for responsibility. If we are only able to choose from among limited options that God has left for us to choose, then we are not responsible for our choices. Obviously that is not the biblical position. In every encounter with the presence of God we are, in fact, accountable for our choices.
 So how are we to reconcile these seemingly contradictory ideas? How is it possible that God can "hem me in" and yet at the same time not hem me in?

One possible resolution is found in the opening verse: "You have searched me and known me."

Parents who have more than one child know all too well that trying to treat all children exactly the same is not practical. If all children in a family were exactly the same in personality and temperament, it might be possible, but that is not usually the case. Some children are extroverts, some introverts. Some respond to positive reinforcement, others only to negative reinforcement. Attentive parents must find out, usually through trial and error, what works with their child.

The same is true with God. God wants us to make good choices. God wants us to do well. But God is not going to override our freedom in order to make us what God wants us to be.

Since God knows us better than anyone, even better than we know ourselves, God is able to work in our lives and in our world in just the right way, so as to give us the best position to make the best choice. Do we always make the right choice? No. Sadly, we do not. God is always faithful to make sure the best choice is available to us in a way that is uniquely designed for us to understand it.

God "hems us in." Not in a constraint that allows no freedom, but in a carefully constructed moment of opportunity that allows us to see or hear or feel what is right. God can do this because God has searched us and known us.

—J. E.

Epiphany 3/Ordinary Time 3

Psalm 62:5-12

"[God] alone is my rock and my salvation, my fortress; I shall not be shaken" (Psalm 62:6). This may seem, to our ears, a strange title for God. After all, "rock" does not rank high, for most of us, on our list of things of value. But consider the people who first coined the phrase. The Hebrew people began as desert wanderers: shepherds, and hunters, gatherers of wild berries and edible plants.

They lived a hand-to-mouth existence, dependent on the goodness of the earth to sustain them.

Sometimes the earth was not good. Sometimes the desert sun waxed hot and unrelenting. In such a time, a large rock provided welcome shade.

Sometimes there were wild animals, or other enemies round about; a rock could be a point of defense.

Sometimes there was flash-flooding: a terrifying, rushing torrent of muddy water, that threatened to carry away shepherd and sheep alike. Then, a rock provided firm footing, and a place to wait out the natural disaster.

Sometimes a traveler was lost in the wilderness. The only landmark, then, might well be a rock — either a natural formation, or the type of stone set upright in the ground by someone who had gone that way before: a little shrine to the God who comes to shepherds in the gloom of darkest night, and reminds them that all will be well.

C. S. Lewis was once asked to speak to a company of the Royal Air Force about Christianity. At the end of the lecture, a tough old officer stood up and said:

> *I've got no use for all that stuff. But mind you, I'm a religious man, too. I know there's a God. I've felt him out alone in the desert at night. That's why I don't believe all your neat little dogmas and formulas about him. To anyone who's met the real thing, they all seem so petty and pedantic and unreal.*

It's not possible to find God, the rock, in a book of theology, or in a self-help group, or within the walls of a favorite church. God does not reside in such places; though God may occasionally be found there. No, the wonder and the glory of it is that in our wilderness journeys, God finds us. God reaches us. God touches us at the moment we most need it, and in the way we most need it. Then, we look around, and know there is no rock like our God.

— C. W.

Epiphany 4/Ordinary Time 4

Psalm 111
(See Proper 15/Pentecost 13/Ordinary Time 20, Cycle B, for an alternative approach.)

The first verse of Psalm 111 says the Lord is to be praised, and the rest of the psalm explains why. Structurally, this psalm is based on the 22 letters of the Hebrew alphabet, with the first word in each measure beginning with the next letter in order, with a total of 22 measures.

This is a psalm of individual thanksgiving, probably belonging together with Psalm 112. It's worth noting that the wisdom reference in verse 10 — "The fear of the Lord is the beginning of wisdom, and all who practice it have a good understanding" — not only sets the theme for Psalm 112, but also abruptly introduces the notion that praising the Lord and obeying his commands are not just for purposes of worshiping the Creator and living righteously, but also makes sense. In other words, it's good advice because the righteous do better in life than the wicked.

We might argue that last point based on empirical evidence from our own day, but allowing that the psalmist and his contemporaries believed it, we are tempted to ask whether that misses the point. We know of people who live by the Golden Rule — mentioned by Jesus in the Sermon on the Mount — because it makes sense, but that misses Jesus' intention. In the Sermon on the Mount, Jesus isn't running a seminar on how to have a happy and healthy life; he is talking about how to live righteously.

So a sermon on "The Motive For Bible Reading" or "Seeing Biblical Benefits As Secondary" or something similar might grow out of Psalm 111. It has nine verses devoted to worshiping God because of who God is, and one verse devoted to worshiping the Lord because there is a payoff for the worshiper — and maybe that balance is about right. We would hope that we follow the way of Christ mostly for the highest motives.

— S. P.

Epiphany 5/Ordinary Time 5

Psalm 147:1-11, 20c
(For an alternative approach to vv. 12-20, see Christmas 2, Cycle A.)

This is our second encounter with Psalm 147 in recent weeks. Verses 12-20 comprised the Psalm Reading for the Second Sunday After Christmas. There we noted that this psalm was likely written for the people of Jerusalem after their return from exile (see vv. 2-3) and that it is intended to remind the hearers that the same God who runs the cosmos also cares for Israel. That theme continues in these verses as well.

We can imagine this psalm being sung as Zerubbabel's temple was dedicated (see Ezra 6:16-22), especially when we're told that as part of that dedication, the people "with joy ... celebrated the festival of unleavened bread seven days; for the Lord had made them joyful ..." (Ezra 6:22).

A sermon might be built on verse 4, which tells us that God determines the number of the stars and names them. The longer we study the skies, the more we realize that both the numbering and the naming of the stars are beyond human capability. As recently as January 1996, scientists discovered, thanks to the Hubble Space Telescope, that our universe was at least forty billion galaxies larger than previously known. The psalmist, of course, couldn't have known about all that, but even the sky he saw with his naked eye was stunningly large and amazingly star-filled.

One direction such a sermon could go is emphasizing that we worship a God so much bigger than the foolishness of astrology, which claims that a few named and relatively close stars determine our destiny.

While God can name the stars and name us, we cannot name God. We use names to refer to the Creator, but none of them succeed very well. When the current *United Methodist Hymnal* was being assembled, the hymnal revision committee extended an invitation to thirteen writers for lyrics using alternative metaphors and descriptions of God, just as the Bible itself does. The resulting hymn, "Source And Sovereign, Rock And Cloud," contains

39 different terms for God — and the songwriter started with a list of over 200, all drawn from scripture! No one of the 39, or of the 200, or the sum total of them all is adequate for all that God is; but by using several, we at least give some sense of how much greater God is than any name — or all names — can contain.

— S. P.

Epiphany 6/Ordinary Time 6

Psalm 30
(For alternative approaches, see Easter 3, Cycle C, and Proper 9/ Pentecost 7/Ordinary Time 14, Cycle C.)

The heading in my copy of the NRSV labels Psalm 30 as a "Thanksgiving for recovery from grave illness," and verse 2 affirms that. Because the psalmist's plea for deliverance has been answered, he brings this psalm as an offering of praise.

One sermon theme this immediately suggests is the matter of remembering to thank God for answered prayers. This was pounded into me again and again by the church of my youth, which placed great emphasis on thanking God. I knew of one pastor who even kept a prayer journal in which he recorded all his prayer requests, and beside them he wrote how and when they were answered. Then, in his subsequent praying, he made it a point to thank God for those answered petitions. That practice is too mechanical and too much a scorekeeping approach for me, but there is something to be said for the principle.

Following the rescue of nine Pennsylvania coal miners from a collapsed mine, the *Wall Street Journal* ran an editorial (August 2, 2002, p. W13), about how some people saw the rescue as an answer to prayer, citing a sign in a restaurant in the miners' town that read, "Thank you God, 9 for 9." After reviewing the usual questions of whether praying changes God's mind and why God would save some and not others, the editorial referred to Thomas Aquinas and Paul Tillich and their shared view that God is "infinite consciousness, wisdom and bliss, underlying and supporting the material cosmos." In this view, the editorial said, "answers to prayer" are not "instances of a supernatural being putting an arbitrary number of requests into his 'Yes' box ... but are responses of this cosmic spirit to the desires and intentions of all finite spirits."

There are other theological explanations of "answered prayer" (not to mention "unanswered prayer"), and there are too many of them to include in a single sermon. A more fruitful avenue arises from the pattern of alternation that underlies this psalm. That pattern is set in verse 2: "I cried to you for help"/"you have healed me," and repeats in other verses. We see it clearly in verse 5 — "His anger is but for a moment; his favor is for a lifetime" and "Weeping may linger for the night, but joy comes with the morning" — but the pattern is present elsewhere as well (see especially v. 11).

A sermon on this text could focus on how prayer and praise are the twin tools for dealing with the experiences of life, both the hard and the gladsome ones. The pastor who kept the prayer journal did not view his practice as any kind of tally sheet. To him, it was simply evidence of how actively God is involved in our lives. His point is right — our response to the activity of God in life ought to be prayer and gratitude.

— S. P.

Epiphany 7/Ordinary Time 7

Psalm 41

This psalm is often identified as a prayer of individual thanksgiving but it reads more as a plea for help. The prayer comes from one so sick that his continued survival is in jeopardy. We cannot help but wonder, however, if his illness has made the psalmist somewhat paranoid (see vv. 5-9).

Yet, whether the machinations of enemies were actual or the product of feverish imagination, the psalmist's feeling that his life was threatened was no doubt real enough. Serious or prolonged illness can have that effect on any of us. An upbeat young woman I know who has nothing of the hypochondriac in her, but who has been afflicted by one real illness after another, tries to live her life positively, giving no quarter to the diseases. But recently, after an injury from an ordinary fall drifted into a rare and thorny complication, she said, "Okay. This is enough! Why am I being singled out?"

If we believe that God is actively involved in the nitty-gritty of our lives, then that is a fair question. It's unanswerable, but fair nonetheless.

This psalm could be the basis for a sermon that acknowledges not only how helpless illness and other vicissitudes of life can leave us feeling, but also how they can make us feel persecuted. There is an old Yiddish proverb addressed to God that says, "Thou hast chosen us from among all the nations — what, O Lord, did you have against us?" On a personal level, a lot of us feel the same.

Is there a way we can help people acknowledge their paranoia about God without leaving them feeling condemned for it? Rather than try to argue such feelings away, we may do better to accept them as reasonable, and then talk about how faith operates in that circumstance. I no longer remember the title, author, or plot of a spy-thriller I read some years ago, but one scene has stuck with me. The protagonist is visiting in a private residence in Moscow, in what was then still the Soviet Union. While he talks with the woman in the home, the woman's aged father is over in the corner praying. The novelist said something to the effect that the old man prayed every day to the God whom he blamed for everything, but whom he trusted implicitly.

In his book, *A Room Called Remember* (HarperSanFrancisco, reissue edition 1992), Frederick Buechner writes of the great pain he feels because of the illness of someone he loves, and moves on to share what it might be like to truly love God:

> *I loved him because there was nothing else left. I loved him because he seemed to have made himself as helpless in his might as I was in my helplessness ... so the farthest reach of our love for God is loving him when in almost every way that matters we can neither see him nor hear him....*

— S. P.

Epiphany 8/Ordinary Time 8

Psalm 103:1-13, 22

This is one of those psalms whose words have become so familiar from liturgical usage that they run the risk of evading our consciousness. How many spoken assurances of pardon have included the words, "The Lord is merciful and gracious, slow to anger and abounding in steadfast love" (v. 8).

Yet they are words that bear repeating, as well as careful study. Within the central portion of this psalm, verses 8-13, are some of the most powerful and profound statements in Hebrew thought concerning the attributes of God — although verse 8 wraps it all up in one tight package.

Let's see what this verse teaches about the nature of God:

1. The Lord is *merciful* (sometimes translated "compassionate") — transgressors can return to God again and again, confessing their sin, confident that the one who judges them also loves them, and will temper judgment with kindness.

2. The Lord is *gracious* — with respect to the penitent, there is no longer any keeping of score, no tally of sins; God is not an accountant of human transgressions.

3. The Lord is *slow to anger* — although some may be troubled by the thought that the Lord gets angry, in fact this is good news, in that the Lord first seeks out every possible alternative to wrath. In the larger context of the verse, divine anger is but one attribute of God, pointing to God's abiding justice — but in the end it is tempered by mercy, grace, and love.

4. The Lord abounds in *steadfast love* — this rich Hebrew concept of *hesed* is difficult to translate in all its fullness. It communicates a sense of deep, reliable caring and protection. While human beings are fickle in their love for each other and for their God, the Lord is utterly reliable.

Does our culture believe these things about God? Not really. Shallow versions of Christianity that see the Lord as either a benignly supportive therapist, or a harsh and terrifying judge, abound. The God described in Psalm 103:8 has some similarities to these superficial views, but this verse bears powerful witness that they in no way exhaust the meaning of the divine. The Lord is both to be feared and loved, and with good reason — but the good news is that, for those who approach the judgment seat in faith, mercy, grace, and love will always triumph over retribution.

In the words of Roman Catholic theologian Hans Küng:

> *From the first to the last page of the Bible, it is clear that God's will is aimed at our well-being at all levels... God's will is a helpful, healing, liberating, saving will. God wills life, joy, freedom, peace, salvation ... both of the individual and of humanity as a whole. And this is the meaning of all that Jesus proclaims.*

— C. W.

Epiphany 9/Ordinary 9

Psalm 81:1-10

This song, written in call-and-response style, summons the people to worship, then treats them to an address by none other than God. Verses 1-5a are the call to worship, and verses 5b-10 are God's reassuring response.

Verses 11-16 (omitted from this week's lesson, but short enough to include in a scripture reading all the same) contain a change in key. God's address to the people continues, but now mentions the people's unfaithfulness. There is little mention of divine retribution, however. On the contrary, God yearns for the people's repentance and full devotion. The psalm eventually ends on a note of reassurance, with the Lord's promise to feed the people with "the finest of the wheat," and to satisfy them with "honey from the rock" (v. 16).

The context of this psalm is undoubtedly some kind of religious festival, very likely the Festival of Booths decreed in Numbers 29 and Leviticus 23. A look at Numbers 29:1-9 will reveal several elements alluded to in this psalm, particularly the sound of trumpets and feasting.

Verse 7 refers to "the waters of Meribah," the water that emerged from the rock when Moses struck it with his staff (Exodus 17). In verse 16, the Lord promises not merely water, but honey from the rock.

This psalm — particularly the omitted section, verses 11-16 — reveals an unusual side of God. We hear the Lord calling the festival participants to renew their faith, to take their place again in the wilderness as their ancestors did of old. This time, however, they will not despoil the Lord's generosity through their complaining, but will in all purity and trust open their mouths wide for the Lord to fill them (v. 10). At this festival, they will not simply subsist on emergency rations, but will feast on the finest wheat and the richest honey. In the Lord's appeal to the people, we come to understand something of God's yearning to be in relationship with us. Who are we to hold back?

— C. W.

The Transfiguration Of Our Lord/ Last Sunday After The Epiphany

Psalm 50:1-6
(For an alternative approach to vv. 1-8 and 22-23, see Proper 14/ Pentecost 12/Ordinary Time 19, Cycle C.)

In the lectionary scheme, the psalm for the day is considered to be a response to or meditation on the First Lesson, but this week, that connection is not obvious. The First Lesson for this Sunday is the translation of Elijah into heaven via the chariot of fire and a whirlwind. It's true that Psalm 50:3 says that a "devouring fire" precedes God as he comes, but that correlation is flimsy. And to further complicate things, the Revised Common Lectionary has whacked the older Common Lectionary's offering of this psalm in half (formerly, it was 50:1-15).

The psalm pictures God holding a trial. In the longer version, we hear the charges God brings, having to do with a crude reliance on animal sacrifices — but in the RCL pruning of the psalm, all we get is the convening of the court. (The RCL does list verses 7-15 as the alternative psalm for Proper 5/Pentecost 3/Ordinary Time 10 in Cycle A, but that's a long way removed from this Sunday.)

The verses we are given first show God sending out the summons for the trial (v. 1). The summons goes to the earth itself. Second, they tell us who the defendants are: "the faithful ones who made a covenant with me by sacrifice" (v. 5). And third, they affirm the righteousness of the Judge, "God himself" (v. 6).

So we are left with the set-up for a trial, but none of its transcript. If we are to preach from these verses, it may be wise to base the sermon on verse 3: "Our God comes and does not keep silence." There are plenty of times when God does keep silence, or seems to, and those are challenges to our faith; yet, perhaps, more troublesome are the times God's voice is heard, as the divine judge convenes the court and tries us "faithful ones who made a covenant with [him] by sacrifice" [of Jesus Christ].

Is that a surprise? If our sins are covered by the sacrifice of Jesus, then what charges can be brought against us? Only this one: that, after receiving forgiveness, we fail to live as though God's love and grace matter in our present conduct.

Consider the case of a wife who wholeheartedly loves her husband. He claims to love her, too, but in ways that really matter, he is unfaithful to her. His wife knows nothing of his infidelity, but each time she tells her husband she loves him, he feels like a skunk because he knows he is betraying her love. In that sense, the wife's genuine love becomes a judgment on her husband, whether or not she ever learns of his unfaithfulness.

In the same sense, God's love is the measure of what God calls us to be, the judgment on us. But divine love also invites us to love God back. God's love tells us that genuine, ongoing commitment covers sin's residual effect, casts out fear, and gives us bold confidence on the day of judgment, whatever form that day may take.

—S. P.

Ash Wednesday

Psalm 51:1-17
(Occurs in all three cycles of the lectionary; see Ash Wednesday, Cycle A; Lent 5, Cycle B; and Proper 13/Pentecost 11/Ordinary Time 18, Cycle B.)

Lent 1

Psalm 25:1-10
(See Advent 1, Cycle C, for an alternative approach.)
In a study on the Psalms, (*Seeing the Psalms: A Theology of Metaphor* [Louisville: Westminster John Knox, 2002], William P. Brown asserts that while there are many metaphors used in the psalms, two overarching ones are "refuge" and "path." Both are equally important, says Brown, and both are metaphors for Torah. Refuge symbolizes both the home and destiny for the righteous aspects of Torah while path connotes movement and direction, the response to God's Torah, the kind of conduct prescribed by the Torah. Psalm 25 gives us opportunity to talk especially about that path.

The psalmist prays, "Make known to me your ways, O Lord, teach me your paths. Lead me in your truth ..." (vv. 4-5a). And again, "He leads the humble ... All the paths of the Lord are steadfast love and faithfulness ..." (vv. 9a, 10a).

The psalmist's "path" is the way of living prescribed by God. Did the first-century Christians have the psalm metaphor in mind when they called Christianity "the way"? (Acts 9:2; 18:25-26).

For sermonic treatment, consider what Psalm 25 tells us about the godly path.

First, it is not necessarily a way that people know intuitively. Why else the petitions: "Make me know" and "teach me" (v. 4)?

Second, it is not a route we walk alone. That's why the psalmist prayed, "Lead me" (v. 5). Note that this is "Lead me," not "Carry me." This is not a maudlin "Footprints in the Sand" story!

Third, it is a path sinners are invited to walk (v. 8), with the understanding that walking the path leads away from sin and toward the good and upright Lord.

Fourth, all the ways of God are characterized as steadfast love and faithfulness, for those who keep Torah (v. 10).

— S. P.

Lent 2

Psalm 22:23-31

(See Good Friday, Cycle A; Good Friday, Cycle B; and Proper 23/Pentecost 21/Ordinary Time 28, Cycle C, for alternative approaches.)

We will meet Psalm 22 in its entirety on Good Friday, but here the lectionary designates just verses 23-31. The lectionary psalms generally illuminate the week's First Lesson, which in this case is about the covenant initiated by God with Abraham and Sarah in Genesis 17. The nine verses from this psalm, while not inappropriate, nonetheless leave us looking for an obvious connection with the First Lesson.

Structurally, the entire psalm falls into two parts. Verses 1-21a are a prayer for help, and verses 21b-31 are a song of praise for help given. In this second part, the one who has been delivered comes to offer praise for deliverance, and to arrange to pay whatever vows have been made (v. 25) during the plea for help.

Perhaps a connection with the First Lesson text can be drawn between vow-keeping and covenant-keeping: although, in biblical practice, vows tend to be made in connection with specific events whereas covenants tend to describe a whole way of living. Nonetheless, it can be useful to talk of vows today.

One reason to do so is that some people think of vows in terms of "bargains" with God. "Just let my wife get better, O Lord, and I will give up smoking," or "Help me out of this one jam, O God, and I promise never to lie again." While the Old Testament does give an example of that kind of vow making (Genesis 28:20-22), more often vows are freely made into promises that are not necessarily *quid pro quo* (though once made, they are considered binding). In the New Testament, Jesus condemns the abuse of vow making (Matthew 15:4-6; Mark 7:10-13).

In any case, it is worth challenging people on this matter of attempting a bargain with the Almighty. While it is certainly an understandable reaction when faced with the serious illness of oneself or a loved one, or when contemplating the unpleasant consequences of one's misdeeds, it is also a way of making God too small.

Recently, a man told me of how he prayed during his young son's struggle for life following a freak accident. The man, though a professing Christian, also viewed pornography from time to time, but in the face of his son's hospitalization, vowed to God to give up the pornography if only God would spare his son. A few weeks later, but before his son's outcome was certain, it came to the man while in prayer that he had no business treating God as someone to be bargained with. And so, while he continued to pray for his son's recovery, the man turned his son's well-being over to God and changed his vow to be that whether his son recovered or not, he would give up pornography. He would do that out of his devotion to God. As it happened, the son made a full recovery, and the man kept his promise, but he told me that he was prepared to do so in any eventuality. The vow had been made.

—S. P.

Lent 3

Psalm 19
(See Proper 22/Pentecost 20/Ordinary Time 27, Cycle A.)

Lent 4

Psalm 107:1-3, 17-22
(For an alternative approach to vv. 1-7 and 33-37, see Proper 26/ Pentecost 24/Ordinary Time 31, Cycle A.)

Psalm 107 provides vocabulary for four different groups of people to give thanks to God for deliverance: those rescued from the desert (vv. 4-9), those delivered from prison (vv. 10-16), those healed from sickness (vv. 17-22), and those who survived storms at sea (vv. 23-32). All these have been redeemed from their trouble, so the psalm opens by advising, "Let the redeemed of the Lord say so."

The portion of this psalm designated for today refers to the deliverance of the sick, and though it speaks from the old view that sickness is the result of sin (v. 17), its description of the misery of the ill is right on: they "endured affliction" (v. 17) and "loathed any kind of food" (v. 18). The point of this part of the psalm, of course, is that God should be thanked for their healing.

The connection between this text and the First Lesson is strong. In the Numbers reading, the people of Israel were healed from the venomous bites of the fiery serpents by looking at the brass serpent on the pole. While it is strange that God permitted such an object among people who had been given the second commandment, the point of the story is that it is God who provides the cure.

A physician who cared for our family in a previous town had a sign in his waiting room that increased my confidence in the doctor himself. The sign read, "We dress the wound, but God heals." This psalm is a reminder that no matter what the procedure or medicine or therapy that saves or extends life, healing is God's realm.

Talking about divine healing always leads to questions about the many who are not healed. Those questions are generally unanswerable, and it's not a lot of comfort to conclude that God chooses not to heal, or accepts self-imposed limits. Nonetheless, the reality is that when we call on the name of the Lord, God's help generally does not mean an immediate fix of the problem or a once-for-all disposal of the pain. But it does mean something real that enables us either to change the outcome in some way or to view it differently if we can't change it — and to know, through all that happens, that we are loved by God and never beyond God's care.

And for those many times when healing does occur — even circumstances as simple as the healing of a minor wound — we know whom to thank.

— S. P.

Lent 5

Psalm 51:1-12
(See Ash Wednesday, Cycle A, and Proper 13/Pentecost 11/Ordinary Time 18, Cycle B, for alternative approaches.)
This psalm is traditionally ascribed to David as his prayer of repentance following his sin with Bathsheba. Whether or not he is actually the author, we cannot know. Nor can we be certain of the circumstances that led to its creation. However, the inclusion of this prayer in the book of Psalms indicates that regardless of its authorship and origin, it served in Israel as a model of how to pray following a significant act of sin.

It serves that purpose for us as well, and the usual approach to preaching this psalm is to indicate the lines that show each of the elements of repentance. These include recognition of the sinfulness of the act (v. 3), confession that the sin is ultimately against the holy God (v. 4), contrition (harder to nail to a specific verse, but more in the overall mood of the psalm), a plea for cleansing (vv. 2, 7), a plea for restoration (vv. 10-12), and a readiness to witness to the grace of God (vv. 13, 15).

The problem with that approach, of course, is that it reduces repentance to a formula. ("Let's see — I have acknowledged my sin, I am contrite, I have asked for forgiveness — now what?") But though the psalm does contain the abovementioned elements, it is more an outpouring of a contrite heart. And more basically, unlike many other psalms, 51 does not ask God to improve a single circumstance in the penitent's life. Instead it says, "I am the problem. Fix me."

In his book, *Prayers*, French priest, Michael Quoist, offers a prayer titled "Sin." In part, it says, "Lord ... I knew you were right near me ... but temptation blew like a hurricane, and instead of looking at you I turned my head away ... When the wind died down ... all of a sudden I found myself alone, ashamed, disgusted, with my sin in my hands."

Quoist's prayer goes on to reveal the depth of the penitent's shame, but at the end there is a reply from God: "Do you think that there's a limit to God's love? ... Ask my pardon and get up quickly. You see, it's not falling that is the worst, but staying on the ground."

It is good and necessary for our congregations to be reminded from time to time of the need for this type of prayer. They (and we) need to hear afresh that even committed Christians sometimes step off the right road, and sometimes quite a way off. And we need to hear also that there is a way back.

— S. P.

Psalm 119:9-16

The reason for this alternate lectionary selection, culled from the longest of the psalms, is undoubtedly the line, "I treasure your word in my heart" (v. 11a). This line matches up nicely with the First Lesson for the day, which is the beloved New Covenant passage in Jeremiah 31. That passage includes the corresponding line, "I will put my law within them, and I will write it on their hearts" (Jeremiah 31:33b).

The taking of God's Word into the heart is an essential part of faith-development. It was true for Israel as a people, and it is true for each of us as individuals. For Israel, that decisive stage of growth did not occur until after the formative experience of the Babylonian exile. For us as individuals, it does not typically occur until our faith is tested in some way, and we emerge from the crucible of that experience as changed people.

When the Hebrew people speak of the heart, they mean something very different than what we do. The heart, to us, is the seat of the emotions. In Jewish thinking, it is more than that. The heart is the place where our very personhood is centered: all the things that we mean by "the heart," yes, but also many of the things we mean by "the mind" and "the will." To say "I treasure your Word in my heart" means that, for the person speaking those words, obedience to the law has become second nature. We most effectively follow the law not because we fear God, but because we love God.

Christian novelist Walter Wangerin tells of an incident from his own life, from his experience as a parent. The Wangerins were going through a difficult time with their son, Matthew, who was on the threshold of adolescence. He seemed to be rebelling against every value the family held dear. On more than one occasion, the boy had been caught stealing comic books from a local store. With the latest incident, Walter was in despair. Feeling he had run out of every other alternative, he resorted to a technique he had not used with his son for years: he gave him a spanking.

The father performed the act gravely, deliberately, almost ritualistically. When it was finished, he was so upset that he ran from the room and wept. After pulling himself back together, he went back in to his son, Matthew, and hugged him, long and hard. Nothing more was said, by father or son, about the incident: but Matthew never stole another comic book.

Years later, Matthew, the grown man, and his mother were doing some reminiscing, and the subject of the comic-book incident came up. "Do you know why I finally stopped?" he asked his mother.

"Of course," she said. "It was because Dad finally spanked you."

"No," replied Matthew, "it wasn't the spanking at all. It was because Dad cried."

It was only when he saw his father cry that Matthew Wangerin experienced the writing of God's Law on his heart.

— C. W.

Palm Sunday/Sunday Of The Passion

Liturgy Of The Palms
Psalm 118:1-2, 19-29
(Occurs in all three cycles of the lectionary; see Liturgy Of The Palms, Cycle A; see also The Resurrection Of Our Lord/Easter Day, Cycles A, B, and C for vv. 1-2, 14-24.)

Liturgy Of The Passion
Psalm 31:9-16
(Occurs in all three cycles of the lectionary; see Liturgy Of The Passion, Cycles A and C, for alternative approaches; see also Easter 5, Cycle A, for an alternative approach to vv. 1-5, 15-16.)

We have visited this psalm before, as it is the designated psalm for Passion Sunday for all three years of the Revised Common Lectionary. The words are the cry of a person in agony and serve as a kind of commentary on the suffering of Jesus. Although the lection stops at verse 16, verses 9-18 comprise a complete unit within the psalm (verses 1-8 are another complete prayer and verses 19-24 are a praise unit).

Within this middle section, verses 9-10 refer to troubles petitioners experience inside themselves, and verses 11-13 those that come from others. Aren't those always the twin sources of problems? We sometimes act as though all our problems arise outside ourselves. If only God — or someone — would fix those, all our troubles would disappear. But then we learn that we too need fixing.

Coming at it from the other way, however, those who first bring their inner persons to God find a peace that lets them deal with the outward turmoil. That's certainly what our suffering Savior did.

In verse 15, the psalmist says, "My times are in your hands," an acknowledgment that it is God "in whom we live and move and have our being" (Acts 17:28). And that is what Jesus said, in essence, from the cross when he cried, "Into your hands I commit my spirit." My times, my life, in this world and the next, are in your hands, O Lord.

Let me tell you about Don. Several years ago, Don and his wife, Nancy, having no children of their own, decided to adopt, and over the course of time, they have welcomed three children into their home. They accepted children from some other countries, saving these kids from a bleak future. Then, sometime later, Nancy experienced a mental collapse and entered a dark period of her own. Though she now has recovered, she is not the same woman. She can no longer handle crowds and her emotional life is precarious. Periodically, she has to return to the hospital to get herself stabilized again.

The two older children have done well, and are now typical teenagers, but the third child, Michael, who came to Don and Nancy's home at age two-and-a-half, brought very tough challenges. He failed to bond with the family and he seemed to have no conscience and no concern for consequences. He stole from the family, mistreated his siblings, and kept things in an uproar. Finally, when his diagnosis revealed deep psychological problems, Michael had to leave home — first to a treatment center, and then to a home with a "professional parent."

But Don visits Michael every Saturday, spending time with him.

"How do you keep hope alive?" I asked Don one day.

"You play the cards you were dealt," he said, modestly.

That's what Don says because he's not one to complain, but that's not really his whole answer. In his Sunday school class, he occasionally shares his worry and concern with a few of us. People in the class pray for Don and his situation. People offer words of support. In short, Don doesn't keep hope alive all by himself. The church community rallies around him and helps him nourish his hope. It's not the only factor, but it is one that helps Don not to give up hope — that keeps him believing that his life, and Nancy's life, and Michael's life are in God's hands.

It may be faith that helps us find the path of life, but it is only the knowledge that our lives are in God's hands that keeps us on that path.

— S. P.

Maundy Thursday

Psalm 116:1-2, 12-19
(Occurs in all three cycles of the lectionary; see Cycle A for an alternative approach; see also Easter 3, Cycle A, for an alternative approach to vv. 1-4 and 12-19.)

This is a thanksgiving psalm. It both celebrates God's answer to the psalmist's prayers for help (vv. 1-2) and declares the psalmist's intention to go to the temple and "return to the Lord" those things the psalmist had promised while praying the prayers (vv. 12-14).

The connection of this psalm with the First Reading (the first Passover) and with Jesus' Passover meal with his disciples on Maundy Thursday is through verse 13: "I will lift up the cup of salvation and call upon the name of the Lord...." In fact, Psalm 116 is often read as one of the sequence of psalms still used in the Passover observance. Obviously, too, the psalm functions just as well for the new meaning Jesus gave the cup at the first Lord's Supper.

In the psalm, the mention of lifting up the cup is given as one answer to the question posed in verse 12: "What shall I return to the Lord for all God's bounty to me?" (The other answer is in 14: "I will pay my vows to the Lord.")

How often do we think of our participation in communion as an act of giving something back to God? More likely, we come conscious of our own needs, and we come expecting to receive. But it is also an act of obedience, and that always is an appropriate gift to God. Obedience is not a popular word in our culture today, but obeying God remains a primary expression of our faith. That's especially critical for those of us not given to emotional responses, those who aren't particularly moved by worship and who don't really get excited by some new idea presented in the sermon. We do not need to worry, for obedience to God alone is a sufficient faith response.

— S. P.

Good Friday

Psalm 22

(Occurs in all three cycles of the lectionary; see Good Friday, Cycle A; Lent 2, Cycle B; and Proper 23/Pentecost 21/Ordinary Time 28, Cycle C, for alternative approaches.)

It's obvious why Psalm 22 is designated for Good Friday for all three years of the lectionary: Jesus uttered its opening words from the cross (Matthew 27:46). The entire psalm describes the suffering of a righteous person in terms that fit the crucifixion of Jesus, including verse 16, "They have pierced my hands and feet" (RSV) and verse 18, "For my clothing they cast lots." In all, five quotations from or allusions to Psalm 22 appear in the gospel passion stories.

One thing this psalm reminds us of is that Jesus did not suffer in total silence. He quoted this psalm and spoke a few other sentences as well. The very idea of the "seven last words," often used as an outline for the three-hour Good Friday services, is testimony that Jesus had things to say while dying. And, of all that he spoke from the cross, the words from Psalm 22 are the most bleak, the sentence we can most clearly recognize as the sound of suffering. The sentiment of Jesus' cry from the cross — "My God, why have you forsaken me?" — is one many sufferers can identify with, whether they voice it or not themselves.

I have a quote in my file attributed only to a Eugene Smith, who, I suspect, is the legendary photojournalist, W. Eugene Smith, noted for the way he worked to capture the essence of humanity in his shots. I don't know the circumstances behind the quote, but it stands well on its own:

> *We are never adequately aware of human suffering, because sufferers are often silent. Those who suffer most intensely do not shriek, for they have not the energy. Between our breakfast and our lunch, thousands will die of starvation. We enjoy our comforts only because we live in an eerie silence protected strangely by the soundlessness of so much suffering. If the amount*

> *of human suffering experienced at this specific moment were to be caught in one shriek, that would become a sound wave of such dimension as to destroy this building and kill each of us in it.*

On the cross, Jesus spoke for the silent sufferers, reminding us of the absolute horror of it.

— S. P.

The Resurrection Of Our Lord/ Easter Day

Psalm 118:1-2, 14-24
(Occurs in all three cycles of the lectionary; see The Resurrection Of Our Lord/Easter Day, Cycles A and C, for alternative approaches; see also Liturgy Of The Palms, Cycle A, for an alternative approach to vv. 1-2, 19-29. Another portion of this same psalm was assigned for Liturgy Of The Palms, Cycle B.)

"I shall not die, but I shall live, and recount the deeds of the Lord." This line from verse 17 is undoubtedly the reason why the lectionary editors have selected Psalm 118 as the Psalm for Easter Day. For its ancient Hebrew author, however, this line clearly does not mean the same thing we commonly understand it to mean, based on our 20/20 Easter hindsight.

The Hebrew people did not have a conception of an afterlife. If there is any persistent human life after death, in their way of thinking, it can only be a shadowy existence in the ghostly realm of Sheol. Consequently, the psalms celebrate earthly life, and view a long, abundant life as the ultimate blessing from God. "I believe that I shall see the goodness of the Lord in the land of the living," says Psalm 27:13.

"I shall not die, but I shall live." That line from Psalm 118 cannot apply to Jesus — for if there's one thing the Passion accounts declare, it's that Jesus really did die. The resurrection is not a rescue from death, but is rather a journey straight through it to victory.

The gospel writers all take pains to point out that Jesus did die. Then they go on to report, with equal emphasis, that the life to which he returned was a real, human life — not some ghostly apparition. Matthew tells how the disciples "took hold of his feet, and worshiped him." Mark has the angel announce that Jesus has gone ahead of his disciples into Galilee — not to some celestial realm, but into the dusty streets of his old neighborhood. Luke includes the homey detail of how the risen Jesus ate a piece of fish. As for John, there's that touching scene in the garden, as Jesus and Mary Magdalene physically embrace — not to mention the scene when Thomas touches his Lord's wounds, to see for himself.

The author of Psalm 118 is a king of Israel, perhaps King David himself. This kingly psalm writer knows what it's like to wait, on the eve of battle, with terror sitting like some cold, lead weight in his gut — knowing the enemy forces are vastly superior to his own. "They surrounded me," he writes, "surrounded me on every side ... They surrounded me like bees; they blazed like a fire of thorn ... I was pushed hard, so that I was falling, but the Lord helped me. The Lord is my strength and my might; he has become my salvation" (vv. 12-14). A little later, the psalmist proclaims in relief, "I shall not die, but I shall live, and recount the deeds of the Lord." There is an awe and wonder to his words, that can only come from a man who has looked death in the face, and has returned to tell the tale. "To be saved does not just mean to be a little encouraged," writes Karl Barth; "it means to be pulled out like a log from a burning fire."

The perspective of the psalmist is in some ways similar to that of today's death-denying consumer culture. In both worldviews, God's blessing means little more than a richer, fuller human life. Death, however, is the invincible adversary, so the only thing to do is to deny it. The good news of Easter, by contrast — that death is real and will prevail for a time, but cannot triumph in the end — comes as an audacious and glorious surprise.

— C. W.

Easter 2

Psalm 133
(See Proper 15/Pentecost 13/Ordinary Time 20, Cycle A.)

Easter 3

Psalm 4

This psalm is familiar to those whose liturgical traditions include an evening, or Evensong, service — for its last line often appears in sung liturgy: "I will both lie down and sleep in peace; for you alone, O Lord, make me lie down in safety" (v. 8).

The "peace," of course, is shalom — that deep, abiding inner peace that penetrates to every part of the human personality. It allows the writer of this psalm to sleep at night.

Being able to sleep at night is a condition that is much sought-after by people of our culture — at least if the plethora of ads for pharmaceutical "sleep aids" is any indicator. The psalmist is able to sleep at night because his soul is at peace.

From whence does such peace come? It comes, he is saying, from personal integrity — from an awareness that we have not compromised our most essential ideals, that we have remained true to who we are and to whom God calls us to be.

Going back to the beginning of this poem, we find the psalmist is crying out for God's help in dealing with a certain problem. He has been wronged by some kind of falsehood. Changing his focus from God to other people, he cries out in agony, "How long, you people, shall my honor suffer shame? How long will you love vain words, and seek after lies?" (v. 2).

This is the cry of someone who has been slandered in some way. The details are unknown to us, but we can feel his pain. No one, evidently, believes him when he protests his innocence. But he takes refuge in the conviction that God hears him, and knows him to be a person of integrity (v. 3).

The writer, Janet Malcolm, observes, "We are all perpetually smoothing and rearranging reality to conform to our wishes; we lie to others and ourselves constantly, unthinkingly. When occasionally — and not by dint of our own efforts, but under pressure of external events — we are forced to see things as they are, we are like naked people in a storm." The psalmist knows God's gift of *shalom* because he is not like this. He is a truth-teller, and the Lord has blessed him for it.

There is a certain conventional wisdom that sees truth as fragile and weak, and lies as the product of strength and cleverness. Those who perpetually lie for a living — certain politicians, CEOs, public-relations agents, advertisers, and others — imagine themselves as being very smart, masters of their own destiny. But they are not. For there is nothing more fragile, at the end of the day, than a life built on falsehood. "Truth," on the other hand — as Oliver Wendell Holmes has put it — "is tough. It will not break, like a bubble, at the touch, nay, you may kick it about all day like a football, and it will be round and full at evening."

In the evening, only those who cherish the truth know God's *shalom*.

— C. W.

Easter 4

Psalm 23
(See Lent 4, Cycle A, and Easter 4, Cycle C, for alternative approaches.)

If asked how many images of God this most familiar of all psalms includes, most people would probably say one, that of shepherd. (And, while saying it, there's a good chance they'd actually be picturing Jesus with a lamb in his arms, thanks to the famous painting of that scene hanging in Sunday school rooms all over America.) But, in fact, there are two images of God in this psalm — the shepherd (vv. 1-4) and the host at a banquet in the temple (vv. 5-6).

Both images of God are appropriate and important, and, since many Christians already address this psalm to Jesus, it's worth noting that they are not mistaken to think of Jesus as both shepherd and host as well.

This psalm can certainly be used to support today's Gospel and Epistle Readings — both of which speak of the shepherding work of Christ — but the psalm could also be used to invite people to think of what the hosting work of Christ is. It has to do, of course, with the invitation to the communion table, but Christ is also the one who invites us to enjoy the hospitality of the kingdom, to sit down at the great feast, the celebration that conveys the joy of the kingdom.

One of the great hospitality stories of recent times comes from the events of 9/11, when the country was reeling from the terrorist attacks in New York and Washington. As the airspace over the U.S. was shut down that day, many flights already aloft were forced to land elsewhere. Some of these planes were rerouted to Newfoundland and grounded there for many long hours. The hospitality those passengers received from the citizenry of Newfoundland has been celebrated in email accounts that circulated widely, and was even described in the *Wall Street Journal* (November 7, 2001, p. A1.) One of the stranded passengers, Thomas Werk, was quoted in the *Journal* article. He said, "We realized that everything was totally out of our control, and that we were at the mercy of ... strangers. They did everything for us." That is human hospitality, and it shone brightly during that emergency. Surely divine hospitality is all the greater, for we are given not just a home away from home, but an eternal home, where goodness and mercy will surely follow us.

— S. P.

Easter 5

Psalm 22:25-31
(See Lent 2, Cycle B.)

Easter 6

Psalm 98

(See Christmas Day, Cycles A and B, for alternative approaches.)

Psalm 98 gets a lot of play in the lectionary cycles. It is the psalm for Christmas Day all three years of the lectionary, and the psalm for the Easter Vigil for all three years as well. It appears here on Easter 6 in Cycle B. It is the psalm for Proper 27/Pentecost 25/Ordinary Time 32 in Cycle C in the semi-continuous readings option and for Proper 28/Pentecost 26/Ordinary Time 33 in Cycle C for the paired reading option. Thus those wishing to preach from the psalms often will have to dig deeper each time 98 comes along.

For this sixth Sunday of Easter, verse 3b — "All the ends of the earth have seen the victory of our God" — connects with the theme of Christ being offered to the Gentiles, which occurs in the Acts lection for today.

But for those wishing to go in another direction, consider verse 1b: "His right hand and his holy arm have gotten him victory." This expression is a military one and is an image of God's power in battle (see Exodus 15:6 and Isaiah 52:10). The image of God's hand appears more than 250 times in the Bible, and often the point is that deliverance comes not because of human activity but because of God's.

Military images of God do not seem politically correct today, but we should not forget that one name of God that appears often in the Bible is *Yahweh Sabaoth*, usually translated as "Lord of Hosts" (235 times in the Old Testament). Note that although this is a composite name, nothing is taken away from either name by the linking of it to the other. *Yahweh Sabaoth*, is, first of all, fully Yahweh: the God who entered into covenant with Abraham and his seed. *Yahweh Sabaoth* is the God of Israel and the God who made the heavens and the earth.

The addition of *Sabaoth* takes nothing away from the name of God, but instead expands how God wished to be understood in those days. And *Yahweh Sabaoth* translates as "the one who will be armies."

This is not to suggest a sermon promoting actual warfare, but we can at least understand that it gives us room to talk about spiritual warfare. Being a Christian is a lot more than being a nice person. It also means fighting against the powers and principalities, in whatever new form they take in each new age.

Back in 1986, when the United Methodists were preparing a new hymnal, a great brouhaha arose in the church when the hymnal committee proposed leaving out the hymn "Onward Christian Soldiers." The committee voted to delete it, feeling it was overly militaristic and was thus inconsistent with the church's goal of the eradication of war and the establishment of world peace.

The reaction of the rank and file in the church, however, eventually forced the committee to reverse this decision. Between mid-May, when the deletion was announced and July 1, the committee's office received over 11,000 pieces of mail, of which only 44 supported the committee's decision. So many phone calls came in about the matter that the staff was forced to make their outgoing calls on pay phones in the lobby! Six days later, the committee voted to restore the hymn.

Afterward, the committee studied the correspondence and discovered that the letters gave one or more of four reasons for keeping the hymn. One of those is significant here: that "militaristic metaphors within hymns should be construed in reference to spiritual warfare, which has a firm biblical base." (Carlton R. Young, *Companion to The United Methodist Hymnal* [Nashville: Abingdon Press, 1993], p. 136.)

— S. P.

The Ascension Of Our Lord

Psalm 47
(Occurs in all three cycles of the lectionary; see The Ascension Of Our Lord, Cycle A.)

Psalm 93
(Occurs in all three cycles of the lectionary; see The Ascension Of Our Lord, Cycle A, for an alternative approach.)

This psalm celebrates God's regal bearing: "The Lord he is king, he is robed in majesty" (v. 1). But it is the powerful imagery of God's throne "established from of old" (v. 2) that draws this psalm into use on Ascension Sunday. Early Christian confessions assert that Jesus ascended to the "right hand of God." This imagery presumes a throne room with a right and left hand of power. Among ancient Eastern monarchs, the place at the right hand of the king was regarded as the most privileged place, second only to the throne itself. It was reserved for that one person who most pleased the king.

Living in the modern world, and especially in the United States, does not offer us many parallels for understanding the significance of all this royal imagery. Even the American president, with the awesome power at his command, still does not touch the sovereign character of ancient kings.

The psalmist, however, offers images that are helpful in making appropriate connections. The psalmist links God's kingship with creation. The reference to the "floods" and the roaring waters most certainly refer to the primeval waters upon which God moved and brought the earth into existence (Genesis 1). The power of God is no where more potently demonstrated than in the administration of the universe.

This is where our view of the modern world helps us. What we know about the scope of the universe makes the confession of God as creator truly astounding. The sheer depth and breadth of our universe reveals a God of immense power and creativity. If that is what the Bible means when it declares that God is king, then God is a king truly glorious and worthy of praise and devotion (v. 1).

The universe, as we understand it, is an immense and complex order. Imagining a living force which stands outside this universe, or acts upon this universe — not to mention bringing it into existence — certainly implies a higher order of administrator. While we may not have a frame of reference for the meaning of king, anyone who can build and sustain such an organization is a creative force worthy of awe and respect. And if Jesus is seated at the right hand of this amazing creative force, then his role as King of kings certainly takes on a universal significance.

The psalmist responds to his own recognition and understanding of God as king by singing a song of praise for the "majesty" of God. How can we do less?

—J. E.

Easter 7

Psalm 1
(See Proper 20/Pentecost 18/Ordinary Time 25, Cycle B, and Epiphany 6/Ordinary Time 6, Cycle C.)

The Day Of Pentecost

Psalm 104:24-34, 35b
(Occurs in all three cycles of the lectionary; see The Day Of Pentecost, Cycle A, for an alternative approach.)

After composing a long list detailing the processes of the earth, both of nature and commerce, the psalmist writes, "When you send forth your spirit, they are created; and you renew the face of the ground" (v. 30). It is this reference to sending forth the spirit, renewing life and creating new life that draws this psalm into service on Pentecost Sunday in all three years of the lectionary cycle. The poem provides a powerful backdrop to the great Pentecost event when the arrival of the Spirit gave new life to the young church.

This is an important activity God performs for us. There is much in life that saps our energy and enthusiasm. Without a way to be renewed and restored, or in some instances re-made, life and its many turns can soon become a burden.

For instance, those who are involved in giving of themselves in acts of kindness for others are always in danger of giving out. The relentless demands on those who provide care for others in need — especially those who attend to the chronically ill, disabled, or the elderly — often create challenges that seem to have no end.

Also, there are struggles with our own pain and disappointment or even failure. The difficulties that are our own can easily result in sagging spirits and depleted energy.

Even success has its dangers. As we expend energy and creativity into our various life projects and then succeed, that success is sometimes followed by an empty feeling: a sort of, "Well, now what?"

The psalmist would have us believe that the presence of God in the form of the Spirit has the power to reanimate and reinvigorate. A renewal of our experience of God's presence can be a source for renewing our energy and our passion for our calling, or even for life itself.

How many times have we seen a football team that is behind and beaten suddenly execute one big play? As if by magic, players start running and jumping as if they weren't tired or behind at all. One play turns the whole team around, and suddenly the team that was playing poorly starts playing with confidence and verve. One play, one good play, and the team that was losing begins to win.

It is not enough that we are doggedly committed to some task. Unless there is passion and purpose, the redundancy of life will suck the joy right out of us. But if we can believe again in our purpose, in our cause, in our calling with a renewed passion, redundancy gives way to creativity, and every day becomes a new day. That is what God's Spirit can do. And when it happens, we can declare with the psalmist, "I will sing to the Lord as long as I live; I will sing praise to my God while I have being" (v. 33).

— J. E.

The Holy Trinity

Psalm 29
(Occurs in all three cycles of the lectionary for The Baptism Of Our Lord/Epiphany 1/Ordinary Time 1; see The Baptism Of Our Lord/Epiphany 1/Ordinary Time 1 Cycles A and B for alternative approaches.)

Though I quite understand the danger of thunderstorms, they do not terrify me. I believe this is because of my childhood memories of my mother going out on the porch during storms to watch and listen to them. One of my first recollections about hearing thunder is my mother telling me it was the sound of angels bowling. But as I grew and came to know my mother better, I realized that she was a deeply committed Christian, and that she considered storms expressions of God's glory (and this despite the fact that an acquaintance of hers had been killed by lightning during a storm).

So does the author of Psalm 29. It is essentially a song praising God's glory as revealed in thunderstorms. The "voice of the Lord" in verses 3-9 is thunder.

The psalmist views the natural phenomenon of the storm as an epiphany of Yahweh — something we, in an era when meteorology is "science," are not likely to do. We can explain, at least in broad strokes, why storms occur, and so have a harder time hearing anything about God's glory in the rumble of thunder. At the same time, when we view the damage and destruction storms can do, we may not want to associate them with God's glory.

What we should not forget, however, is that whether or not we identify storms with the glory of God, the Creator can use any medium as a channel to speak to us. My mother heard God in storms where others found only anxiety. We can explain storms, prepare for them, hide from them, get caught in them, clean up after them, and so on, but we cannot say that heavenly beings never shout, "Glory!" in them. (In v. 1, the author calls on "heavenly beings" to lead the praising of God, so maybe my mother's reference to angels wasn't that far off!)

In his excellent book on the psalms in the *Interpretation* commentary series, James Luther Mays points out the danger of reducing the natural phenomenon entirely to "the dimension of our reason and needs." He then quotes Calvin: "It is a diabolical science which fixes our contemplations on the works of nature, and turns them away from God ... Nothing is more preposterous than, when we meet with mediate causes, however many, to be stopped and retarded by them, as by so many obstacles, from approaching God." (Mays, *Psalms*, in the *Interpretation* series [Louisville: John Knox Press, 1994], pp. 138-139.)

— S. P.

Proper 4/Pentecost 2/Ordinary Time 9

Psalm 139:1-6, 13-18
(See Epiphany 2/Ordinary Time 2, Cycle B. For an alternative approach to vv. 1-12, 23-24, see Proper 11/Pentecost 9/Ordinary Time 16, Cycle A.)

This psalm embodies the tension between a God who knows and a God who acts. The first part, verses 1-18, is the most familiar. The words of imprecation in the second part, verses 19-24 ("I hate them with perfect hatred") are shocking, and as a result have not become a favorite devotional piece, as the first part has.

Yet the two are linked. The psalmist takes comfort in the fact that the Lord has searched him and knows him, that there is nowhere he can flee from God's presence (vv. 1-12). But then, in verses 19-24, he takes God to task for not doing something about the evildoers, whom God surely knows just as thoroughly.

In between are verses 13-18, which form the heart of this week's lectionary reading (vv. 1-6, which precede them, serve as a sort of introduction). As is often the case when the lectionary dismembers a passage and presents it to us in several pieces, it pays to take a look at the whole, before getting down to interpretation.

Verses 13-18 are the conclusion of the first section of the psalm, the full development of the psalmist's meditation on how well God knows him. He reflects on the miracle of human gestation: how, in the mysterious darkness of the womb, a human body becomes infused with life and gradually takes shape. While the psalmist cannot have seen the same images of *in utero* fetal development we have — the product of modern medical science and advanced photographic technology — he must know in general terms something of what goes on in the womb. God, to his mind, tenderly watches over this entire process.

There is a sense of predestination to this passage: "Your eyes beheld my unformed substance. In your book were written all the days that were formed for me, when none of them as yet existed" (v. 16).

This is reminiscent of the famous words of Jeremiah 1:5: "Before I formed you in the womb I knew you, and before you were born I consecrated you; I appointed you a prophet to the nations."

We may be "fearfully and wonderfully made," but it is also a fearsome and wonderful thing that God knows us so deeply. There are consequences to this, in how we choose to live our lives. As for those who do not recognize this truth and form (or mis-form) their lives accordingly, that is a mystery — and God's decision to let them be, to persist in their evildoing, is every bit as mysterious.

— C. W.

Proper 5/Pentecost 3/Ordinary Time 10

Psalm 138

Attempting to use mere language to discuss and describe the workings of God is not an easy task. God, for all the obvious reasons, quickly exhausts our meager language. But that doesn't keep us from trying. The writers of the psalms were constantly using extreme language, pushing words and syntax to their limits, in an effort to describe their awareness or experiences of God.

Psalm 138 is a good example. Set in the context of praises to God for answered prayer, the psalmist takes us far beyond the realm of his personal situation. The God he knows has a name "above everything" (v. 2).

The psalmist wastes no time in getting to the point of his poem. "I give you thanks" are the first words he writes. The expression of thanks becomes the overriding theme for everything else that is offered. As the psalmist pours out praises from a grateful heart, his imagination soars with the wonder of God's greatness.

God is greater than all other gods. God is greater than kings. God's presence, God's name, God's Word are all greater — "above everything."

We have all heard people say they would like to find and commit themselves to something "bigger than they are," or "larger than life." Although saying these things has a certain clichéd quality about it, the sentiment nevertheless describes a common human need and aspiration. We sense intuitively that human life is about more than just personal survival. We were made for greater things, for more lofty purposes. We sense that we will only find the true meaning of our lives by giving ourselves to something larger than ourselves.

This desire to connect with something larger than ourselves becomes particularly important in times of suffering and distress (v. 7). If we have as the focus of our lives the preservation of our lives, then death becomes our constant fear. We live only to stay alive. And any threat of death, such as illness or calamity, serves not only to increase our fear, but also raises the specter of meaningless. In other words, the fulfillment of our aspiring need to connect to something larger than life is also the remedy for the fear that accompanies a life that we know is short.

If all this is true, then the psalmist has us on the right path. He seems to have found something not just larger than life, but larger than kings and even other deities. Meaning for him has been found in the name that is above every name. With that as his reason for living, the psalmist declares, "The Lord will fulfill his purpose for me" (v. 8).

—J. E.

Proper 6/Pentecost 4/Ordinary Time 11

Psalm 20

Among the greatest political speeches ever written is Abraham Lincoln's *Second Inaugural Address*. His brief *Gettysburg Address* is more famous, but those who take the time to read the *Second Inaugural Address* will come away impressed not only by Lincoln's rhetorical skills, but also with his probing philosophical mind and deep piety.

Lincoln wrote these words as the Civil War was drawing to a close. Victory had not yet been achieved, but the South had become so worn down by years of bloody fighting that the triumph of the North was inevitable. Yet, in his big moment in the national (and even international) spotlight, Lincoln resists the easy path to triumphalism. With remarkable humility for a national leader, he struggles with the thorny theological question of whose side God is on:

> *Both read the same Bible, and pray to the same God, and each invokes His aid against the other. It may seem strange that any men should ask a just God's assistance in wringing the bread from the sweat of other men's faces, but let us judge not that we be not judged. The prayers of both could not be answered. That of neither has been answered fully. The Almighty has his own purpose ... Fondly do we hope, fervently do we pray, that this mighty scourge of war may speedily pass away. Yet, if God wills that it continue until all the wealth piled by the bondman's two hundred and fifty years of unrequited toil shall be sunk, and until every drop of blood drawn with the lash, shall be paid by another drawn with the sword, as was said three thousand years ago, so still it must be said "the judgments of the Lord are true and righteous altogether."*

The prayers of neither side have been answered fully. Such is the realistic assessment of a Christian believer, after the dreadful scourge of war has exerted its price. At the beginning of armed conflict, there is typically greater optimism and an easy assurance of God's favor.

Such is the sunny assessment of Psalm 20, a prayer on the king's behalf, imploring God for help on the eve of war. These words are addressed to the king: "May [the Lord] grant you your heart's desire, and fulfill all your plans. May we shout for joy over your victory, and in the name of our God set up our banners" (vv. 4-5a).

Verse 6 goes on to declare, without equivocation, that the Lord will be on the king's side in the coming battle. But then, in verse 7, is planted the seed for a broader, more universal view: "Some take pride in chariots, and some in horses, but our pride is in the name of the Lord our God. They will collapse and fall, but we shall rise and stand upright" (vv. 7-8).

God does not take sides in war. Far more important is whether or not we take God's side.

— C. W.

Proper 7/Pentecost 5/Ordinary Time 12

Psalm 9:9-20

Psalm 9 was probably once joined with Psalm 10, for the letters of the Hebrew alphabet appear in order, half in Psalm 9 and half in Psalm 10. That is, each second verse begins with the next letter of the alphabet.

There is much in this psalm that we have heard in others, but we pause now over verse 11, which advises us to "Sing praises to the Lord" and "Declare his deeds among the peoples." In other words, this psalm calls us to witness to the presence of God in our lives.

Some of us, in our less-than-faithful moments, may be tempted to fantasize about deleting certain verses from the Bible — because, if those verses were deleted, being a Christian would suddenly become easier. If we could drop the verse about loving our neighbor, for example, there would be fewer unpleasant people we would have to tolerate. Or perhaps we would fantasize about omitting the verses about tithing or turning the other cheek.

In my fantasy, I might choose Psalm 9:11 and some other verses that say much the same thing about glorifying God in the marketplace. I'd be a lot more comfortable if I wasn't expected to witness to my faith. I'd rather just preach to those who come to church expecting to hear it than have to "declare ... among the peoples." Witnessing about our faith to people who don't want to hear it is tough. And it can be embarrassing.

But of course, we don't have the option of deleting this verse, and more importantly, we can see the logic and the importance behind it. Christianity needs to be shared, if it is to continue through upcoming generations. Paul put it plainly in Romans (10:13-14): "For, 'everyone who calls on the name of the Lord shall be saved.' But how are they to call on one in whom they have not believed? And how are they to believe in one of whom they have never heard? And how are they to hear without someone to proclaim him?"

And so Christians have to think of ways to build bridges to nonbelievers in order to share their faith. In a baccalaureate address to a senior class, Nathan Perry, former president of Harvard, said, "The finest fruit of serious learning should be the ability to speak the word 'God' without reserve or embarrassment. And it should be spoken ... with reverence and joy."

The key, however, is knowing when to speak that word. The practice of randomly engaging strangers in conversations about Christ is sometimes called "buttonhole evangelism." The problem with that — aside from the fact that doing it would make most of us quake in our boots — is that it treats the person being buttonholed as a "target," a soul to rack up for Jesus. United Methodist Bishop William Grove once said that "buttonhole evangelism that doesn't even take time to discover the person's name is an offense to God." Thankfully, there are some people with the gift of mass evangelism who can talk to crowds about Jesus, and there are others who have the gift for one-on-one evangelism, who can approach a stranger and engage him or her meaningfully in conversation about Christ.

Where some of the rest of us fall down is when a natural invitation occurs in normal conversation to be honest about our faith. Consider the people in our workplaces. If we have worked beside them long enough, they should have some idea that we are committed to Christ. Most of our conversations with fellow-workers deal with routine, everyday things. But as we develop relationships with others, there sometimes come moments when something more serious comes up. Perhaps the other person may even be asking for our opinion about something or wanting to talk about a personal problem. Sometimes, those are situations that are best served by a natural expression or explanation of our faith.

For most of us, being a faithful witness doesn't mean going out to the street corner and buttonholing strangers, or using gimmicks to start unnatural conversations with them, or holding prayer meetings at work. It does mean that when those moments come where another person has opened up his or her life and invited us in, that we be willing to tell about the Lord who means so much to us.

— S. P.

Psalm 133
(See Proper 15/Pentecost 13/Ordinary Time 20, Cycle A.)

Proper 8/Pentecost 6/Ordinary Time 13

Psalm 130
(See Lent 5, Cycle A, for an alternative approach.)

Because the organizing principle of the lectionary is that the psalm is supposed to be a meditation on the First Lesson, we may be forgiven for puzzling about the pairing of Psalm 130 with 2 Samuel 1. The two readings match in neither subject nor tone. The 2 Samuel lection gives us David's lament over the death of Saul and Jonathan, while Psalm 130 is a penitential prayer and a plea for help (and no, we don't buy that mourning over the death of a loved one is akin to mourning over one's sins).

Be that as it may, the psalm offers its own preaching possibilities. It comes as a prayer "out of the depths" (v. 1). "The depths" literally refers to Sheol, the place of the dead, but the psalmist is probably speaking metaphorically, thinking not so much of his physical death in the future as of his current separation from God, the source of life. This separation is the result of his "iniquities," which, if tracked by God scorekeeper fashion — "If you, O Lord, should mark iniquities" (v. 3) — would doom the psalmist to ongoing alienation from God.

But having asked for restoration and redemption, the psalmist "waits for the Lord more than those who watch for morning" (v. 6) — that is, more than those who for whatever reason have been awake through the long hours of the night and look eagerly for the dawn.

Here is an opportunity to talk about the nature of sin. The psalm defines sin as separation from God. That is a useful definition, but let's put that in a modern context. There are some people who like to play golf. Nothing wrong with that. There's certainly nothing sinful about the game as it stands. Now suppose those people like to play golf so much, they abandon their families every Saturday, despite repeatedly promising to participate in some activity with them. Under those circumstances, could playing golf become a sin?

Or let's suppose some other people enjoy sitting around a restaurant with a group of buddies drinking coffee. No sin in that. But now let's say those people do that when they are supposed to be working at the sort of job where they work on their own recognizance. Is it quite so innocent an activity now? Even further, let's lay that scenario out in a real-life situation:

Back in 1981, an inside concrete-and-steel walkway in the Kansas City Hyatt Regency Hotel collapsed, killing 114 people and injuring many others. When the inevitable investigation took place, a large share of the blame fell on the two city building inspectors who had overseen the Hyatt project. Investigators discovered that these two, along with many other Kansas City building inspectors, routinely falsified work logs so they could spend their time bar-hopping during working hours — merely driving by sites they were supposed to be inspecting.

Were the actions of these inspectors sin? Yes — but not just because, in one case, these actions ended up being a factor in the deaths of many people. It was sin back on the days of the inspections when these men issued the certificates saying everything was safe — without actually checking to see that it was. The sin was present in their overall attitude, not just in the consequences of their actions. Although they probably didn't think of it in so many words, their attitude said, "So I'm supposed to protect my fellow citizens. But I don't care about them. I don't love my neighbor as myself. What I want to do is more important to me. Forget about God's Laws."

At the heart of sin is an attitude that fails to honor God or fails to love our neighbors. Sinful acts are what follow from that attitude. "If you, O Lord, should mark iniquities, Lord, who could stand?"

— S. P.

Proper 9/Pentecost 7/Ordinary Time 14

Psalm 48

Psalm 48 is a song of praise celebrating the presence of God. God's presence is praised in general, but in particular the psalmist wants to celebrate the manner in which God's presence has blessed Jerusalem and its temple. The psalmist does not say it explicitly, but intimates strongly that it is in Jerusalem's temple that God's presence is most profoundly experienced: "Walk about Zion, go all about it, count its towers, consider well its ramparts; go through its citadels that you may tell the next generation that this is God our God forever and ever" (vv. 12-14).

In the Protestant tradition, there may be some squeamishness about invoking this kind of praise for a building. Our utilitarian pragmatism tends to view buildings as mainly functional. How many times have we heard a sanctuary referred to as an "auditorium"? Reading this lavish praise heaped on the temple in Jerusalem suggests something far beyond mere utility.

But for the psalmist the temple and the city where it resides is more than merely a worship place. This is God's house — the dwelling of the Most High on earth. When viewed in that light, how could the psalmist do anything less than sing praises to God's "holy mountain, beautiful in elevation ... the joy of all the earth" (vv. 1-2)?

But let's not lose sight of the underlying motive for this song of praise for Jerusalem and its temple. It is not the temple, after all, that makes God present. On the contrary, it is the presence of God that makes the temple holy.

The psalmist writes: "Within its citadels God has shown himself a sure defense" (v. 3).

It is God's presence that creates and defends the city. It is God's presence that sanctifies the great halls and courts of the temple. It is God's presence that brings security and safety to Israel.

It is in the temple that these blessings of God's presence are remembered and celebrated. And because the temple has been set apart for that purpose, it too is worthy of honor and praise. Not for its own glory, but for the faithful witness it offers to God's goodness.

There is one more piece of this praise song that is truly striking. The psalmist seems to suggest that the magnificence of the worship place stirred awe and fear in those who would be Israel's enemies (cf. vv. 4-8).

What a tribute to a place of worship — that those who would do us harm fear us not because of our military might, but because of the God we worship!

— J. E.

Proper 10/Pentecost 8/Ordinary Time 15

Psalm 24

Psalm 24 celebrates the orderly reign of God over creation. It presupposes a world that has not been disrupted by tragedy or displacement — in other words, the world as it was before the exile of Israel in 587 B.C.

From the vision of an ordered universe, the psalmist takes us to the holy mountain for worship. He poses the question, "Who shall ascend the hill of the Lord? And who shall stand in his holy place?" (v. 3).

The answer the psalmist offers is given in terms of the orderly reign of God over humankind expressed in the Law of Moses — the Torah. The law is to human existence what the shores are to the sea (v. 2). The law provides boundaries that form the shape of human character. It is only in strict observance of the law that worshipers may approach God "with clean hands and pure hearts" (v. 4).

Our Christian sensibilities may be troubled by the idea that only those with "clean hands and pure hearts" may enter into worship. The whole notion of "clean" versus "unclean" is one of those issues rendered irrelevant by the grace revealed in Jesus. Our approach to worship would be more in the spirit of "whosoever will may come."

But there may not be as much conflict here as first appears. The idea of "clean hands and a pure heart" is not necessarily limited to ritual or ceremonial interpretation. Even in Christian worship, there are elements of mental and emotional preparation which precede worship. For example, Paul's instruction to the Corinthian church to "examine yourselves, and only then eat of the bread and drink of the cup" (1 Corinthians 11:28), is a clear indication that certain expectations must be met before worship can take place. The same is true for Jesus' admonition to "be reconciled to your brother or sister" before participating in worship (Matthew 5:23-24).

There is a sense in which we all approach God with unclean hands and impure hearts. We are like Isaiah in the presence of God — people of "unclean lips" (Isaiah 6:5). But God wants us to worship and provides resources for us to become clean and pure. In the case of Isaiah, it was a burning coal that made his lips clean. For the rest of us, it is a cruel cross that opens the door to the sanctuary.

— J. E.

Proper 11/Pentecost 9/Ordinary Time 16

Psalm 89:20-37
(See Advent 4, Cycle B, for vv. 1-4, 19-26.)

Psalm 89 is an example of what some scholars classify as a "royal psalm." These royal psalms typically celebrate the Davidic monarchy. This particular psalm comes from a time when Israel is suffering at the hands of some enemy. The setting for the psalm is not necessarily during David's reign. The royal psalms were used in worship during the reign of successive kings.

The portion of the psalm we are considering (vv. 20-37), represents a poetic version of Nathan's prophecy regarding David's reign (2 Samuel 7:4-17). It serves as a reminder of both God's promise and the king's responsibility.

It is possible that this psalm was actually recited in worship by the Davidic king himself. The effect of hearing the king voice the promise of God to guard the throne for David's descendents would have been very dramatic. It is also possible the psalm would have been recited to the king and the congregation by the worship leader. The king would have heard his people reminding him of God's expectations.

The content of the psalm follows the main points of Nathan's prophecy. God promises to remain steadfast with David throughout his life. God also promises to do great things through the king, not the least of which is to make of his descendants, "the highest kings of the earth" (v. 27).

What God expects from the Davidic line in return is obedience. The use of this psalm with successive kings would have served to remind them that God's promise is conditioned upon the king's continued observance of the law.

The section concludes with a return to the promise. God pledges fidelity to the Davidic line. "I will not violate my covenant, or alter the word that went forth from my lips" (v. 34).

What are we to do with conditional promises? Does God's gracious favor come and go depending on our behavior? We make a mistake if we seek to apply this psalm to our ordinary daily relationship with God. God does not accept us then abandon us when we fail to live up to expectations.

However, if we experience a moral lapse while serving in a position of leadership, we should not be surprised when we are removed from that position. This does not reflect God abandoning us personally. It is, however, and example of a principle Jesus articulated: "From everyone to whom much has been given, much will be required" (Luke 12:48).

— J. E.

Proper 12/Pentecost 10/Ordinary Time 17

Psalm 14

(See Proper 19/Pentecost 17/Ordinary Time 24, Cycle C, for an alternative approach.)

This psalm reflects on what Gerhard Von Rad termed "practical atheism." It's not that there are those who decide, intellectually, that God does not exist. Rather, there are those who in their hearts say, "There is no God." The psalmist has in mind those who act and make decisions as though there were no God to hold them accountable. It is entirely possible that there are those who confess with their lips that God is real, but then act is if God does not exist.

The results of such practical atheism are significant and widespread. Those whose behavior is marked by a lack of accountability "do abominable deeds; there is no one who does good."

The psalmist leaves little doubt that God is watching this behavior. The Lord's desire is to find those who are willing to do what is right. But those who are committed to their own way cannot commit themselves to God's way.

This selfish self-interest has an impact apart from the foolishness engendered by the practical atheism. Those who have time only for their own interests and concerns, and who act out of a sense of personal autonomy, wreak havoc socially. Their behaviors result in social arrangements that "eat up my people as they eat bread" (v. 4). They even fail to offer thanks to God for their meal.

But God will not be confounded by human selfishness. Those who are committed to their own self-interest will find themselves living in fear. This is because "God is with the company of the righteous" (v. 5). Practical atheism threatens the poor by disregarding their needs, "but the Lord is their refuge" (v. 6).

We see the truth of this psalm acted out on the stage of world history every day. Powerful corporations seek to extend their profits regardless of the toll on human life. Communities are threatened by pollution because "the bottom line" is more important than human health. Violent regimes terrorize their citizens, holding them in check with fear.

Only those who say in their hearts, "There is no God," could be capable of doing such things. Their actions reveal a reckless autonomy that seems to belie the idea of accountability — to anyone, but especially to God.

They may be good people who attend church. They may rise and recite the Apostles' Creed. They may sing the great hymns of our faith. But their actions are filled with foolish unbelief.

—J. E.

Proper 13/Pentecost 11/Ordinary Time 18

Psalm 51:1-12
(See Ash Wednesday, Cycle A, and Lent 5, Cycle B, for alternative approaches.)

Psalm 51 is revered as one of the most moving and memorable examples of penitence found in the Bible. The superscription attributes the psalm to David himself at the time when the prophet Nathan confronted the king with his adultery with Bathsheba. Whether or not David wrote (or spoke) these words, they certainly reflect a proper sense of remorse in the face of moral failure.

There are many elements in this psalm that are important. Two themes of special significance deserve consideration. The first has to do with God as the injured party, and the other with the locus of salvation.

The first of these important themes is expressed in verse 4: "Against you, you alone, have I sinned, and done what is evil in your sight."

God is the norm and reason for human behavior. As a result, failure to live as God has directed is an attack on and an affront to God's character. This is not to say that others are not hurt by our sin, but God is the one who suffers most of all. If nothing else, the cross has taught us that.

The other important theme concerning the locus of salvation is expressed in verse 12: "Restore to me the joy of your salvation." The burden of guilt dulls our capacity for joy. Life loses its vitality as our failure erodes our ability to be happy. We seek release from our guilt that the joy might return. Or, as the psalmist puts it: "let the bones that you have crushed rejoice" (v. 8).

However, given our individualism engendered in us by western culture, we anticipate the psalmist's writing, "Restore the joy of my salvation." For us salvation is our possession. We receive it, we have it, we find it, and we lose it, and so on.

But the psalmist will have none of this. Salvation belongs to God. We don't possess it. Salvation is a relationship into which we enter and live.

Both these themes establish the priority of God in the relationship. Our sin is against God. Our salvation is God's. Only the failure is ours, and it threatens to empty our lives of joy and purpose. Thankfully, God is gracious, loving, and merciful. The Lord is quick to restore those who repent.

—J. E.

Proper 14/Pentecost 12/Ordinary Time 19

Psalm 130
(See Lent 5, Cycle A; see also Proper 8/Pentecost 6/Ordinary Time 13, Cycle B.)

Proper 15/Pentecost 13/Ordinary Time 20

Psalm 111
(See Epiphany 4/Ordinary Time 4, Cycle B, for an alternative approach.)

Psalm 111 is a carefully crafted, alphabetic acrostic. The subject of the acrostic is the praise of God, for all that God is and does. This theme is developed by 22 lines of Hebrew poetry, each one of which begins with a successive letter of the Hebrew alphabet. The content of this psalm makes it very clear that it was written by someone who wanted to give thankful testimony about God's goodness to the worshiping community.

The psalmist begins with a call to the community to praise the Lord. This praise is expected to give attention to the way God has blessed those who worship. The psalmist leads the worshiping community through a litany of confession about the great deeds of God.

The psalmist gives significant attention to God's character, which is described as the motivation for the great deeds God does. The Lord is described as "gracious" and compassionate (v. 4). God is also a nurturing presence among the people. The Lord remembers the covenant promises and always works for the well-being of those who approach in faith.

The psalmist is also concerned about the character of the worshiping community. He tells them thanks should be offered with the "whole heart" (v. 1). In order to grasp the full meaning of what the psalmist is calling for here, we would need to add "and our whole mind." The heart in ancient Israel was believed to be the source of human thought.

The main point, of course, is that a God as great as Israel's Lord deserves more than half-hearted worship.

The psalmist also informs worshipers that proper thanksgiving takes place in "the company of the upright" (v. 1). This is not to suggest that worshipers are expected to be morally perfect; that would be impossible. It is possible, however, for the words and actions of the community to have integrity. In order to properly worship a God who faithfully keeps promises and is always attentive to the needs of the people, the least we can do is make sure there is consistency between what we say and what we do.

In fact, the psalmist suggests that when worship of a God with integrity is carried out by people of integrity, the result is a level of spiritual and ethical maturity, or what the psalmist calls "wisdom." In short, worshiping God with integrity leads to wisdom that allows for meaningful living (v. 10).

—J. E.

Proper 16/Pentecost 14/Ordinary Time 21

Psalm 84

This vibrant psalm celebrates the presence of God in the temple built by Solomon in Jerusalem. The psalmist seems to experience the presence of God both as possibility and reality. Like so much of what we experience with God, there is an "already," but also a "not yet."

The psalmist begins with words filled with awe and wonder. He praises the splendor and beauty of the temple: "How lovely is your dwelling place, Lord of hosts" (v. 1).

As the psalmist gazes all around the temple, he catches sight of a small bird flying through one of the great courts. The bird has built a nest somewhere in the upper reaches of the temple complex.

The psalmist finds this an occasion for praise. Even a small bird can find a home for herself and her young in God's own house. The sentiment is similar to Jesus' reminder that God has regard for even the small birds that occupy the world. If God cares for the birds, how much more does God care for all of us (Matthew 10:29)!

This theme of nurture and security continues throughout the remainder of the psalm. The writer celebrates the manner in which worship in the temple gives strength to those who attend to God's ways. "Happy are those whose strength is in you" (v. 5), and "They go from strength to strength; the God of gods will be seen in Zion" (v. 7).

The psalm concludes as it began — praising the place where God is worshiped. The psalmist employs dramatic imagery to describe the significance of worship and its effects on us. He writes that he would rather be a menial servant standing only in the very entrance of God's house than a full resident and owner in "tents of wickedness" (v. 10). The blessings of being in God's house are so great that simply standing in the doorway is a rich and satisfying experience.

The final issue in the psalm is about trust. Faithfully attending to worship is a visible and practical demonstration of trust in God. Those who make time to worship on a consistent basis are acknowledging that life is not their own, it is God's. Faithful worship also demonstrates that the continuance of life depends on God. In worship we declare that we do not make or maintain our own lives. We are given life by God, and we trust God to keep us safe, even as the Lord watches over the birds that fly through the air.

—J. E.

Proper 17/Pentecost 15/Ordinary Time 22

Psalm 45:1-2, 6-9

(See Proper 9/Pentecost 7/Ordinary Time 14, Cycle A, for an alternative approach, emphasizing 45:10-17.)

Psalm 45 is a royal wedding song composed as a tribute to the king and his bride. There is nothing quite like this psalm anywhere else in the Old Testament. The language is sometimes difficult, which may be an indication of an ancient origin for the poem.

Despite this technical issue, however, the festive character of the psalm comes through with clarity.

The psalmist begins his song of praise with a sort of dedication. His heart, he writes, "overflows with a goodly theme" (v. 1). This overflow manifests itself in the song the psalmist is about to offer. "I address my verses to the king; my tongue is like the pen of a ready scribe" (v. 1).

From there the psalmist launches into praise for the king. He praises the king's attractive appearance but also his gracious character (v. 2). The king is a blessed and brave man on whom God has shown great favor.

With that the psalmist moves deftly from focusing on the king to the real power behind the throne. In fact, with extremely artful phrasing, the psalmist reminds the king that the throne on which he sits is in fact God's throne (v. 6). The king is reminded as well that even the office he holds is the result of God's power. Since the king has served faithfully and has done what is right, God will allow him to continue as king: "Therefore God, your God, has anointed you with the oil of gladness beyond your companions" (v. 7).

It is an important comparison and contrast the psalmist achieves. On the one hand there is the joy of the wedding and the praise of a good king. Alongside of this, however, stands the eternal God. God judges all our endeavors — they must meet God's standards. It is God alone who endures. We are temporary, and all we do and have is always transitory.

The wedding, therefore, serves as an object lesson. Two transitory people come together before God to form a union that will only last the length of their lifetime. God's expectation, however, is that the content of their marriage will be as though it would last forever.

The same is true for the good king. Though he reigns only for the duration of his life, it is in the presence of the eternal that he serves. The king must be sure that his actions are consistent with what God will continue doing even after all of us are gone.

— J. E.

Proper 18/Pentecost 16/Ordinary Time 23

Psalm 125

Psalm 125 celebrates the presence of God during times of distress. The psalmist offers comfort to those whose faith is in the Lord in times of oppression or difficulty. He assures them that their faith makes them like Mount Zion itself, strong and secure.

Most scholars identify the historical circumstances the psalmist addresses as the difficult period of post-exilic reconstruction of Jerusalem. Of course, that is far from certain. The psalm's content is general enough to address any time of distress or difficulty.

If the setting is post-exile, the psalmist's beginning point is a courageous assertion. It would mean, possibly, that the psalmist was asserting the strength of Mount Zion with the rubble of Solomon's Temple still on the ground.

If that is the case, the psalmist is demonstrating great pastoral insight with this approach. When things fall apart, when dreams fail, when suffering comes, it is easy to be led to a place where we say, "God does not care for me." The psalmist takes his readers to the place of their greatest disappointment and assures them God does care for them and is with them.

Of course, that is the essence of faith. When we are able to persist in committed belief even in the face of disappointing results, then something genuinely faithful has taken hold in our lives.

This may be one of the reasons Jesus was so impressed with the Gentile woman who seeks healing for her daughter (Mark 7:24-37). She refuses to be rebuffed even when it appears that Jesus is insulting her. She is committed to her belief that there is help for her child in Jesus and she will not be turned away. Because of her persistent faith she finds the peace and healing she seeks.

The power of the psalmist's assurance is not dependent on the temple being in ruins, of course. The writer could have been addressing some other contemporary difficulty in which case his allusion to an intact Mount Zion serves as a reminder of the enduring presence of God.

There is hope for us either way. If we are facing the rubble of our broken dreams, whether the source is bad choices or bad luck, the promise of God is that we can endure. The foundation of faith in our lives serves as the bedrock on which God will rebuild our dreams and restore our hope.

If the trouble we face is not broken dreams, but rather an assault on our confidence or sense of security, that same foundation of faith, adorned with our spiritual disciplines and practical life experiences, stands as a strong bulwark against whatever may come our way. "As the mountains surround Jerusalem, so the Lord surrounds his people from this time on and forevermore."

—J. E.

Proper 19/Pentecost 17/Ordinary Time 24

Psalm 19
(See Proper 22/Pentecost 20/Ordinary Time 27, Cycle A.)

Proper 20/Pentecost 18/Ordinary Time 25

Psalm 1
(See Epiphany 6/Ordinary Time 6, Cycle C, for an alternative approach.)

Psalm 1 has long been considered as a possible prologue to the rest of the psalter. In fact, in several ancient Hebrew manuscripts, this psalm is not numbered as are the others in the collection. The content of the psalm also has something of a "foreword" quality about it. Many of the themes that are developed at length in the rest of the psalms are touched upon in this first one.

As for type, Psalm 1 belongs to a group of poems referred to by scholars as "wisdom psalms." These psalms adopt an instructional tone and seek to encourage obedience to God's Law, the Torah.

The psalm begins with a blessing on those who "do not follow the advice of the wicked." These blessed ones do not stand in the path of sinners nor linger near the dwelling place of scorners. All of these images — lingering, standing, dwelling — are metaphors for learning. The blessed ones have one source for their wisdom: God's Law.

A life lived in commitment to God's truth results in a stable and vital existence. The psalmist compares this existence to a tree that is planted near a sustaining source of water. The tree lives and flourishes because it is rooted near the source of its nourishment.

Those the psalmist identifies as "the wicked" have exactly the opposite life experiences. They are unstable in all their ways. Instead of being like trees nourished by God's truth, the wicked are like the dry chaff that is left after the grain has been removed from a stalk of wheat. So light and airy are these chaff-like people that even the slightest breeze can blow them away.

There are many possible applications of the principles of this psalm. Our culture's preoccupation with wealth, power, and success offer a stark contrast to the simple virtue suggested by the psalm.

The issue of where these values come from is also critiqued by this psalm. What is the water that feeds our souls? Do we dip from the well of greed, or are we refreshed and made strong by the moving water of God's truth? Like the strong tree in the psalm, a faithful life is rooted in serving others. The quest for glory and honor is a fickle dream that is easily blown away with a passing wind.

The psalmist brings the poem to a close, making explicit what was implied in the opening line: The Lord watches over the righteous while the wicked perish. It is not necessary to resort to eschatology to interpret the meaning of this idea. There is a practical truth revealed here that does not require end-time scenarios to understand.

In general terms, those who seek to live meaningful lives of industry and generosity can expect to find great satisfaction in life. This does not mean they will never fall or experience disappointment. It does mean that when those situations do occur, the same resources that fill life with meaning in ordinary times will help them get through the extraordinary.

On the other hand, those whose lives are marked by poor choices and bad habits often find themselves miserable. This happens all along the socioeconomic scale. These people struggle with daily normalcy, and really struggle when something unexpected happens. God does not have to throw them down; the decisions they make and the values they follow often carry their own sorrow with them.

— J. E.

Proper 21/Pentecost 19/Ordinary Time 26

Psalm 124
(See Proper 16/Pentecost 14/Ordinary Time 21, Cycle A, for an alternative approach.)

Psalm 124 takes us deep into the thorny issue of claiming to have God on our side. The matter has come up repeatedly, in recent years, during the war in Iraq. Prayers have been offered, from both sides of the conflict, petitioning God's help in defeating "our" enemy and protecting "our" troops.

There is a slightly different nuance in this psalm. For one thing, instead of seeking God's favor in some pending conflict, the matter is already resolved and the psalmist is giving thanks for God's protection. Israel had suffered attack from some enemy and had prevailed. The psalmist interprets this outcome as God's saving power at work. Despite this minor variation, the theme is clear: Israel prevailed because God was on their side.

This is a predictable response for a person or community of faith. When good fortune comes our way — or, as in this case, salvation — it is our natural tendency to give God the credit. There is not any necessary sense of privileged position, but rather a general acknowledgment of thanks for a blessing that has touched our lives.

Claiming to have God on our side, however, does become a problem when we begin to take action based on the assumption. Once we assume a position of divine prerogative, the designations "us" and "them" can become severely problematic. If "we" are the Lord's and the Lord is on our side, then "they" are not only our enemy, but also the enemy of God. The gospel offers us a different perspective on this issue (cf. Mark 9:38-50). Jesus turns conventional wisdom on its head by telling us, "Whoever is not against us is for us."

We want to be able to say with the psalmist, "It was the Lord who was on our side." Sensing God's presence in times of trouble, acknowledging God's goodness in times of blessing, these are appropriate expressions of faith.

What we do not want to say, however — and probably cannot honestly say — is that "it was the Lord who was on our side exclusively." Once we make this claim, the hope of bridging the distance that exists between us and other human beings all but disappears. In the absolute claim of God's exclusive patronage, fellowship dies.

The tendency to divide the world into "us" and "them" is rooted deeply in our innate insecurity and fear. Hopefully, the love of God can set us free from that fear and suspicion and allow us to see what Jesus saw — that "those who are not against us are for us." Of course, in the full realization of God's intent for us, all reference to "us" and "them" vanishes. In its place is an ideal vision of human community that may sound something like this: "We found each other as we gathered together on the Lord's side. It was there that we discovered that the Lord was for all of us equally."

— J. E.

Proper 22/Pentecost 20/Ordinary Time 27

Psalm 26

Themes of justification and vindication run powerfully through this psalm. The psalmist cries out, "Vindicate me, O God, for I have walked in my integrity ..." (v. 1).

This plea is his whole purpose in writing the psalm. The psalmist wants the Lord to decide his case and declare him just. We are not told exactly what issues in the psalmist's life are in question. Apparently, some untruth has been spoken about the psalmist or perhaps about Israel in general. Regardless of the particulars, however, the psalmist seeks God's vindicating judgment in order to prove the accusation false.

The basis for the plea is the psalmist's claim that he has "walked in [his] integrity." The psalmist asserts he has been faithful to do what was expected under the Law of God. This is not a claim to moral perfection, a notion that did not even exist at the time of this writing. The abstract idea of perfection, much less moral perfection, would not appear in human consciousness until the rise of modernism.

The psalmist's claim is "blamelessness." To be blameless in the sight of the Lord means that everything the psalmist knows he should have done has been accomplished. Fulfilling all obligations to God and neighbor is the biblical definition of "righteousness."

The psalmist cries to the Lord: "prove me, try me, test my heart and mind." In Hebrew this is literally, "kidneys and heart." These organs were believed to be the seat of reason and emotion. The idea the psalmist is putting forth is that not only has he behaved properly, observing the letter of the law, but his thoughts and emotions have also followed the Lord's way. "Walked in my integrity" means the psalmist's interior motivation has been to please God, and not to pursue some other purpose.

This continues to be a struggle for people of faith. What is our motivation for appropriate behavior? Do we do the right thing out of fear? Do we observe strict behavioral standards out of fear that "the wrath of God" will fall upon us? Or do we seek some personal glory, some standing in the community? Jesus frequently criticized self-serving faithfulness as "hypocrisy."

The better way is the way of integrity — doing the right thing for the right reason. If we walk in integrity, we can call out in confidence for God to vindicate us against false charges. However, it may be that God's vindication is not necessary. Quite often persons of integrity are vindicated by their virtue.

But even when that is not the case and false charges come, those whose actions are not driven by the need for approval — either from God or others — will be able to face the accusations with courage and conviction. Their walk in integrity not only leads them to do right, but also to stand strong.

— J. E.

Proper 23/Pentecost 21/Ordinary Time 28

Psalm 22:1-15
(See Good Friday, Cycle A; Good Friday, Cycle B; and Lent 2, Cycle B, for alternative approaches.)

Psalm 22, perhaps more than any other text in the Bible, gives eloquent expression to the loneliness and isolation which comes from experiencing God's absence. We can debate the reality of a theology of abandonment, arguing back and forth whether or not God ever actually does abandon us. But whether God moves or not, there are clearly times in life when we feel completely alone. This psalm gives voice to that feeling.

Of course, we are most familiar with the opening verse of this psalm in connection with the crucifixion. Jesus' utterance of these words from the cross has led to some intricate musings on why God turned his back on the Son. As we read the psalm in its entirety, however, it may be that Jesus was pointing us to something other than hopeless abandonment.

The main theme is a plea for salvation. The psalmist cries out for help from the depths of his pain. We are drawn to the plaintive cry of the lowly as having great authenticity. Not that the rich and powerful are immune from suffering. After all, money can buy many things, but not always peace of mind, or peace in the soul, or a sense of the presence of God.

Interestingly, the verses in the psalm selected for this reading (vv. 1-15) leave the matter of God's presence unresolved. We are left with the psalmist "in the dust of death" (v. 15). We are tempted to press on in the psalm and read down to the place where the psalmist gets past his feelings of abandonment and can say, "for he did not despise or abhor the affliction of the afflicted ..." (v. 24).

But we are wise not to rush too quickly to the comfort of a confessional stance that "God is always near." The path out of pain and despair is often *through* pain and despair. It is much better to have a genuine sense of God's presence after we have lived through a difficult time, than it is to adopt a "God is with me" stance, whether we feel the Lord near or not.

Having the ability and willingness to give voice to our feelings of despair and isolation is part of our healing. This is certainly part of what Jesus meant when he said, "Blessed are they who mourn, for they shall be comforted." He might just as well have said, "Blessed are they who can mourn." It is only through honest and thorough mourning that we are able to progress from pain to comfort. And in comfort we find God. The gift of God's comfort is in God's presence.

By leaving the matter in "the dust of death," we have a chance to stand with the psalmist in his feelings of abandonment. If his words can become our words, if our suffering can take on the tenacious faithfulness that waits for the genuine presence to manifest itself in our lives, we may eventually find ourselves with God at 22:24.

— J. E.

Proper 24/Pentecost 22/Ordinary Time 29

Psalm 104:1-9, 24, 35c

Psalm 104 begins and ends with a unique call to praise. Instead of calling on others to praise the Lord, the psalmist instructs himself: "Bless the Lord, O my soul." This psalm and Psalm 103 are the only places in the Bible where this particular expression occurs. What are we to make of this unusual phrase?

The occasion of this call to praise is a celebration of God's great creative power. In fact, Psalm 104 follows both the content and the sequence of the creation account found in Genesis 1:1—2:4. In this regard we might characterize the psalm as a meditation on the meaning of creation.

This reflection leads to an awareness of the greatness of God. This greatness is made manifest in the marvelous act of creation (v. 24). Standing in awe of the glories of God's handiwork, the psalmist cannot find any better way to express this feeling but in exuberant praise.

The psalm provides a fitting backdrop to discuss praise as an element of worship. When we are stirred spontaneously to deep feelings of awe or gratitude or wonder, it is appropriate for those deep experiences to emerge in words and gestures of praise.

It is worth noting, however, that while it is possible for all these feelings of joy to arise spontaneously, they cannot arise in a theological vacuum. The psalmist is able to see the majesty of God in creation because he is looking for it, and — by orientation and tradition — has some idea what to look for. This is the significance of addressing the self. Worship and praise are the results of intentional acts of disciplined and informed worship.

In other words, the psalmist's praise is not a case of manufactured wonder. The emotions have not emerged by chance. Because the psalmist has carefully meditated on the meaning and scope of creation, he has been drawn step-by-step into an awareness of the profound intricacies of God's creative power. And since this awareness comes from deep reflection and not shallow emotion, the praise takes on a singularly meaningful dimension.

By instructing the self to "bless the Lord," the psalmist is demonstrating a disciplined and careful attention to all things sacred. This intentional discipline results in the humble awareness that the glory of God is not ours to exploit, but rather to enjoy. It is a choice we make for ourselves: whether we will experience this glory, or only hear about it from others. The psalmist wants it for himself, and is determined to find it. "Bless the Lord, O my soul" expresses this conviction of his heart.

—J. E.

Proper 25/Pentecost 23/Ordinary Time 30

Psalm 34:1-8 (19-22)
The writer of this psalm begins with an assertion and an invitation to the gathered company of worshipers. He announces his intention to "bless" the Lord all the time, to praise God with a continual song. In fact, the boast of his life is to be "in the Lord," and he calls upon all who are oppressed (NRSV "humble") to hear what he has to say.

Offering praise to God "all the time" is a formidable commitment. When things are going well, praise makes perfect sense. When our lives are touched by God, it is natural to be grateful and full of thanksgiving. The psalmist, however, is concerned to let us know that not only is God worthy of praise for what has already been accomplished, but also for what the Lord will accomplish. The psalmist writes, in effect, "God has done this for me" (v. 4); "rest assured God will do it for you."

The call to the "humble" or "oppressed" to praise God even in the midst of their suffering is a difficult challenge. It is one thing to exult in God's goodness after we have what we need, or our pain has ceased. It is a different level of faith altogether that exults in God's goodness even while we wait for our suffering to end.

The psalmist is not suggesting some sort of mind-over-matter exercise. We are not being asked to believe that because God is going to do something in the future we are free from pain now. The pain of the moment is real. Likewise, the psalmist is not saying that healing or the end of suffering will come because we have praised God — as if our praise somehow obligates God to act on our behalf.

On the contrary, the psalmist's words are intended as a profound statement of confidence in the goodness of God. We can praise God now, even while we struggle, because we know that God will act eventually on our behalf. Our praise will not be in vain because God does not fail (vv. 20-22).

This is a tough call. In the middle of difficulty, our tendency is to offer prayers of lament or complaint. Prayers of this type are perfectly acceptable and are well-attested in the psalter. But this psalm offers us another option. Beyond lament and complaint, there is patient confidence that leads to praise. There is expectation that God will come and heal and restore. Believing deeply that the matter will be fully resolved at some future moment, we celebrate the Good News to come and give thanks to the God who will bring it to pass.

What will praise do to our suffering? Probably not much. But what it will do for our ability to hope is profound.

— J. E.

Proper 26/Pentecost 24/Ordinary Time 31

Psalm 146
(See Advent 3, Cycle A, for an alternative approach to vv. 5-10.)

This psalm appears several times in the lectionary, with different applications during the Christian year. It is used in two different years in connection with All Saints. What makes the psalm applicable in many settings, including All Saints, is the theme of God's love for the righteous (v. 8). There is tremendous value in remembering and celebrating the contribution of those who have gone before us. The act of remembering helps keep us faithful to the sacrifices and acts of kindness accomplished on our behalf. Celebrating the memory of those who have gone before takes on special significance as we acknowledge our belief in God's blessings and care for these faithful ones.

This psalm also includes an important insight regarding the character of the people we choose to place our trust in. The psalmist warns us, "Do not put your trust in princes, in mortals in whom there is no help" (v. 3).

This insight actually cuts two ways. On the one hand we are called to be responsible for finding and following "mortals" who are helpful. The psalmist is not warning us that all mortal humans fail to offer help, only that some do. If being mortal disqualified everyone from being a mentor or teacher, we would all be lost. We must find those good role-models and follow them. These are the teachers and role-models who shape us and mold us. These are the ones whose life and memory we will celebrate throughout time.

The other side of this, of course, is the recognition that not all mortals are helpful. The psalmist zeroes in on "princes." The reason why should be obvious. What was true in the ancient world is also true now. People of wealth and power can take on a "larger-than-life" status. In our day these people would include politicians and pop stars.

They walk among us as giants. If we are not careful, we will grant them respect and awe beyond what they really deserve. More than that, because of their stature, we may allow them to shape us and mold us into their own image.

People who seem larger than life often have influence that far outreaches their character. This is mostly our own fault. We often have difficulty distinguishing the path that leads to wealth and success from the path that leads to wisdom and integrity. The psalmist offers a subtle warning that we should not be overawed by people in the limelight. They are mortals like the rest of us and are not necessarily the best teachers.

Instead we are challenged to join in a song of praise celebrating God's goodness. God cares for the weak and oppressed. God cares for the prisoner and sets them free. God gives sight to the blind (vv. 8-10). In other words, while we are standing star-struck by the "princes" who walk in our midst, God is standing with the poor and the needy. God stands where the righteous before us have always stood, and where we are challenged to stand as well.

—J. E.

All Saints

Psalm 24
(See Proper 10/Pentecost 8/Ordinary Time 15, Cycle B.)

Proper 27/Pentecost 25/Ordinary Time 32

Psalm 127

It is not possible in a single sermon — or even a psalm — to answer the question, "What is the meaning of life?" That is one of those complicated and complex questions that require a lifetime of reflection, prayer, study, and some trial and error. However, it is possible to ask and answer a different question that may be just as important. The writer of Psalm 127 seems to be trying to answer such a question: "How do we find a life that is really worth living?"

In order to answer this question, the psalmist draws on the imagery of a "house." He identifies several necessary activities that are essential to successfully building a house: building, protective care, and meaningful work. While these are important, there is a central component that is absolutely essential: "Unless the Lord builds the house those who build it labor in vain" (v. 1).

But what does that mean — that the Lord must build the house? If the Lord builds the house, does that mean we are called to a life of passive and idle waiting? Are we merely the raw materials of an actual house? Are we the boards, bricks, and mortar, which lie inanimate until the builder comes for them? Is that what the psalmist means by "the Lord builds the house"?

It seems not. There are "builders" who are seemingly at work with the Lord in doing the building. The Lord builds with the builders. What are we to make of that?

Several years ago, my wife and I built our first home. We hired a general contractor who in turn hired subcontractors — carpenters, brick masons, painters, electricians, plumbers, and so on. All these workers were employed to "build" our house. However, it was the general contractor who supervised their work. Everything the builders did had to first meet his approval. Any work that did not measure up to what the general contractor was looking for was not accepted and had to be re-done.

That is what the psalmist is trying to say. God is the general contractor and we are the subcontractors. We are the builders of our own lives using the raw material provided to us by God. We are free to build any sort of life we want. We can take our time and build something lasting and beautiful. We can create a lasting structure of faithfulness, wisdom, and integrity. Or we can take shortcuts and end up with something less than what God has in mind for us.

God remains the critical standard. If what we build does not measure up to the blueprint God has in mind for us, our lives will be less than satisfying. Building a life without resort to God's goodness and wisdom is a monumental waste of time.

—J. E.

Proper 28/Pentecost 26/Ordinary Time 33

1 Samuel 2:1-10

Hannah's song is probably best-known and most frequently associated in the liturgy as an accompanying reading for the celebration of the angelic visitation to Mary (Luke 1:39-57). When the text is used in this manner, Hannah serves as a type of Mary, with her song echoing themes and expressions to be found in Mary's song.

In doing this, however, the meaning and beauty of Hannah's song becomes obscured, even subordinated to Mary's song. This is not to say that Mary and Hannah serve equal functions in the history of faith. Obviously the birth of Jesus is far more critical to the life of the church than the birth of Samuel. However, it is still a mistake to simply collapse Hannah's song into the Magnificat. Doing this neglects an important yet subtle message found in Hannah's song: A message that can only be heard if she sings her own song.

There are several significant differences between Hannah and Mary. Mary is a young, vibrant woman. Her whole life is before her. She is marriageable, and filled with the possibility of bringing life into the world.

Hannah is none of these things. Hannah is barren. In the ancient world, barrenness was a legitimate cause for divorce. Of course, Hannah's husband did not exercise this prerogative, but in fact pledges his love to her in spite of her barrenness. Unfortunately, this was not enough. To be without children, no matter how much her husband loved her, placed Hannah in a psychological and even theological quandary. Hannah knew that in the pecking order of wives and women, her barrenness rendered her second-rate. And in the prevailing theology of her day, she could only conclude that the source of her condition was God.

When filtered through the lens of Hannah's suffering and exclusion, her song sounds quite different from Mary's. When Hannah sings that God has remembered the weak and lowly, the message has a poignant, personal application. Mary may have been poor and had some sense of what life is like among marginal people. But prior to her pregnancy, she was not a marginal person as a woman. Hannah was not poor, yet was oppressed by a social and theological system that regarded her barrenness as a curse.

In other words, when God granted Hannah's prayer and allowed her to bring a tiny life into this world, she experienced the gift of that son out of the depths of her own despair. The birth of Samuel was not just an answered prayer; it was also a validation of Hannah's very existence.

Her song functions, therefore, as a poetic celebration of God's ability to bring life out of death. It is a reminder of God's persistent desire to lift the fallen and the lowly. It is also a powerful example of God granting voice to one who had no voice. In other words, the song of Hannah celebrates just the sort of thing God finally does with the cross. Not that Mary's song fails to do this, for certainly it does. But when Hannah sings of God bringing life out of death, we know she has someone in particular in mind.

—J. E.

Christ The King/Proper 29

Psalm 132:1-12 (13-18)

This psalm is a poem of public worship, celebrating the Davidic kingship. It recalls God's promise to protect David's name and to keep an heir of David on the throne. Reciting these promises, the psalmist asks the Lord to bless and to redeem David in the midst of all his "hardships" (v. 1). Of these troubles, only one is specified.

The psalm recounts David's passionate desire to move the Ark of the Covenant to Jerusalem. The Ark, of course, was the central religious symbol for the people of Israel. The Ark was the great symbol for the abiding presence of God in the midst of the people.

Of course David was not merely interested in moving the Ark to Jerusalem and leaving it there in its movable tent. David wanted to build a permanent resting place for the sacred object. His desire to do this was so great that he took a vow not to sleep until his purpose was accomplished.

The poem also recounts the Lord's decision not to allow David to build a resting place for the Ark. Instead the Lord "swore to David a sure oath from which he will not turn back ..." (v. 11). The oath of the Lord refers, of course, to the establishment of the Davidic dynasty. The Lord promised that so long as David's descendents remained faithful to the covenant, an heir of David would sit on the throne in Israel.

The actual conduct of the monarchy in Israel fell far below these lofty expectations. The kings who followed David were a mixed bag of faithful and unfaithful. In time, according to the biblical account, it was the unfaithfulness of the kings that led to the collapse of Israel and Judah. The exile marked the effective end of Davidic dynasty.

In an effort to make sense of God's promise that David's line would be eternal, Israel's hope shifted to focus on a future "anointed one" who would restore Israel to prominence and who would reign in the spirit of his ancestor, David. This "anointed one," or Messiah, would save not only Israel, but also the world.

Christians believe that Jesus of Nazareth is the fulfillment of this messianic hope. In Jesus, God has not only kept the promise made to David, but has also established a universal kingdom with Jesus at the head. This kingdom offers citizenship and life to any who will enter and accept Christ as king.

In Christ we have a king who faithfully accomplishes God's will. In Christ we have a king who keeps the covenant made between God and the people of Israel. But Jesus as anointed king reigns not only in Zion but also at the right hand of God. Because of his saving work on the cross, and because of the resurrection, Christ occupies this most privileged of places of honor. From there he offers salvation freely to all who will accept it.

—J. E.

Thanksgiving Day

Psalm 126
(See Advent 3, Cycle B.)

Cycle C

Advent 1

Psalm 25:1-10

(See Lent 1, Cycle B, for an alternative approach.)

There are two important features about this psalm that should not be overlooked. First, like a few other psalms, this one is an alphabetic poem, known as an "acrostic." This means that the psalm follows the alphabet with each successive verse starting with the next letter of the Hebrew alphabet. Writers who employed this technique were not simply trying to be clever. Ancient Hebrews believed even the very letters of words used to worship and honor God were sacred. Arranging the verses in this creative and thoughtful way was just another attempt to show reverence and respect to the Lord.

The second feature to note is that the psalm is a lament. The lament is the most prevalent type of psalm in the psalter. Over forty of the psalms in the canon are laments. In general, a lament was a prayer or plea offered to God in times of distress.

The lament of Psalm 25 was originally written to be used in a service of worship in which an individual's needs or suffering was the focus of the service. It is this feature that finds this psalm used several different times throughout the Christian lectionary cycle, especially during Lent and Advent.

In both these significant seasons in the Christian year, the psalmist's plea is important: "Do not let those who wait for you be put to shame" (v. 3). Faithful waiting is the main emphasis in both Advent and Lent. Both seasons call for a disciplined wait for fulfillment. We wait for the birth of the Messiah. We wait for the child to become a man. We wait for the man to die on a cross. We wait for his resurrection. We are waiting for his return.

Being put to shame can have two points of focus. As we wait faithfully for the Lord to act on our behalf, we hope not to be humiliated or oppressed by circumstances. Nothing is a greater challenge to our faith than to suffer in the midst of, or because of, our obedience. Waiting is inevitable, but as the Lord taught us to pray, we can ask that the Lord "deliver us from evil."

The other focus of shame has to do with the character of our faithfulness. The temptation during the long wait for the Lord to appear is to lose heart and to break trust. In a fit of despair we cry with the fool, "there is no God" — or, what amounts to the same thing, we claim there is no hope. In this sense, the psalmist is praying that when the Lord appears we will be found faithful, that we will not be shamed by our disobedience or by our surrender to despair.

In the case of the psalmist, the wait is marked by suffering — but isn't that always the way? If there were no pain in life, no tension, no challenges to our morality, there would be no longing for the Lord to appear. It is because our world is fallen and we are constantly bombarded with messages to give up or give in that our waiting takes on such a critical function. In a broken and cruel world marked by violence and death, we wait for the arrival of the Prince of Peace.

— J. E.

Advent 2

Luke 1:68-79
(See Christ The King/Proper 29, Cycle C, for an alternative approach.)

The *Benedictus*, the prophecy and song of blessing voiced by Zechariah after the birth of his son John (the Baptist), falls into two parts. The first (vv. 68-75) praises God for the coming messiah and Israel's deliverer. "He has raised up a mighty savior" (v. 69). The second focus of Zechariah's song is thanksgiving to God for the forerunner who prepares the way for the Messiah to come (vv. 76-79). After all, it is the occasion of John the Baptist's birth and the significance of his life revealed to Zechariah by the Angel Gabriel that inspired the song in the first place.

Interestingly, even while Zechariah is speaking directly to his son about the role he will play (v. 76), he continues speaking about the significance of the coming Messiah. John's role, while important, would always be secondary to the work of the anointed one. In the language of the Gospel of John, the Baptist would have a recurring role to play in the drama of redemption, summed up in the prophet's own words: "he must increase, I must decrease." Even though he is called the "prophet of the most high," he nevertheless declares himself unworthy to even untie the Messiah's sandals.

The theme at work here, of course, is "preparation." John announces the Lord's coming so all may be ready to receive him. As we celebrate John's role as the one who prepares the way of the Lord, we learn to appreciate the significance of those who stand in the background. As we prepare ourselves for Advent, John's secondary role becomes an important one for helping us understand our own role in God's work.

A popular country gospel song from several years ago observed, "No one wants to play rhythm guitar for Jesus anymore." In the world of country bands, the rhythm guitar player is not the star. It is the lead guitar player who makes all the dramatic licks and runs. It is the lead guitar player who carries the melody. The rhythm guitar is just in the background, providing the basic chords from which the lead player makes the music.

The notion that "No one wants to play rhythm guitar for Jesus," recognizes how easy it is to move Jesus into the wings of our lives, and move our own desires onto center stage. If we are not careful, even Advent can become about what we want, instead of about who Jesus is.

In other words, we are followers of the Messiah along with John the Baptist and others. In that position we are called upon to follow John's example and say in regard to Jesus' presence in our lives, "I must decrease, he must increase."

As we learn to say those words, we also join John the Baptist in his work of preparing the world to receive its king. As we prepare to receive him into our own lives, we may find that we are helping others benefit from our efforts to put Jesus first in the season.

—J. E.

Advent 3

Isaiah 12:2-6
(See Proper 28/Pentecost 26/Ordinary Time 33, Cycle C, for an alternative approach.)

The theme of joy is highlighted in this reading from the prophet Isaiah, which is why the text is frequently employed during Advent. The poet sings, "With joy you will draw water from the wells of salvation" (v. 3) and "Shout aloud and sing for joy ... for great in your midst is the Holy One of Israel" (v. 6). The key to joy is those closing words in verse 6, in which the prophet celebrates the presence of God in the midst of the worshiping community.

Joy is different from happiness. Being happy has to do with circumstances. We are happy when life goes the way we want or expect it to go. We are happy when we get a raise or promotion. We are happy when the diagnostic test for cancer comes back "negative."

We are unhappy when we get downsized. We are unhappy when a loved one dies. We are unhappy when the diagnostic test comes back positive.

But joy is different. Joy is not tied to circumstances. Joy is tied to our awareness and participation in the presence of God. Joy is possible in both the happy and the unhappy moments of life. In fact, joy can be the undercurrent that sustains us in times of great distress and difficulty.

This peculiar aspect of joy can be seen in many areas of life, but perhaps nowhere more clearly than at some funerals. The death of a loved one, no matter what age or circumstance, is never a happy occasion. However, there are instances in which the funeral of certain people, because of the character of their lives — faith, service to others, longevity, creativity, and so on — becomes both a time of mourning and a celebration of a life well-lived. The emotion that drives that celebration in the funeral setting is joy.

In the setting of Advent, our joy is in response to the fulfillment of a promise — the promise of God to send the Messiah. Throughout Advent, as we have disciplined our worship with waiting, anticipating, and preparation, we are ready to engage in vibrant celebration of the gift of God's Son. That calls for joy.

The fact that joy is possible regardless of circumstances becomes particularly important during the Advent season. Regardless of how hard we work or how hard we shop, sometimes happiness eludes us during this time of year. In fact, the season from Thanksgiving to Christmas is for many people one of the most difficult and even bleak times of the entire year. Psychologists call it seasonal depression.

Cultivating a sense of joy that is grounded not in personal circumstances but in faith and a sense of God's presence can provide a powerful remedy for this seasonal depression. Not that we are able to manufacture happiness simply because it's Christmas; rather, we are able to embrace a hope that is deeper and more profound than a mere holiday celebration. Out of this hope comes the possibility of joy.

—J. E.

Advent 4

Luke 1:47-55
(See Advent 3, Cycle A.)

Psalm 80:1-7
(See Advent 4, Cycle A; Advent 1, Cycle B; and Proper 15/Pentecost 13/Ordinary Time 20, Cycle C.)

Christmas Eve

Psalm 96
(Occurs in all three cycles of the lectionary; see Christmas Eve, Cycles A and B.)

Christmas Day

Psalm 97
(Occurs in all three cycles of the lectionary; see Christmas Day, Cycle A; see also Easter 7, Cycle C, for an alternative approach.)

Psalm 98
(Occurs in all three cycles of the lectionary; see Christmas Day, Years A and B, and also Easter 6, Cycle B.)

Christmas 1

Psalm 148
(Occurs in all three cycles of the lectionary; see Christmas 1, Cycle A; Christmas 1, Cycle B; and Easter 5, Cycle C, for alternative approaches.)

Psalm 148 is a magnificent hymn of praise that moves with sweeping stanzas and evocative language through the orders of creation — from angels to humans — calling on all of creation to praise God. Not only does the psalm begin and end with a call to praise, but this call is repeated ten additional times in the body of the song. The reasons for the praise are given only at the end of each of the two sections of the psalm, when the poet has satisfied himself that — in symbol at least — he has left no being and no thing, whether in the heavens or on the earth, uninvited to praise.

This sort of exuberant behavior is reserved in our culture for sporting events and live entertainment. We are accustomed to seeing football fans, clothed in outlandish costumes, standing and cheering with all their might. We are also familiar with the fans of rock stars screaming at the top of their lungs as they express adulation for their heroes.

Ironically, faith traditions that feature loud music and animated actions on the part of worshipers are often derided as being part of "the faith fringe." We in the mainstream pride ourselves on doing things "decently and in order," and look upon over-excited vocal expressions of joyfulness as distractions rather than genuine elements of worship.

In other words, the call to unrestrained praise suggested by this psalm has to be toned down to a more acceptable liturgical level in order to be performed in many churches.

This is not to suggest that all congregations should immediately adopt charismatic or seeker-style worship services — obviously, too much of even a good thing can be too much. However, there is an important lesson to be learned from this psalm, and the more reserved we are in worship the harder it is to hear.

We are called as people of faith to engage in lavish and energetic worship — worshiping God with all we've got. Certainly there are moments when solemnity and reflection are needed. Certainly there are times when awe and reverence should be observed. Even silence has its place in worship.

Yet, as the psalm suggests, there are also times when praise — exuberant, heartfelt praise — is the order of the day. If we really believe what we confess about God and the work God has done in Jesus the Christ, how can we in good conscience remain silent as we apprehend the goodness and grace of God?

I have a friend who is highly regimented in his daily routine. He runs at the same time every day and eats breakfast, lunch, and dinner right on schedule. His meetings start and stop on time, and he is always early with his deadlines.

I told him once, "Bob, you need some spontaneity in your life, some free, creative time." He looked at me seriously for a moment and said, "I could schedule some of that."

We are called to praise the Lord. If necessary, let us "schedule" a time in our service, or in our lives, when we let down our guard and our reservations and praise the Lord with all we have.

— J. E.

Christmas 2

Psalm 147:12-20
(Occurs in all three cycles of the lectionary; see Christmas 2, Cycle A.)

The Epiphany Of Our Lord

Psalm 72:1-7, 10-14
(Occurs in all three cycles of the lectionary; see The Epiphany Of Our Lord, Cycles A and B; see also Advent 2, Cycle A, for vv. 1-7.)

The Baptism Of Our Lord/ Epiphany 1/Ordinary Time 1

Psalm 29
(Occurs in all three cycles of the lectionary; see The Baptism Of Our Lord/Epiphany 1/Ordinary Time 1, Cycles A and B, and The Holy Trinity, Cycle B.)

Epiphany 2/Ordinary Time 2

Psalm 36:5-10
 If we wanted to give a name to this psalm, we might call it "A Song of Exuberant Praise." The psalmist is unrestrained in voicing his praise to God. And the list of things for which God is praised is impressively exhaustive. Within the scope of five short verses, God is praised for steadfastness, faithfulness, righteousness, judgment, and salvation. These divine qualities affect not only human existence but also extend to the heavens, clouds, mountains, the great deep, and even animals.

The true significance for the psalmist, of course, is the way in which these qualities of divine character affect human life. The range of God's character creates a shelter, like the wings of a great bird, under which her young might hide and find protection or comfort. God's love and grace create a feast that nurtures human life and creates hope. God's goodness is the very source of life itself. And God's great power provides protection from anyone who would seek to disturb the faithful. Salvation is for God's people. They are the focus of all God's goodness.

It is not that other parts of creation are unimportant. We ought to know by now the interrelated nature of our existence with the natural order. We do not stand alone as living beings on this planet. Our life is part of a life system that we ignore or damage at our peril, but the psalmist draws ever-narrowing lines from the far reaches of creation to a focal point in human existence. The salvation God offers is offered to us.

Of course, there is good reason for this narrowed focus, both theologically and scientifically. God has given humankind a singular role to play in creation. It is human beings who bear the image of God. It is human beings who have been entrusted with the care and stewardship of the earth. This is what is meant by "dominion" (Genesis 1:26). God wants us to care for the earth, not dominate it.

Because of this unique calling and relationship to the created order — at least the part of it we occupy — it is necessary to first redeem the human mind and spirit, so the other beloved features of God's creation may also be cared for. God reveals in Jesus what human life is supposed to look like. Our commitment to this vision redeems us and restores our broken humanity. Once we are healed, then it becomes possible for us to work for the fulfillment of the psalmist's vision, that God can "save humans and animals alike" (v. 6).

—J. E.

Epiphany 3/Ordinary Time 3

Psalm 19
(See Proper 22/Pentecost 20/Ordinary Time 27, Cycle A.)

Epiphany 4/Ordinary Time 4

Psalm 71:1-6
(See Proper 16/Pentecost 14/Ordinary Time 21, Cycle C, for an alternative approach.)

The power and importance of the psalms lies partly in their honesty. The elements of worship represented in the psalms include the kinds of things we would expect: praise, joy, devotion, prayer, and so forth. However, within the context of worship, the psalms are also able to contain emotions and experiences that we do not often hear in our worship services. The psalmists of old felt the freedom to offer complaint, lament, protest, and even despair. Psalm 71 is an example of this sort of honest worship. It is the lament of an individual who cries out for God's help (vv. 1-4) but at the same time expresses affirmation and trust in God's goodness (vv. 3-5).

The cries for help dominate the first four verses: "deliver me ... rescue me ... save me ... rescue me...." This repetition may suggest the degree of suffering that the psalmist is experiencing.

If that is true, then the repetition of God's qualities also represent the degree of trust and faith the psalmist has in God. God is variously portrayed as "rock of refuge ... strong fortress ... my rock ... my fortress."

Clearly, the psalmist understood, perhaps firsthand, the destabilizing power of distress. Pastoral care specialists point out that when a person is in crisis their entire body can change. Sleep patterns can become disrupted, appetite may increase or decrease, blood pressure sometimes goes up, and so on. Living through a traumatic event or crisis may create a sense that the whole world is shifting under our feet.

The psalmist addresses this sense of shift and instability by portraying God as a safe and solid refuge. The whole world may shake and fall apart, but the shelter of the Lord is immovable. We remain safe under his care.

This psalm, with its promise of shelter, is used three times in the lectionary cycle — once during Holy Week and once during Epiphany. This makes perfect sense. As God is revealed in Jesus, the promise of a shelter, safe and strong, is not rooted in some abstract image of God high above the heavens, distant and removed from our hurts and fears. God becomes known to us in a most concrete fashion — as the Word made flesh.

The Word made flesh becomes the stabilizing influence not only for our individual lives but for the whole world. The Word also becomes part of the focus of our praise and adoration. And, if we have the honest courage, the Word made flesh also becomes the one to hear our complaints and our laments. Or as the prophet noted, "He has borne all our sorrows."

—J. E.

Epiphany 5/Ordinary Time 5

Psalm 138
(See Proper 5/Pentecost 3/Ordinary Time 10, Cycle B.)

Epiphany 6/Ordinary Time 6

Psalm 1
(See Proper 20/Pentecost 18/Ordinary Time 25, Cycle B for an alternative approach.)

The writer of Psalm 1 has created a timeless image of human existence as a tree. The image of a tree allows the poet to proclaim in graphic terms the effects of having, and not having, a viable relationship with God. The tree, as a durable life form, symbolizes well the significance and importance of seeking and living a faithful life.

The good tree, according to the psalmist, is positioned by an abundant source of water. Having good soil and plenty of water, the tree thrives and grows. The psalmist points to the tree and says to us, "This tree can be a picture of your life — rooted, productive, truly alive, beautiful."

"How can we do that?" we ask. "How can a life have all these dimensions?"

The psalmist is ready with an answer. First, there are things to avoid. People whose lives are rooted and growing don't follow the advice of the wicked, they don't take the paths sinners take and they don't associate with cynics and scoffers (vv. 1-3). These are habits and practices and relationships that take us away from good soil and good water.

For the psalmist, the path to a happy life, nurtured and blessed by God, requires only the observation of one discipline: Those whose lives are flourishing, whose lives are truly happy, are the ones who take "delight in the law of the Lord."

Translating the Hebrew word, "Torah," as law is sometimes misleading, even though it is by far the most common rendering of the word. The problem comes, however, when we use our American connotation of what "law" means to interpret what Torah means — they are not the same. Law in our culture consists of statutes, ordinances, prohibitions, and directives. And there is certainly some of that in the Hebrew Torah. However, if we limit our understanding of Torah only to enforceable do's and don'ts, we miss the significance of what the psalmist is trying to tell us. Life does not flourish simply because the rules are kept.

The idea of Torah, while including do's and don'ts, is really about learning God's way of doing things. Law is meant for instruction rather than enforcement. No one has ever forced anyone to live a meaningful and happy life. These are things we learn.

Understanding the word, "law," this way helps to highlight the contrast the psalmist has set up between the "advice" of the wicked and the "path" of sinners as opposed to God's "teaching," God's way. It also helps to complete the image of the tree. The water and the soil that enriches life and makes it whole is not blind obedience to a set of rules. It is when we are nurtured on God's truth, and we learn God's way that true happiness and wholeness become the fruit of our faithfulness.

— J. E.

Epiphany 7/Ordinary 7

Psalm 37:1-11, 39-40

Some years back, there was a best-selling book that got a lot of attention in the church, one written by a rabbi, Harold Kushner. The book was called *When Bad Things Happen to Good People* (HarperCollins, 1982). It is an honest attempt to grapple with the problem of evil. Why is it, Rabbi Kushner wants to know, that good and faithful people sometimes have to suffer?

There is another variation of this problem that sometimes troubles us — in fact, it is the exact opposite of Rabbi Kushner's book title. This alternative form of the question is: "Why do good things happen to bad people?" In a certain sense, that form of the question can be even more troubling: "Lord, I try hard to be a person of faith. I don't always succeed, but I do always want to do the right thing. Just look, though, at that person over there — that person has never so much as darkened a church door. He lives by lying, cheating, and generally taking advantage of others. What a big car he drives! What a huge boat sits in his driveway! He has so much more of the things of this world than do I. Lord, it doesn't seem fair!"

The author of Psalm 37 struggles with this question as well: "Do not fret because of the wicked; do not be envious of wrongdoers, for they will soon fade like the grass, and wither like the green herb" (vv. 1-2). While evildoers may seem to triumph in the short term, in the long term they are doomed. For when the Lord's final justice comes rolling in, all that lush grass will dry up and die.

The point, here, is not to condemn individual people. In the psalms, the category of "the wicked" is an abstract concept. While we ought to be appropriately cautious about relegating any individual to that category, the purpose of the category is to teach us that moral evil truly does exist, and is a perilous trap for the faithful. The thing that makes faithful believers vulnerable to that trap is the sin of envy, which is always to be avoided.

The antidote is stated in verse 7: "Be still before the Lord, and wait patiently for him...." The believer's attention is more appropriately directed towards God, not toward evildoers. The word "fret," used in verse 1 and in the second part of this verse, literally means "burn." "Do not allow yourself to be consumed with anxiety over the wicked" is what the psalm is saying. Truly, emotions like envy and jealousy — that we imagine are focused on others — are just as much directed at ourselves, and can cause terrible damage.

— C. W.

Epiphany 8/Ordinary Time 8

Psalm 92:1-4 (12-15)
(See Proper 20/Pentecost 18/Ordinary Time 25, Year B, for an alternative approach.)

This psalm — which, like so many others, contrasts the wicked with the righteous — relies on an agricultural metaphor that would have been familiar to most early readers, but which may be less familiar to those living in urban areas today. The metaphor is the contrast between grass and trees.

Those who dwell in arid regions, in particular, would have been familiar with the phenomenon of desert grasses: tough species that require little water, and which grow and die very rapidly. A flash flood roars through a desert *wadi*, scrubbing the little canyon nearly clean. Pools of water linger for a time, and shortly afterward give birth to swaying, green grass. This grass gives an illusion of fecundity, when in fact its existence is precarious. It will not be long before the water in the soil dries up, and the grass with it.

Yet there is another sort of plant growing in that *wadi*. When the floodwaters come, they swirl around the trunk of a wizened, ugly little tree. The waters are not strong enough to carry the tree away. When the scorching desert sun comes out and dries up the grass, its rays are not hot enough to reach deep into the earth, where the tree's roots are sunk. Those roots reach into hidden, subterranean streams of water: a source that is far more constant and reliable than the capricious floods that periodically refresh the ground's surface.

"The righteous flourish like the palm tree, and grow like a cedar in Lebanon" (v. 12). Palm trees, in the Middle East, are the distinctive trees of desert oases. Not only do they provide welcome shade, but also provide dates, a staple food. As for the famed cedars of Lebanon, they are a notably tall and straight tree, suitable for the most magnificent of construction projects. Trees, of course, are particularly long-lived: "In old age they still produce fruit; they are always green and full of sap ..." (v. 14).

Our culture is in love with the passions of the moment. Advertisers hawk the pleasures of the latest gadget or luxury item, and value the trendy over the reliable. People of faith know better. They know life is a distance race, not a brief sprint. They know the Lord blesses those who are in it for the long haul, who cherish divine values more than the merely worldly.

—C. W.

Epiphany 9/Ordinary 9

Psalm 96:1-9
(See Christmas Eve, Cycles A and B.)

The Transfiguration Of Our Lord/ Last Sunday After The Epiphany

Psalm 99

(See The Transfiguration Of Our Lord/Last Sunday After The Epiphany, Cycle A, for an alternative approach.)

One of the greatest of all Christian hymns is Reginald Heber's powerful and beautiful "Holy, Holy, Holy." The hymn is based on Revelation 4:8-11, which depicts heavenly creatures singing praises day and night, celebrating God's holiness and glory.

Psalm 99 also offers a triple "holy, holy, holy." "Holy is he" (vv. 3-5) and "Holy is the Lord our God" (v. 9). The key to this psalm, obviously, is understanding the meaning of the word, "holy."

The basic idea behind the word translated "holy" (Hebrew *qadosh*) is "apart" or "separate." A location may be holy because it is "set apart" by God's presence or appearance there. Moses' encounter with God and the injunction to remove his sandals because he is standing on holy ground is a typical example (Exodus 3:5). This understanding may be extended to clothing, objects, animals, and of course, people.

To say that God is holy is to acknowledge that God is set apart. God is different from us. God is separated in both a qualitative and quantitative sense. God is different from us in terms of righteousness, goodness, judgment, mercy, and so on. God is also apart from us in occupying a place "in the heavens."

This sense of separation does not negate the biblical idea of God's presence, nor the ability of God to engage in meaningful relationships with us. It does, however, strongly suggest that since God is so different from us and so far removed from us, the only way we can have a relationship with God is for God to take the initiative and bridge the distance.

The Bible records many instances of God taking the initiative. These acts of God make up some of our favorite biblical stories. Interestingly, the Bible offers no instances of humans storming the gates of heaven or in some other way establishing a connection with God, without God making the first move.

Unfortunately, ideas of holiness, of separation and distance, often deteriorate into discussions of clean and unclean, pure and impure. While it is true that God is morally superior to us, and that our sin is "an abomination," God is not put off by these things. Though holy beyond imagination, God is nevertheless interested in our redemption. The New Testament declares that while we were yet sinners, God took steps to redeem us.

God's holiness, therefore, is not an obstacle to God's embrace of us. That is certainly one reason Jesus worked so hard to break down the clean/unclean class system that existed in first-century Palestine. God wants us to be holy, and certainly calls us to a life of holy living. Holiness is not about moral superiority; it is about living distinctively in the world. It is not about separatism or exclusive spirituality; it is about exemplary living in the midst of our neighbors.

— J. E.

Ash Wednesday

Psalm 51:1-17
(Occurs in all three cycles of the lectionary; see Ash Wednesday, Cycle A; Lent 5, Cycle B; and Proper 13/Pentecost 11/Ordinary Time 18, Cycle B.)

Lent 1

Psalm 91:1-2, 9-16
(See Proper 21/Pentecost 19/Ordinary Time 26, Cycle C, for an alternative approach to vv. 1-6 and 14-16.)

We immediately recognize a portion of this psalm as part of the dialogue between Jesus and the devil in the temptation narratives. In the well-known scene, the devil suggests to Jesus that if he jumped from one of the high towers of the temple, God would not allow him to be injured. The devil assures Jesus that no harm will come to him because "he will command his angels concerning you ... on their hands they will bear you up" (vv. 11-12).

It surely does not come as a surprise, but the devil uses these words grossly out of context. The psalmist does not envision a situation where we can expect God's protection even though we are acting in a reckless manner. In fact, the promise here has nothing to do with protection from any sort of injury. The psalmist merely describes one of the benefits which accrues to a life faithfully lived.

The opening verses establish the boundaries of this faithful life: "You who live in the shelter of the most high ... My God in whom I trust." Faithfulness is about trusting God. It is also about worship, and it is about commitment. The expectation is that we will make God our single focus, our reason for living.

We should not, and cannot, say that faithfulness always affords protection from harm — that, simply because we have done what we should, that "angels will bear us up" out of harm's way. That is not always possible and it is not always true. Even the most faithful of followers occasionally must face and endure suffering. Sometimes being faithful — as is the case with the cross — is the cause of our suffering. There are times when escape from a difficult situation is actually an instance of unfaithfulness.

So what does the psalmist mean? What is he talking about here?

The psalmist is not suggesting escape or protection from pain. The benefit the psalmist describes is for God's help for those who must go through difficult or painful situations.

The devil really got it completely backward. It is not that we are able to leap from some lofty perch of spiritual privilege in the arms of guardian angels. What is closer to the truth is that as we stumble while carrying our burdens and nearly fall to the ground, God's grace keeps us from going all the way down. It is not a fall from a spiritual high in which we are caught; it is the moment just before we surrender to despair, having walked bowed toward the ground for a long time.

—J. E.

Lent 2

Psalm 27
(See Epiphany 3/Ordinary Time 3, Cycle A, for verses 1, 4-9.)
There are two themes flowing through this psalm. These themes are connected, a part of each other, like two sides of a coin. But they are also separate, especially as they manifest themselves in human experience. While existing closely together in thought, they diverge dramatically as they work themselves out in life.

The first theme is fear. The psalmist addresses the fear of his audience directly. He knows the fear as one who shares it with his fellow worshipers. The fear is named: *enemies, evildoers, armies.* These realities create other fears, whose names are *despair, hopelessness, anger, bitterness.*

But the psalmist, while knowing and naming the fear that plagues his audience, also knows the name of the one who can overcome the fear. He calls out the names of this fear-buster: *the stronghold, the shelter, the savior, the gracious one, the good one, the Lord.*

This is where we find the second theme — hope. The fear is present reality. They fear now. The confidence that the psalmist offers as a remedy for the fear is a hope. It is an outcome that will only be found at the end of a disciplined path. The psalmist names the path: *I asked of the Lord, I seek after, I will offer, I will sing, I cry aloud, teach me, I believe.*

The psalmist assures his audience that in following the disciplined path, their fear will give way to something wonderful. Something life-giving will emerge in the place of the fear. He names this assurance: *my heart shall not fear, I will be confident, my head is lifted up, I will be strong, I will have courage.*

This is important wisdom for anyone who fears. Fear evokes in us all those qualities that ultimately work against our best interests. Fear makes us defensive, violent, untrusting. But the disciplined path suggested by the psalmist cultivates in us those particular human qualities that benefit not only our individual existence, but the lives of those around us as well. When we are confident and trusting that God's way is the best way, we resist violence, we refuse despair, we embrace our neighbor.

This is not a mind-game the psalmist proposes. This is not a form of self-hypnosis, whereby we convince ourselves that we are not afraid when in fact we really are. And this is not a form of denial. The psalmist is not proposing that we ignore the evil of our world or acquiesce to its power. In fact, he offers the very opposite of acquiescence. He offers us a way to resist the evil in our world in a way that the evil may be transformed.

The root of all fear is the threat of loss. We fear we will lose our lives, our homes, our purpose, our standing. The disciplined path the psalmist describes offers us a new identity — an identity that is not shaken, even should the world in which we live cease to exist. Our purpose and being is not tied to any particular social or economic reality. Our identity comes from a constant that does not change and does not yield to the comings and goings of power. As we tap into that eternal constant, our fear begins to ebb.

And how do we tap into that eternal constant? What is the key to finding and staying on the disciplined path? The psalmist names the way plainly: *Wait. Wait for the Lord.*

— J. E.

Lent 3

Psalm 63:1-8

Psalm 63 is particularly well-suited for helping Christians take stock of their commitment. Oftentimes, as we take a long, inward look, we become aware that we have lost or laid aside some of our passion for God. This does not necessarily mean we have left the church. There are many who sit in the pews week after week, visibly faithful and plugged in, who are nevertheless spiritually fatigued.

The psalmist gives poetic expression to this fatigue. Drawing upon the common experience of those who live in an arid region, the psalmist compares waning spiritual passion to thirst. "My soul thirsts for you," he writes, "as in a dry and weary land" (v. 1).

The loss of spiritual passion, often called burnout, actually has many causes. For instance, spiritual drought can result from doing too much: too many committees, too many jobs, too many roles. If we are not careful, God gets crowded right off our calendars by all the things we are doing for God.

A barren spiritual life can also be the result of doing too little. We are aware that there are legitimate things we should be doing — maybe just the basics of prayer and worship. Maybe it's some calling, some task for which we are uniquely suited. It could be something we agreed to do but then failed to do it, or failed to give it our best effort. The guilt that comes from doing too little can have an eviscerating effect on our souls.

We can become barren from success. Consider what happened to Elijah after defeating the prophets of Baal on Mount Carmel (1 Kings 18). After his astounding accomplishment, he was apparently so spent that the feeble threat of Jezebel sent him scurrying to the wilderness to hide and die. There is a strange deflation that may occur after we get what we want. Finishing a task can leave us feeling that we can do nothing else, or that we have nothing else to do.

And, of course, failure can leave us feeling barren and dry. When we make an effort, do the best we can, but fall on our faces — it can wipe us out. The pain of failure can create in us such a sense of powerlessness and incompetence that we may be tempted never to try again.

Regardless of the way we get to spiritual drought, whatever it is that makes us thirsty, the psalmist reminds us that it is God for whom we are really thirsty. It is not busyness, or success or failure that really makes us dry — it is the absence of God in our lives. In order to find all God's refreshing and life-giving potential, we must be willing to find God in the way God wants to be found.

"So I have looked upon you in the sanctuary, beholding your power and glory" (v. 2). It is not in busywork that God is found, but in worship. It is when we stop and focus mind and heart in devotion and adoration that we can expect renewal to come.

And if it is failure that has dimmed our hope, it is in the sanctuary that we will find forgiveness. We must school ourselves to believe that God's "steadfast love is better than life" (v. 3). Once we learn that, we will be able to say with the psalmist, "I will lift up my hands and call on your name" (v. 4), and "My soul is satisfied" (v. 5).

— J. E.

Lent 4

Psalm 32
(See Lent 1, Cycle A, for an alternative approach.)

In the powerful 1995 film, *The Mission*, Robert De Niro plays a violent slave trader who has killed his own brother. Though not a religious person, De Niro's character nevertheless turns to a local priest to help him deal with the terrible guilt of his awful deed. The priest, it turns out, is a missionary to the very tribe of natives that De Niro, the slave trader, has raided over the years. As part of his penance, the priest tells De Niro he must serve the very natives he has previously preyed upon. As an additional element of penance, De Niro takes all his implements of war — his sword, shield, armor, and so on — ties them in a huge net bag and drags the heavy bundle through the jungle on his way to the mission.

In order to get to where the tribe lives, De Niro must climb a sheer cliff. The burden of his implements of violence nearly pulls him off the cliff several times during the climb. As he reaches the top, tribal leaders recognize him as the slave trader who has captured many men from their group. They ask the priest why he has brought this dangerous man into their midst.

The priest tells them De Niro is repenting of his violence and is not a threat to them. When they point out the swords, knives, and armor, the priest tells them it is part of De Niro's penance — to carry the very items of death that have killed his brother.

One of the tribal leaders thinks about this for a moment and then does an amazing act of kindness. Taking his own knife from its sheath, the tribesman cuts the rope that ties the heavy bag to De Niro's weight. The heavy burden crashes down the cliff. De Niro, realizing he has been set free by the very people he has oppressed, begins to weep uncontrollably.

The visual symbolism of the slave trader suddenly being freed from his sins is stunning. It is possible to feel vicariously the moment of release and the flood of gratitude he expresses.

The psalmist's words do much the same. He deftly describes the effects of guilt on the human soul. As we hold our failure in, it makes us weak; we feel the heavy weight of its presence.

But, when we are able to experience the forgiveness of God, the burden slips away. We feel relief and release. A sense of euphoria sweeps over the psalmist as he contemplates his new state of being. "Happy are those whose transgression is forgiven, whose sin is covered" (v. 1).

Most people who are aware of their failures know the agony of guilt. But weighted down with guilt is a poor way to live. Better to admit our failure (v. 5). God already knows anyway. The psalmist believes that, as we confess our sin to God, we release the hold our guilt has on us. And as we accept God's forgiveness, we discover that we have been set free in the depths of our lives.

— J. E.

Lent 5

Psalm 126
(See Advent 3, Cycle B.)

Palm Sunday/Sunday Of The Passion

Liturgy Of The Palms
Psalm 118:1-2, 19-29
(Occurs in all three cycles of the lectionary; see Liturgy Of The Palms, Cycle A; see also The Resurrection Of Our Lord/Easter Day, Years A, B, and C for vv. 1-2, 14-24.)

Liturgy Of The Passion
Psalm 31:9-16
(Occurs in all three cycles of the lectionary; see Liturgy Of The Passion, Cycles A and B for alternative approaches; see also Easter 5, Cycle A, for an alternative approach to vv. 1-5, 15-16.)

Psalm 31 is an eloquent testimony to the grinding force of grief and pain. That is one reason this psalm is so appropriate to be read at the beginning of Passion Week. It is not hard to imagine Jesus experiencing the feelings the psalmist has described for us. Since the gospels offer us virtually nothing of the inner life of Jesus, his private ruminations, we are forced to rely on others who have known suffering to help us understand and appreciate the inner agony that must have been the Lord's.

The psalm also serves as a sort of blueprint or a map of the process that begins with grief but ends in comfort. For all those who suffer, there is a hopeful message offered here: that what begins in lonely agony can end with a sense of peace and the assurance of God's presence. For those who are themselves at the beginning of a journey of pain, that hope can become an important source of encouragement.

There is great sermonic value in approaching the psalm in these two ways. First, we kindle the imagination and allow the psalmist to help us understand Jesus' suffering. Then, we move directly from Jesus' agony to our own as we allow the words of the psalmist to trace the path of our own suffering.

In pulling these two themes together we are able to establish a basis for beginning to understand what Paul means when he writes about "sharing in the sufferings of Christ" (Philippians 3:10) and when he writes, "I am completing what is lacking in Christ's afflictions" (Colossians 1:24).

In other words, this psalm allows us to be drawn into the passion narrative. Jesus not only suffers for us, but also with us — and us with him, and just as his sufferings are redemptive, so ours may be as well.

Obviously, we must take care at this point. This is not an invitation to martyrdom or for injury to be inflicted on the self in search of some greater glory. The idea is not to induce suffering, but rather to offer meaning and hope in the face of suffering that is already at work.

The psalmist gives us words that allow us to express the depths of our pain: "My eye wastes away from grief ... My life is spent with sorrow ... my bones waste away ... I have become like a broken vessel" (vv. 9-12). The psalmist also gives us words that direct us toward our comfort: "Be gracious to me, O Lord ... I trust in you ... My times are in your hand ... Let your face shine upon your servant ... save me in your steadfast love" (vv. 9, 14-16).

It is the gospel that gives our suffering meaning. Our pain is part of the suffering that God undertakes for us and with us. In the heart of God there is a cross that is filled with the agonies of human suffering. Out of that pain flows a torrent of gracious love that sweeps away our sinfulness and makes possible a life of purpose and dignity.

Our sufferings are part of that. Whether our pain is psychological or physical, whether it comes from our actions or the acts of others, whether our pain has an understandable cause or exists in us as a mystery, the meaning of it is found in the cross of Christ. It is there that we will be able to say with the psalmist, "Save me in your steadfast love."

—J. E.

Maundy Thursday

Psalm 116:1-2, 12-19
(Occurs in all three cycles of the lectionary; see Maundy Thursday, Cycle A and Maundy Thursday, Cycle B; see also Easter 3, Cycle A for an alternative approach to vv. 1-4 and 12-19.)

Good Friday

Psalm 22
(Occurs in all three cycles of the lectionary; see Good Friday, Cycle A; Lent 2, Cycle B; and Proper 23/Pentecost 21/Ordinary Time 28, Cycle C.)

The Resurrection Of Our Lord/ Easter Day

Psalm 118:1-2, 14-24
(Occurs in all three cycles of the lectionary; see The Resurrection Of Our Lord/Easter Day, Cycles A and B for alternative approaches; see also Liturgy Of The Palms, Cycle A, for an alternative approach to vv. 1-2, 19-29.)

The climactic verse in the Easter reading of Psalm 118 (v. 24) can easily serve as an appropriate anthem for celebrating the goodness of God on any given day. Every day is the day that the Lord has made. But there is poignancy in using this verse in reference to the day we celebrate the resurrection of Jesus. It would be effective to construct a sermon around verse 24, using the rhythm of the litany already established by the verses leading up to it.

The Resurrection was not an afterthought, or a "Plan B." God had it in mind all along. Death would be defeated once for all in our lives by the raising of Jesus from the dead. This is the day God made to accomplish this incredible act — let us rejoice in it and be glad!

The sorrow that follows on the heels of all our losses, the lonely separation from loved ones by death, is certainly one of the most difficult burdens we bear. But because of God's gift of eternal life demonstrated powerfully by raising Jesus from the dead, we are not doomed to carry the burden of loss without hope. We can find comfort in the knowledge that we will see our loved ones again. This is the day the Lord has created for this great purpose — let us rejoice in it and be glad!

Of course, death is not only about the loss of life. People in our world daily face the death of their dreams. It may take the form of the loss of a home or career. It may come as a divorce or a debilitating illness or injury. Suddenly, without warning, the world we thought we knew turns on us, and we are laid bare with distress.

But God has unleashed a powerful principle of renewal in our world. God can take that which is dead and breathe new life into it. The Lord can take shattered dreams and lost hopes and make them alive again. We can experience resurrection in our hearts and in our minds as God works with us to creatively find ways around and through our disappointments. Just when we think the world has ended, God makes a new world. And this is the day the Lord has made where that sort of renewal of life can happen — let us rejoice in it and be glad!

More often than not, it is the daily grind that robs us of our joy, fills us with boredom, and tempts us to apathy. It is the mind-numbing routines that mark our days and sap our energy that we come to resent. Without any specific event, with no particular tragedy, we yet find ourselves grieving a life that is not snatched away, but rather slips away. We stand looking back over twenty, thirty, or fifty years and wonder where the time went.

But there is a cure for this malaise. It is the recognition that God has chosen to infuse life with a constant source of newness. We can, if we choose, live in the light of a new day every day. This is that day that the Lord has made for us to live in. Today, let us rejoice in it and be glad!

— J. E.

Easter 2

Psalm 118:14-29
(See Liturgy Of The Palms, Cycle A, and The Resurrection Of Our Lord/Easter Day, Cycles A, B, and C.)

Psalm 150

Psalm 150 offers eloquent testimony to the power of repetition. Opening with a call to praise, this psalm hammers the joyful notion that our business in this world is to praise God with everything we can imagine.

There are several good reasons for the repeated use of the command to praise. For one thing, the repeated use of a theme is a particular form of Semitic rhetoric. The ancient Hebrews used repetition as a way of expressing superlatives. Instead of saying, "That man is a good farmer," the ancient Hebrews would find ways to repeat either the man's name or the qualities of his farming skill — something like, "Old Joe is like two farmers."

The psalmist's repeated use of "praise" in this psalm would immediately be recognized by the audience as a call to a quality of praise: a superlative praise. The psalmist is not encouraging us to praise God simply by saying the word "praise" a bunch of times in succession (which is what it appears he has done), but rather to offer a heartfelt acclaim that is worthy of the one being praised.

There is another significant use of repetition. The repeated use of the word "praise" makes the case, within the context of worship, that acclamation is a viable alternative to any other response. The poem acknowledges no distinctions in the attitudes of the worshipers. The psalmist does not say, "If God has been good to you, praise the Lord. If your crops came in on time or your flocks are multiplying — praise God for it. If your child survived a dreaded illness, praise God with all your being." There is none of that. The condition of those called to offer praise is not a factor.

It is almost as if the psalmist is anticipating objections and meeting them with the repeated call for praise.

"Praise the Lord," the worship leader says.

"But I just lost my ..." we begin to stammer.

"Praise God in his sanctuary."
"But I...."
"Praise him for his mighty deeds."
"But...."
"Praise him according to his surpassing greatness."
Silence.
"Praise him with trumpet sound."

As the crescendo of praise builds in the service, we are swept up in the emotional whirlwind of gratitude and adoration, and even though our situation in life has not changed, the repeated call to praise has forced us to view our circumstances in a new light. We are drawn by the call to praise into a posture of trust.

Suddenly, without realizing it, we have joined our voices with those around us in singing a heartfelt, "Praise the Lord."

This is not self-hypnosis, nor some attempt to numb our pain through mindless chanting. The repetition of the call to praise is an assault on despair. It is a stubborn, hymn-like effort to subvert darkness and death. It is a relentless assault on hopelessness. We will not give in to our doubts about God; instead we offer praise with everything we can get our hands on.

Praise the Lord!

— J. E.

Easter 3

Psalm 30

(For alternative approaches, see Epiphany 6/Ordinary Time 6, Cycle B; and Proper 9/Pentecost 7/Ordinary Time 14, Cycle C.)

The main theme of this psalm is captured profoundly in the movement within a single verse: "Weeping may linger for the night, but joy comes with morning" (v. 5). Casting life experiences between light and dark is not unique or novel, of course, but the poet's treatment of these themes offers some fertile ground for reflection.

The psalmist gets right to his awareness of the perils of "the night." He calls them "foes" — the darkness of conflict and violence. Then there's the "pit," the dark place of the dead, *Sheol*. The psalmist may be referring to a close encounter with death, either from the hands of a foe or maybe an illness. Either way, he has seen the face of death and it is a face made of shadows.

But the psalmist does not leave us alone in the dark. There is light in the morning that comes in the form of joy. In the morning we are "lifted up" (v. 1). In the bright light of a new day we can see God's face. In the light of a new morning our grief gives way to dancing and we are "clothed with joy" (v. 10).

All this may give the impression of an emotional roller coaster. We are pitched back and forth, up and down, alternately steeped in despair or happiness. Obviously, there are times when life is just like that.

But the psalmist may just as well be giving expression to something more recurring, more regular. There is a rhythm to life that is not so much the violent rocking of a roller coaster as it is the gentle ebb and flow of a tide.

Over the course of a lifetime we are likely to spend a considerable amount of time "in the shadows." Facing the loss of loved ones, dealing with dramatic changes brought on by aging (in ourselves or those we may provide care for), loss of jobs, accidents, natural catastrophes — all these and more are portals to what the psalmist describes as "the pit."

But over that same span of time, there will be many bright and shining mornings. There will be births and graduations, weddings and anniversaries, birthdays and homecomings. There will promotions and retirements, mortgages paid off and diseases cured.

These are the normal events of life that all of us experience to one degree or another. Sometimes they come like roller coasters, dramatic ups and downs, but not always. Sometimes the shadow and sunlight meander along together in the course of a life. We move from one to the other gradually, over time, with one occasionally giving way to the other.

If this is what the psalmist has in mind, then the message of the psalm could not be more important. This recurring pattern, this rhythmic moving from shadow to morning, leaves no room for us to become stuck in despair. As we find ourselves in the shadows, we must know and believe that the morning's light will not be far behind.

The psalmist offers a practical and helpful pattern of behavior as we move from shadow to light. In the shadows as we face the threat of "the pit," we give voice to our pain. "To you, O Lord, I cried, and to the Lord I made supplication." As we face the shadow times of our existence, we discipline ourselves to seek the Lord's help, and wait for that help to come.

When it does come, we remember to give thanks. "O Lord my God, I will give thanks to you forever."

— J. E.

Easter 4

Psalm 23

(See Lent 4, Cycle A, and Easter 4, Cycle B, for alternative approaches.)

This well-known psalm, rich in so many themes and images, is drawn into service during the Easter season primarily because of its shepherd imagery. Jesus says, "My sheep hear my voice. I know them and they follow me" (John 10:27). The psalm details in marvelous language what, as Christians, we have come to celebrate and what it means to follow Jesus as the Good Shepherd.

But the psalm had life before the advent of Jesus. The shepherd imagery was associated with God before Jesus personified the image of "the good shepherd." In fact, it can even be argued that the psalm gave definition to Jesus' work, rather than Jesus giving particular meaning to the psalm.

There are many compelling themes in the psalm but none more evocative than the phrase, "even though I walk through the darkest valley ... you are with me." It is this promise of God's presence even at the extremes of our existence that has made this psalm a regular feature at funerals or in hospital visits.

Which may be unfortunate, as the psalm clearly seems to be more about how we should live rather than how we should die. The psalm is a steady reflection on the blessings that come to a life focused on God. As we allow God to guide us to "good pastures" and "still waters," a healthy stability begins to emerge in our lives. We experience a sense of purpose, perhaps renewed purpose — as though our very souls have "been restored."

Following God as shepherd means God leads us down "right paths." This is more than just a nod toward moral and virtuous living, though it certainly includes that. Following right paths means living for and wanting the right things. As we walk with God, we begin to understand something about God. We begin to notice how God deals with people. We begin to appreciate God's commitment to justice and kindness.

Following God as shepherd allows us to develop a certain confidence about life. The psalmist declares that God has prepared a table "in the presence of my enemies." Those who follow begin to experience a sense of having been set aside, of having been carefully and lovingly chosen (anointed).

It is in the context of following God as Shepherd that the psalmist's words about "the darkest valley" begin to be fully understood. God's presence with us at those moments of great stress and despair are not like an emergency-room scene where an injured person is wheeled into the presence of the doctor for aid. The image, rather, is of a shepherd and a sheep that suddenly falls or becomes threatened. The shepherd turns to aid or defend. The shepherd does not come from somewhere else to the place where the sheep falls. The shepherd is there to help, the moment it happens.

It is in the darkest valley that the shepherd most needs and uses the rod and staff — the rod for guidance, the staff for defense.

The psalm concludes with a vision of a life continuing in God's blessing, continuing in God's care, continuing in God's presence. The shepherd, once the sheep are in the fold, is careful not to lose them.

— J. E.

Easter 5

Psalm 148
(See Christmas 1, Cycle A; Christmas 1, Cycle B; and Christmas 1, Cycle C for alternative approaches.)

The theme of this psalm is the glory of God. The praise is extravagant and unrestrained. The psalmist makes good use of repetitive themes to drive home the central message of the psalm, namely that God is worthy of praise. The psalmist, with great deliberation, leads worshipers through a litany of causes and effects that demonstrate the praiseworthiness of God.

Starting with the lofty places where God resides, the poet moves us from heavenly heights where angelic hosts are called to praise, all the way down to the birds of the air and the creeping life upon the earth.

The psalmist moves the call for praise into the human realm and begins again to move, in descending order, from kings all the way down to the very young and the very old.

The psalmist concludes this sweeping litany of praise with the reminder of a hope. God has given life to (raised up) a "horn for his people." The word "horn" is a symbol of power and leadership. The gospels take up this refrain as we hear Jesus say, "God is glorified in me." Jesus is the horn God has raised to provide life and hope for God's people. He is God's glory and God is glorified in him.

The themes and the movement of this psalm create a unique opportunity to understand something that is intrinsic to the gospel. While moving resolutely to the fulfillment of God's promise to save God's people, the psalm allows us to follow the movement of praise from the heights to the depths. The gospel message, particularly in John's Gospel, does the same thing. Jesus is the one who leaves heaven to embrace the pain of creation. He leaves the heavenly realm, to the praise of the heavenly host, and descends to the earth. There, among God's creatures, Jesus discloses God's plan of redemption. As the heavenly hosts praised Jesus on his descent, so do the lowly creatures of this world — including us!

In the realm of humankind, the psalm continues to anticipate the movement of the gospel. Starting again at the top of the human order, kings praise the salvation of God. This praise continues all the way down to the lowliest among us: the very young and the very old.

The gospel message heralds this descent away from political power and wealth toward the lowly and the weak. God's "horn" is for all people, but in the real world good things often go to those who have the money to buy them — or the power to take them. The weak and poor are often left with only leftovers. But this is not the way it will be in God's new economy. There will be praise from every quarter, because there is salvation and hope for every person.

In this, Jesus said, God is glorified.

— J. E.

Easter 6

Psalm 67

The opening verse of this psalm echoes the blessing of Aaron found in Numbers 6:24-26: "The Lord bless you and keep you; the Lord make his face to shine upon you and be gracious to you; the Lord lift up his countenance upon you, and give you peace." The presence of the blessing in this psalm signals a theme that will be expanded in the remaining verses. The priestly blessing celebrates the presence of God and what that presence means to God's people — and to others!

The psalm was probably composed to celebrate the harvest. The blessing of Aaron was invoked to remind worshipers that the true source of the harvest is God. The fruit of their labor and the land should be seen as a reminder of God's desire to bless God's people and care for them. The harvest is a symbol of God's bountiful care.

But this bountiful care is not just for the people of Israel alone to celebrate. God desires that all the people of the earth should praise God's goodness (v. 3).

The people of God have a vital role to play in making this praise possible. With the bountiful harvest comes a reminder of God's commitment to justice. The psalmist reminds us that God "judges the peoples with equity." In the context of Aaron's blessing, this equity takes on the force of an ethical imperative.

God blesses the people with a bountiful harvest. There is enough to eat, and more than enough. As a result, God's bountiful harvest allows God's people to accumulate wealth and substance. Unfortunately, there are always present in the world those who are hungry and homeless. We enjoy our prosperity in sight of their poverty.

God's equity indicates that God desires all people to share in the bounty God provides. In the same way Israel sees the harvest and is moved to praise God, so may those who benefit from our bounty come to believe that God has blessed them through us. As the poor experience God's bountiful harvest, they are moved to praise.

That means, of course, that our failure to share God's desire for equity has both economic and spiritual consequences. If we keep the harvest all to ourselves — either by force, or by means of economic arrangements that favor us while allowing poverty and hunger to exist — not only do we deprive the poor of food, but we may also deprive them the opportunity to experience the fullness of God's bounty. Our greed obscures the goodness of God and deprives God the praise of the poor.

Aaron's blessing in this psalm serves as a challenge to us. The "you" in the blessing becomes more than just the nearest member of our own kin or community. The "you" of the blessing becomes our neighbors who live on the edges of, or outside, our community. May the Lord bless "you."

— J. E.

The Ascension Of Our Lord

Psalm 47
(Occurs in all three cycles of the lectionary; see The Ascension Of Our Lord, Cycle A.)

Psalm 93
(Occurs in all three cycles of the lectionary; see The Ascension Of Our Lord, Cycles A and B for alternative approaches.)

Easter 7

Psalm 97
(See Christmas Day, Cycle A, for an alternative approach.)

A genre of movies that's become popular in recent years is disaster films. Whether it is invaders from another galaxy, a catastrophic global climate change, or a falling asteroid, Hollywood loves to fill the nation's big screens with images of destruction.

The idea did not originate with Hollywood. Psalm 97 is something of a disaster psalm: "Fire goes before him, and consumes his adversaries on every side. His lightnings light up the world; the earth sees and trembles. The mountains melt like wax before the Lord, before the Lord of all the earth" (vv. 3-5).

(It would be interesting to see the cinematic wizards of Pixar or Industrial Light and Magic try to reproduce that imagery!)

The point of the psalm, of course, is to celebrate the Lord's might and majesty. It does so from the standpoint of a cosmology we no longer hold as our own. God is very much "up there" in this psalm — enthroned above the upturned bowl of the firmament, the vast planetarium-screen on which are displayed the heavenly lights that proclaim God's righteousness (v. 6). From this vantagepoint high above the heavens, God periodically casts down lightning bolts to wreak havoc on unsuspecting adversaries (vv. 3-4). The Lord's throne is the highest of all; it is higher than the thrones of any other gods (v. 9). And what other gods might these be?

There is evidently a pantheon of lesser deities arrayed around the Lord in this psalm — but clearly subservient, as they bow down before the Most High (v. 7).

Is it really true anymore that "all the peoples behold [God's] glory" (v. 6)? There was a time, perhaps, when most humans would look to the starry heavens and see there the imprint of a creator's hand — but that is no longer true of those who exclusively follow a secular scientific worldview. Is it even possible, anymore, to reach an assurance of God's existence through natural theology? Or do we, as Barth and his followers insist, in fact depend only on God's self-revelation in Jesus Christ for all knowledge of the divine?

For many of our people, the numerous disjunctions between the Hebrew worldview and our own make it difficult to get much value out of this psalm. Still, some individual verses offer preaching possibilities:

1. "Righteousness and justice are the foundation of [God's] throne" (v. 2b) — a sermon could focus on righteousness and justice as attributes of God.

2. "All worshipers of images are put to shame" (v. 7) — a sermon on idolatry is always timely, reminding the people of how idolatry goes far beyond mere statues of wood or stone.

3. "Light dawns for the righteous, and joy for the upright in heart" (v. 11) — a sermon on joy as the outcome of faith may speak to people who are jaded and weary from looking for joy in all the wrong places.

— C. W.

The Day Of Pentecost

Psalm 104:24-34, 35b
(See The Day Of Pentecost, Cycles A and B.)

The Holy Trinity

Psalm 8

(See Trinity Sunday, Cycle A, for an alternative approach.)

It's tough being a Christian. First, we are told that because of Adam and Eve, sin has entered the world. The power of sin affects all of us to the extent that Paul is forced to write, "All have sinned and fallen short of the glory of God" (Romans 3:23). As we look closely at the Adam and Eve narrative, we are surprised to discover that their sin was not some gratuitous act to indulge fleshy appetites; their sin was spiritual. They wanted to fully know "good and evil." This is an ancient Hebrew idiom meaning "everything." Adam and Eve wanted to know everything — they wanted to know what God knew.

And so, because of their sin, we sin. Reflecting on this theological assertion, there have been many who have taken it to great extremes. Equating sin with the body, some of these have taken extraordinary steps to literally beat their flesh into submission. Self-inflicted wounds, starvation, prolonged exposure to harsh elements — all these and more have been used by those who recognized they were sinners.

Even among those not so extreme in practice there remains a view of human nature that is less than appealing. Writing in the late nineteenth-century hymn "At The Cross," Isaac Watts ponders within the verses, "Would he devote that sacred head for such a worm as I?" And while the answer to the question is, "Yes" — a tribute to God's grace — the reality expressed in the hymn is that human beings are worms.

The author of Psalm 8 will have none of it. Without apology or restraint, the psalmist sings of the grandeur and power of God. He is aware, of course, of the wide distance that exists between the goodness of the creator and the fallen-ness of creation. He poses the question, "What are human beings that you are mindful of them, mortals that you care for them?"

The answer given is astounding: "Yet you have made them a little lower than God, and crowned them with glory and honor."

Human beings are made just a little lower than God. The KJV translators found this idea completely untenable and translated the offending verse, "lower than angels."

But the psalmist's intent is clear. God loves us and has given us an honored place in the created order. We are co-creators with God, sharing in God's ability to conceive and manufacture. We share God's ability to reason and to love. We are, as it is expressed in the Latin, *imago dei* — in the image of God.

This does not diminish the reality of sin. Nor does it reduce the effect of sin on our character. We can, by means of human evil, seriously distort God's image in us. What we cannot do, however, is so empty human life of value that God does not regard us or have hope for us. We are not worms. We are made in the image of God, only a little lower than God, and it is to that ideal that God calls us to live.

—J. E.

Proper 4/Pentecost 2/Ordinary Time 9

Psalm 96
(See Christmas Eve, Cycles A and B.)

Proper 5/Pentecost 3/Ordinary Time 10

Psalm 146
(See Advent 3, Cycle A, for vv. 5-10; see also Proper 26/Pentecost 24/Ordinary Time 31, Cycle B.)

Proper 6/Pentecost 4/Ordinary Time 11

Psalm 5:1-8

There are several things in the course of a lifetime that have the power to cause us to question our faith. The first is personal suffering and loss. As we experience pain that there does not seem to be a reason for — no obvious connection between our behavior and our suffering — it is hard not to ask, "God, why are you doing this? Where is your protecting hand?"

Next to our personal suffering, perhaps the next greatest challenge to faith is innocent suffering of others. After a massive earthquake in Lisbon in 1755 left thousands of people dead and many more suffering, the French philosopher Voltaire began to seriously reconsider the meaning of God. As we watch the worldwide AIDS epidemic, or as we observe drought and famine in Africa or the poverty and disease of India, it is tempting to ask the classic question of evil: "If there is a God, and that God is good and all powerful, how can God let these things exist? God is either not good, not powerful, or does not exist at all."

In fact, evil itself can pose a serious challenge to our faith. Why do the wicked prosper while the righteous beg for bread? Why does God allow powerful people, acting out of self-interest and greed, to prosper over the weak? Why doesn't God come to our rescue and save us from these evil people?

The author of Psalm 5 is aware of these challenges to faith, in himself and in the lives of other worshipers. But instead of giving in to these challenges, the psalmist decides to push past them and embrace a stance of faith in spite of the challenges to it.

The psalmist portrays God as a careful and caring judge who is always fair and just. God as judge is ready and willing to hear the complaints of the faithful. The psalmist approaches and begins with his own pain: "Give ear to my words, O Lord, give heed to my sighing" (v. 1). The psalmist assumes that God is listening and God cares: "I plead my case to you, and you watch" (v. 3). The psalmist shapes his prayer around this assumption and offers his plea without hesitation.

Because the psalmist believes God is fair, he chooses to remain patient in the face of the evil in the world. He believes that God "does not delight in wickedness" (v. 4) and that God "hates evildoers" (v. 5). While they may prosper for a moment, the justice and judgment of God will eventually right the scales, and those who have worked against righteousness will perish.

For the psalmist's part, he chooses integrity. Even though he suffers, even though there is evil in the world that seems to go unpunished, the psalmist will not be distracted from the right path. Trusting that God will do what is right, and that God really does care, the psalmist believes that until matters are set right, the best place to be is on the side of right.

In this the psalmist does not ignore the problems of evil, nor does he try to explain them. He simply chooses to believe that whatever injustice and unfairness may exist in the world at the moment will not be the final state of things, when God the righteous judge sets things right. His is a path of courageous faith. It is the path we are all called to travel.

— J. E.

Proper 7/Pentecost 5/Ordinary Time 12

Psalm 42 and Psalm 43

Though numbered separately in almost all texts, Psalms 42 and 43 are actually one psalm. Even a cursory reading makes this clear, and a closer reading leaves little doubt that the two poems should be read as one. The central message of the psalm is the presence of God, or more to the point, the absence of the presence. The psalmist draws our attention to the need to be steadfast in our faith with a recurring refrain spread out across the two poems: "Why are you cast down, O my soul, and why are you disquieted within me? Hope in God; for I shall again praise him, my help and my God" (42:5, 11, and 43:5).

The mystic tradition has used, as an image to describe the path to God, the concept of "desire" or even "yearning." The psalmist offers us another path: necessity. As an animal cannot live without water and searches fervently until water is found, so do we pursue God. God is the water of life, without which we cannot live. God is that essential life element that cannot be overlooked or left behind.

Of course, no one in the psalmist's audience would likely dispute that understanding of God. The problem for the psalmist and his audience is not that they fail to recognize the importance of God in their lives; the problem is, they can't find God.

We cannot be sure what has created this problem. The psalmist and his audience may have been part of the exile. There may have been some other national calamity that created a crisis of faith and a sense of God's absence. But even if we cannot know for sure what has created the crisis, we can appreciate the psalmist's advice for dealing with it.

If it were water we were lacking, would we sit on our hands and say, "Well, if that water wants to find me, I'm right here"? Of course not. We must have water to live. And if we don't have it, we go find it. We dig for it, we listen for it, and we smell for it. We put our whole being into focused motion to find that one thing we must have to live.

The psalmist would have us confront the absence of God's presence in exactly the same way. Never mind whatever disruption there has been in life, search for God with all we have. Never mind the pain or disappointments we may have experienced, without God we are nothing — let's go find the Lord.

The refrain that recurs throughout the two poems is a touchstone for us: a reminder that not only do we need to find God, but we *will* find God — if we keep searching and do not lose heart. The moment of doubt and spiritual emptiness will not last. If we will remain faithful and attend to those things we know are right, our efforts will be fruitful and we will again experience the lifegiving presence.

Therefore, "Why are you cast down, O my soul, and why are you disquieted within me? Hope in God; for I shall again praise him, my help and my God."

—J. E.

Proper 8/Pentecost 6/Ordinary Time 13

Psalm 77:1-2, 11-20

There is nothing quite as unsettling as being lost. A sense of weakness and anxiety takes hold as we realize we don't know where we are, or how we got there, or how to get back. There is no one to ask, there are no signs that point the way; there are only miles and miles of unfamiliar landscape. Deep inside, a growing sense of panic begins to take hold, as we consider the possibility that we may never be found.

Then it happens. A landmark comes into view that seems familiar. We stop and take a close look at it. Yes, it is definitely something we have seen before. Then, there's another familiar landmark, then another and another. Suddenly the road that only a moment before had seemed dreadful and threatening now seems safe and familiar and comforting. No longer is it a path leading to our doom; now it's the way home.

The psalmist is trying to help us find some landmarks. Somehow the psalmist and his congregation had gotten lost. We hear his cry: "In the night my hand is stretched out." What a powerful image of groping in the dark, trying to find the way!

Of course, the psalmist is giving voice to the fears of his community. For some reason they are in the dark. They are on a road that does not seem familiar. There is a growing sense of dread that perhaps God has abandoned them, or that they have wandered so far from God, they will never find him again. The psalmist voices their fear, but also their hope.

The psalmist declares: "I will call to mind the deeds of the Lord; I will remember your wonders of old" (v. 11). For the psalmist, helping the people remember will get them back on the right road. They need to remember the stories they know. They need to remember their own blessings from the past. They need to remember the promises God has made.

Of course, remembering also includes acting. They need to remember how to bow in the presence of God. They need to remember the words to use in prayer — and then use them in prayer. They need to remember the sights and sounds and smells of worship.

If the people will remember, they will begin to see familiar landmarks. The road they are on now, even though it seems treacherous and foreign, will suddenly become familiar. Just as in the days of old, they will remember how "You led your people like a flock by the hand of Moses and Aaron" (v. 20).

Then it will happen. They will see one happy landmark after another, until suddenly they will realize they are on the path that leads to home.

—J. E.

Proper 9/Pentecost 7/Ordinary Time 14

Psalm 30

(See Epiphany 6/Ordinary Time 6, Cycle B, and Easter 3, Cycle C, for alternative approaches.)

Anyone who has ever had the experience of losing a friend because of some conflict or dispute, and then has had the friendship restored because of love and forgiveness, has a unique insight into the meaning of this psalm. Although the poem begins and ends with praise, there is in the middle of the poem a brief moment of confession and contrition that puts the praise portions of the psalm in an entirely different light.

The first hint that this psalm is more than just a general praise song to God is introduced with the words, "For his anger is but for a moment" (v. 5). This phrase appears suddenly after many words of praise and exultation. God has saved the poet from suffering and from the hands of an unnamed enemy. The focus is on God, but without verse 5, the impression could be that God has intervened on behalf of a hapless victim of the cruelty of others.

Suddenly the psalmist lets us see that the suffering he endured was self-inflicted. Enemies beset him because he had drifted from God's will. The poet writes, "I said in my prosperity I shall never be moved." Then he writes, "You hid your face; I was dismayed."

The psalmist had apparently once known the comfort and the security of wealth. The statement, "I shall never be moved" rings with tones of self-sufficiency and maybe even pride. Reveling in his wealth and power, the psalmist forgot that God is the source of all blessing — material and otherwise.

It was then that the psalmist realized that God had withdrawn from him. The phrase "you hid your face" powerfully describes the experience of the absence of God. The psalmist's pride and forgetfulness had left him with only his own resources — a realization that did not leave him with a good feeling.

And so he repents. "To you, O Lord, I cried, and to you the Lord I made supplication" (v. 8). The psalmist forsakes his inordinate trust in wealth and power as the source of his security, and returns to the true source of all life. He pleads with God for mercy, with imagery and language filled with irony.

The psalmist asks the Lord, "what profit is there in my death ... will the dust praise you?" (v. 9). In other words, if God follows through with the penalty the psalmist deserves, he will die. But then, who will praise God? It is a clever and subtle way of promising God that, if God spares the life of the poet, the poet will make the goodness and the greatness of God well-known.

The psalm in which this promise occurs, of course, is the fulfillment of that promise. The verses leading up to the confession, and the verses that follow, all focus on God's goodness, mercy, and greatness.

Structurally, the psalm illustrates how life really works. Our failure occurs right in the middle of our praise. Sometimes, in the very midst of exulting in God, we fail. The psalm's message is that the grace of God is present both before and after our moments of foolishness.

That is why the psalmist's mourning has turned into dancing (v. 11), and why the psalmist is determined to "give thanks forever" (v. 12).

— J. E.

Proper 10/Pentecost 8/Ordinary Time 15

Psalm 82

Often, a distinction is made between the pastoral or priestly work of the church and the prophetic work. Pastoral care has to do with the care of souls, the offering of comfort in times of loss. The priestly character of pastoral work seeks to mediate the presence of God to those who are hurting.

The prophetic work of the church, however, involves challenging the faith community to act ethically, and also to speak the truth to the powerful. The prophets of the Old Testament often positioned themselves between the king and the community of faith, and challenged each to faithfully observe their various divine appointments. It is this in-between position, taken by the prophet, which has led to the claim that a prophet cannot function as pastor, and vice versa. A prophet is in the community, but not quite.

Psalm 82 demonstrates that this line of thinking may not be entirely true. The psalmist has created a poem that succeeds in comforting the afflicted, while at the same time afflicting the comfortable.

The psalmist begins by making the claim that God sits at the head of all tables. God is the King of all kings, the Ruler over all rulers. In doing this, the psalmist effectively subordinates the power of earthly kings to the dictates and expectations of God's will. If we are going to speak the truth to the powerful, it's not a bad idea to begin the conversation by putting in proper perspective just how limited the power of the powerful really is.

Once the conversation begins, however, the psalmist moves immediately to the prophetic judgment: "How long will you judge unjustly and show partiality to the wicked? Give justice to the weak and the orphan; maintain the right of the lowly and the destitute."

The judgment continues as an aside, as if God turns to the psalmist himself. "They have neither knowledge nor understanding, they walk around in darkness" (v. 5).

The purpose of the aside is twofold. First, the powerful overhear God's complaint — but the worshiping audience also overhears. The psalmist presents the report of this council meeting in the context of the worship. Those present for prayer overhear God's condemnation and complaint, and in the aside, God speaks to his people about their leaders, telling them that the leaders are in the dark.

This amazing device has the effect of simultaneously subverting the power of the unjust leaders, while at the same time emboldening the community of faith. These words assure them that God is really on their side.

It is also in overhearing the conversation between God and the leaders that the pastoral-care feature of this psalm has its effect. It is among those who have been victimized by the powerful that God condemns their oppressors. It is in the hearing of those who are hurting that God orders the princes of the land to "rescue the weak and the needy" (v. 4).

In the real world, we know that the powerful do not always respond to God's challenge. They forget that, in spite of their great power, they will "die like mortals." In the real world, the powerful often silence the prophets and leave the weak in misery, but what this psalm accomplishes is to give a powerful reminder of whose side God is really on. Even though the wicked may prosper for a season, God will ultimately vindicate the cause of the poor and heal them with love and mercy. In that promise, they are encouraged to keep faith and have hope.

—J. E.

Proper 11/Pentecost 9/Ordinary Time 16

Psalm 52

We are not surprised when we learn about crooks and robbers boasting about "mischief done against the godly" or "plotting destruction" all day long. The image we have in our minds about who "bad" people are, and how they conduct themselves, make such accusations completely plausible. We are less inclined to believe such things about leaders, especially respected leaders among us. We have difficulty believing someone with wealth and power would deliberately plot to do someone else harm. That's why political scandal is front-page news and convenience store hold-ups are found in the metro section on page eleven.

But the psalmist will not allow us this misinformed luxury. The "mighty one" of whom he writes has wealth and power — but is just as much a crook and thief as even the humblest pickpocket.

In ancient Israel, this was startling. Wealth was viewed as the proof of God's blessing. God conferred power on those who deserve it. But the prophets, and many psalmists, did not embrace this accepted wisdom. The wealthy and powerful, because they have greater resources, also have greater responsibility. Their wealth and power are not just for their private use. God expects them to use their resources to care for the weak and the vulnerable. The failure to do so amounts to stealing from the poor that which God intends for their care. The rich are merely caretakers and stewards of God's bounty.

Wealth and power are powerful lures. It takes great integrity to deal with these resources faithfully. Because there is so much power involved with these resources, it is easy to begin trusting in wealth as the true source of life and security. Or, as the psalmist puts it, "See the one who would not take refuge in God, but trusted in abundant riches and sought refuge in wealth!" (v. 7).

Once we lose the perspective created by a commitment to God and God's way, all ethical bets are off. When having and keeping power and wealth become the chief goal of life, a mindset develops that believes it is acceptable to do whatever it takes to maintain a privileged position. That's when the mischief against the godly begins to take form.

The remedy is not to live in poverty, but rather to live in dependence on God's truth. That is the meaning behind the psalmist's use of the imagery of the olive tree. "I am like a green olive tree in the house of God. I trust in the steadfast love of God forever and ever" (v. 8). A life that is rooted in God's truth, in the practices of worship ("in God's house"), and in the ethical practices growing out of worship is a life that is alive, vital, and growing — *green!*

But a life rooted in wealth, power, and self-gratification is a life going nowhere. It is life dependent on constantly manipulating circumstances in order to maintain the *status quo*. Life rooted in God does not grapple for life or sustenance or standing. God's care flows into our life freely and abundantly. We stand in freedom and peace and proclaim the goodness of God's name because "it is good" (v. 9).

— J. E.

Proper 12/Pentecost 10/Ordinary Time 17

Psalm 85
(See Advent 2, Cycle B, for an alternative approach to vv. 1-2 and 8-13.)

In 1988, Southern Baptists held their annual convention in San Antonio, Texas. It was a contentious meeting, as factions within the denomination vied for control of the various agencies and boards. Throughout the week, angry words were spoken across the aisle as various resolutions and officer elections revealed the deep schism growing within the group.

Meanwhile, beyond the halls of the heated convention, most of the rest of the country was suffering the worst drought since the "dust bowl" days of the 1930s. It had been months since there had been any appreciable rain. Livestock and crops were languishing for lack of water.

At the peak of one hotly contested business session during the convention, a pastor stepped up to one of the microphones set up for floor discussions and made a motion that the convention pause and pray for the people affected by the drought — and to pray for rain. His motion received a second and a vote was taken. The result was unanimous. Pausing to pray for rain was the only unifying action taken that entire week.

The writer of Psalm 85 would have appreciated that brief moment of unity. He, too, is concerned about the land. In fact, his psalm opens and closes with a reference to God's favorable stance toward the land. In between, however, there is trouble. Not a drought, but something else. The land of which the psalmist writes is not beset with natural calamity. The land of the psalmist has been beset by God.

Part of the problem, apparently, is that the people have forgotten whose land it really is. It turns out the land does not belong to them. The psalmist makes this clear as he declares, "You were favorable to your land" (v. 1).

Forgetting that the land belongs to God is where most of our trouble begins. The moment we stop recognizing God as the author and sustainer of all life, selfishness, greed, violence, and idolatry will not be far behind. We experience alienation from God as individuals when we forget God's ownership, and we experience exile as a people when we forget that life itself is a gift from God.

But judgment, alienation, and exile are not the last things we hear from God. God's desire is not to punish us forever. The psalmist asks the question, "Will you be angry with us forever?" (v. 5). But the tone is not one of despair. He asks the question in the midst of a plea for forgiveness: "Restore us again, O God of our salvation" (v. 4).

Repentance means to turn, or in this instance to *re*-turn. As we return to a proper understanding of who owns what, and of who is in charge. The forgiveness that we need and the blessing God wants to give will not be far behind.

—J. E.

Proper 13/Pentecost 11/Ordinary Time 18

Psalm 107:1-9, 43
(See Proper 26/Pentecost 24/Ordinary Time 31, Cycle A, and Lent 4, Cycle B.)

Proper 14/Pentecost 12/Ordinary Time 19

Psalm 50:1-8, 22-23
(For an alternative approach to vv. 1-6, see The Transfiguration Of Our Lord/Last Sunday After The Epiphany, Cycle B.)

Imagine the shock of arriving for worship one Sunday morning and finding the doors of the church blocked by a sheriff's deputy.

"I am sorry," the deputy says, "but you cannot enter the sanctuary."

As the congregation gathers at the door, everyone wants to know what the problem is; why can't they enter for worship?

The deputy hands a legal document to the minister. His face becomes ashen as reads it. With a stunned look on his face, the pastor announces to his congregation, "God is suing us for breach of contract!"

As absurd as that may sound to our modern sensibilities, that is precisely what the psalmist is writing about to his congregation. God the righteous judge has a complaint, a legal complaint with the people. God entered into a covenant, a contract, with the people and they have not kept their end of the bargain. Therefore, God has a complaint, a suit. And God plans to be judge, jury, and chief witness: "Hear, O my people, and I will speak, O Israel, I will testify against you. I am God, your God" (v. 7).

But what is the breach? If we return to our scene outside our local church, the minister might continue by saying, "We are being sued for a failure to be faithful."

"But how can that be?" the congregation responds. "We are here for worship, aren't we? We maintain this worship place with our tithes, don't we? We give to missions and benevolence. We teach our children and youth in Sunday school. Where is our failure?"

The minister scans the document and announces, "God's complaint is not what we do in church. His complaint is what we do after church."

The psalmist put it this way to his congregation, "Not for your sacrifices do I rebuke you; your burnt offerings are continually before me" (v. 8). The problem is not the people's ritual worship. The problem is their covenant fidelity.

The psalmist writes, "Those who bring thanksgiving as their sacrifice honor me; to those who go the right way I will show the salvation of God" (v. 23).

Thanksgiving as a sacrifice points to a quality of worship. God does not want mere ritual attendance. God desires the hearts of those who call upon God's name. Simply going through the motions, offering lip service is not enough. God wants us engaged to the point that we are deeply aware of what God has done for us. If we are, we will bring "thanksgiving" as the first fruits of our lives.

And it does not end in the worship place. Worship is but the first step on what the psalmist calls "the right way" (v. 23). What we do in worship, we must also do in life. What we celebrate as truth in prayer, we demonstrate in the daily practices of our lives. We cannot be holy in worship only. We are God's people every day, all day, everywhere we go.

It is what we promised to do when we agreed to the covenant. God will be God, the agreement says, and God is faithful. God does his part, and we are God's people. Our part of the covenant calls us to worship and to observe faithfully the demands of worship. But the covenant also calls us to integrity: to be God's people the way God wants us to be God's people. That means that our words and our lives must show we are God's people.

—J. E.

Proper 15/Pentecost 13/Ordinary Time 20

Psalm 80:1-2, 8-19
(See Advent 4, Cycle A, and Advent 1, Cycle B, for alternative approaches.)

The focus of this psalm is a recurring refrain found in three different verses. The refrain is a petition in which the worshiping community calls upon God to "let your face shine" (vv. 3, 7, 19).

The phrase is a Hebrew idiom that means something like, "to be present with someone with good results." Offering the expression in the form of a blessing, "May God's face shine upon you," has the force of a wish or a hope for someone's well-being and prosperity. But that is not the force of the prayer in this psalm. Psalm 80 is a community lament. In this prayer, we encounter people in pain. Their call for God's face to shine upon them carries a poignant and slightly understated "Again — let your face shine, *again*." This part of the plea is found in the recurring call for God to "restore."

This is a difficult tone for modern Americans to incorporate into our worship services. It is rare, if ever, that a service of worship would include recognition, even a tacit recognition, that the community is in the throes of the absence of God.

We may want to take issue with the tendency in the psalm to equate suffering with God's absence, and prosperity with God's presence. But we cannot deny in our own experience the feelings of abandonment and alienation that are often the result of tragedy or displacement in our world. It matters little whether or not God is "truly" absent, if we cannot — because of our pain — experience "God's face shining upon us."

The psalmist here is not interested in entering into a discussion about theodicy. As the worship leader, he is only interested in connecting the worshiping community with the source of their hope and life. To do that, he leads them in a fervent prayer that God might again bless the people with God's presence.

We may be tempted to see the use of repetition of words and phrases as examples of a cultural literary device, and certainly there is something to that. But at a deeper level, as we ponder the anguish of a community desperate to know again the presence of God through the recurring phrase, "let your face shine" and the word "restore," we also see an illustration of persistence.

The psalmist uses the image of a vine: transported out of Egypt and transplanted in a new land. But the vine has come under siege, and, either by pain or neglect or personal failure, the vine is languishing. We are naive to expect that our way back to health and vitality (back to God's presence) will be an easy one. Only through persistent and disciplined care can we once again experience God's attention. The psalmist would have us pursue and plead with God relentlessly for the restoration of our hope. Every worship hour, every moment in prayer must be directed toward urging God to "turn again," and have regard for the community (v. 14). To do any less might suggest a lack of adequate desire.

—J. E.

Proper 16/Pentecost 14/Ordinary Time 21

Psalm 71:1-6

(See Epiphany 4/Ordinary Time 4, Cycle C, for an alternative approach.)

The old saying, "experience is the best teacher," could serve as a subtitle for this psalm. Written as a prayer for help in a time of distress or oppression, the psalm subtly hints at a recognition and awareness that only comes with time. There is a track record, so to speak, that the psalmist is aware of: God's record of dependability. Based on God's proven record of saving power and grace, the psalmist is able to pray for salvation, but at the same time celebrate the certainty of its arrival.

The phrase that suggests the psalmist has some reservoir of experience from which to draw is this one: "For you, O Lord, are my hope and my trust, from my youth" (v. 5). It is not the sort of thing a young person would say. A young man wanting to affirm an exuberant relationship with God would likely say, "I've always hoped in God."

But when youth is far enough removed from us to allow a perspective on having been a youth, then we begin to reference that time as a separate and unique moment in our development. We hear it comically used in stereotypical scenes where a parent addresses a wayward child with the words, "Well, when I was young...."

That's not exactly what the psalmist means, though it does reveal a certain view of youth as a time gone by. What the psalmist is doing is appealing to God's own record of faithfulness as part of his appeal for help in the present. The psalmist tells God, in effect, "I have a long memory." Since God was faithful and helped in the past, surely God will be faithful again. God, after all, does have a reputation to consider.

Of course, the prayer is offered in the context of worship. It is prayer offered by one who has had some experience with God in the presence of those who may not have had so much experience. In that setting, the prayer is deliberately offered so as to be overheard by other worshipers. In this manner, the prayer becomes a vehicle for engendering hope. It perhaps accomplishes the same effect as an elder lecturing a younger on the way it was "when I was young." Yet, cast in the form of a prayer, these words invite those whose experience does not readily admit to hope to embrace a testimony that affirms the goodness and dependability of God.

In this the psalmist offers his own personal testimony as well. Not only is God dependable as savior and provider, but the psalmist presents himself as a reliable witness to these things. While it is true that the young cannot attain experiences they have not had, they can, if they choose, learn wisdom from those who have had experience. And what is that but the passing along of tradition — which is part of the legitimate function of worship anyway? Instead of creeds or doctrines, however, this psalm offers a vivid example of how we pass along not so much what to believe, but *how* faith itself comes alive.

It is something only learned over time, with much trial and error.

— J. E.

Proper 17/Pentecost 15/Ordinary Time 22

Psalm 81:1, 10-16

The writer of Psalm 81 employs a most interesting mixed metaphor. It is not mixed, however, because the psalmist was careless and neglected his subject matter. On the contrary, it is because of an important insight into human nature that the psalmist has us "eating with our ears."

Verse 10 rehearses what was, and is, the most basic confession of faith for followers of the Lord. God speaks and says, "I am the Lord your God, who brought you up out of the land of Egypt. Open your mouth and I will fill it."

This single confession draws together the full sweep of Hebrew salvation-history: from the great "I Am" of Moses' meeting at the burning bush, to the dramatic rescue out of Egypt, to the daily manna and ultimately the bounty of the promised land. The psalmist skillfully draws us, by means of this confession, into what will be the Lord's complaint with God's people. We are ready for it and we hear it coming. In fact, if we peek ahead to the next verse, we can actually see its opening volley: "But my people...."

The way the psalmist leaves us in verse 10, however, we are expecting some sort of complaint about what God wanted us to eat. The second phrase, "Open your mouth and I will fill it," leaves us expecting God to complain, "But my people would not eat what I gave them." Instead, however, the psalmist writes, "But my people would not listen to my voice" (v. 11).

Why the mixed metaphor? Why set us up for food, then give us words? The clue is given in the final verse, in which the psalmist reintroduces the feeding/food imagery. He writes, "I would feed you with the finest of the wheat, and with honey from the rock I would satisfy you" (v. 16). The key word is "satisfy."

The people have been trying to satisfy their needs. They have gone off on their own trying to find contentment, peace, security, and meaning. Yet in following their own lights, they abandoned the only authentic source for those kinds of things — the Lord's words and way. God tried to stop them, but they would not listen. They wanted what they wanted, and the Lord let them go, to pursue it (v. 12).

God let them go, then waited. God knew that the longer they followed the empty paths of their own counsels, the emptier their lives would become. Sooner or later, they would become hungry for the one truth that truly satisfies. They would need real security from real danger; they would need real help with real problems.

They would eventually realize that their meager diet of self-gratification was killing them, and that they must feed on the sacred words that constituted their existence in the first place.

Then, and only then, would God be able to give them that which would save them. It's not that God was unwilling. The problem was with their appetites, not God's willingness to care for them. Any time they were ready, God was ready with the menu.

"I will fill their mouths," God says, "if only they will open their ears."

— J. E.

Proper 18/Pentecost 16/Ordinary Time 23

Psalm 139:1-6, 13-18
(See Epiphany 2/Ordinary Time 2, Cycle B, and Proper 4/Pentecost 2/Ordinary Time 9, Cycle B; see also Proper 11/Pentecost 9/Ordinary Time 16, Cycle A, for an alternative approach to vv. 1-12, 23-24.)

Proper 19/Pentecost 17/Ordinary Time 24

Psalm 14
(See Proper 12/Pentecost 10/Ordinary Time 17, Cycle B, for an alternative approach.)

The psalm writer has an interesting perspective on the origin of injustice in our world. He begins this psalm with the assertion that those who do not believe in God are "fools." He goes on to accuse them of corruption and of being incapable of doing good. Later on he writes, "Have they no knowledge, all the evildoers who eat up my people as they eat bread, and do not call upon the Lord?" (v. 4).

It's a staggering thought. The greed and selfishness that marks so much of our world — and that most certainly contributes to, and maintains, the massive poverty we see everywhere — is rooted in a failure to acknowledge the presence of God.

Of course, the psalmist is really saying more than just that. For the psalmist, those who say "there is no God" are the ones who have no "knowledge of God." This is not a nod toward a mental affirmation of some abstract existence of a divine being. The psalmist believes that knowing God means experiencing God in a personal, intimate, and disciplined relationship. It's not just saying, "Yes," to the question, "Do you believe in God?" Knowing God means being connected to God, in a relationship in which our entire existence centers on the presence of God.

Failure to do this, the psalmist seems to be saying, is the root of all our problems. It's what makes it possible for us to put money and possessions above people and their needs. Our failure to have a vital relationship with God renders us mentally and spiritually incapable of making appropriate ethical and moral decisions.

This is an important distinction for us to understand. There is a certain religiosity in our culture that is quick to offer verbal affirmations about God. In fact, there is a significant amount of interest in some quarters about the need to "acknowledge God" in our public life. Unfortunately, what this often boils down to is some sort of public display of piety, or some token acknowledgment such as a monument to the Ten Commandments.

But the psalmist will not allow us to empty the meaning out of "knowing God." When we really know God, we know God's people. The psalmist writes, "You would confound the plans of the poor, but the Lord is their refuge." In other words, had we been in the company of God by means of a committed, intimate relationship, we would never have allowed the exploitation of the weak and the needy.

The final verse points to the ultimate hope underlying the psalmist's meditation. The expression, "when God restores the fortunes of his people" could very well be an allusion to the Jubilee year detailed in Leviticus 25. The jubilee celebration was marked by the restoration of all property to those who had become poor through the intervening years.

Common sense would suggest that, were we forced to give land we had held for fifty years back to the original owner, this would be an occasion for anger and resentment. But if we "know the Lord," the coming of the great restoration is an occasion for rejoicing and celebration within the entire community. This response is only possible if we have a lively relationship with God. By means of an intimate connection with God's presence, we learn to want what God wants. We will want what is right and fair.

After all, only fools — who say and act as though there is no God — are comfortable in a world where the poor suffer while the wealthy prosper.

— J. E.

Proper 20/Pentecost 18/Ordinary Time 25

Psalm 79:1-9

This poignant prayer of lament and community grief gives expression to what it feels like to suffer as a person of faith. If we believe we are truly part of God's community, then the destruction of that community — as was the case with Israel in 587 B.C. — becomes a time for doubt, anger, and confusion. Furthermore, if we believe we are individual members of that community, our personal suffering also creates an opportunity for a crisis of faith: "Why didn't God protect me?" Of course, it does not take a national catastrophe to raise those sorts of questions. The cancer wards and surgical suites of hospitals are often settings for prayers of lament.

Once we start asking the question, it's hard to stop. What exactly is going on when we suffer, either as a nation or a community or as individuals? The psalmist assumes, as does the prophetic tradition associated with the exile, that the suffering of Israel was punishment. Israel sinned against God and God's covenant. Israel became unfaithful. Israel forgot the widow and the orphan. For these sins, God sent them into exile.

But for how long? Is the sin so great that the relationship is ended forever? Is it exile or is it abandonment? The people of Israel surely had moments when they wondered whether God had forgotten them.

The psalmist gives eloquent voice to all this, and more, but there is in this psalm an allusion to another fear, a fear that is perhaps greater than fear of divine abandonment. The psalmist hints that there are some who might wonder if God is really up to the task of protecting God's people.

The psalmist writes, "We have become a taunt to our neighbors" (v. 4). What is the content of these taunts? Are these tormentors suggesting that the God of Israel is a weak God, an inept God?

As the taunts ring out, those who are suffering might become aware of their own concerns. Maybe this started out as punishment, but what if God *can't* call it off? God allowed the "nations" to swoop down upon the holy city, but is God capable of turning them back? Does the pain of an extended exile, coupled with the pain of Jerusalem's defeat, really suggest that God can be defeated?

In defiance of this fear, the psalmist directs his prayer to the very heart of God's character. "Help us, O God of our salvation, for the glory of your name" (v. 9). The psalmist challenges God to honor the covenant, even though God's people did not. The psalmist calls on God to vindicate God's reputation in the world by restoring the people of Israel to their place of privilege — even though it was through their own carelessness it was lost.

There is therapeutic value in giving voice to our pain and our fears. It's pretty easy to confess, "I am suffering because I deserve it." It's a bit harder to say, "I'm suffering and I don't know why God is allowing it; why God won't stop it; why it goes on and on."

By calling on God to vindicate God's own reputation, the psalmist offers a profound way to reintroduce hope to a community that may well have been on the brink of losing hope, and may be losing faith. Even if we don't deserve to be saved, God will save us anyway: because that's who God is.

— J. E.

Proper 21/Pentecost 19/Ordinary Time 26

Psalm 91:1-6, 14-16
(See Lent 1, Cycle C, for an alternative approach to vv. 1-2 and 9-16.)

The writer of this psalm deftly employs a striking image, that at once offers us hope in times of trouble — but at the same time, redefines for us what it means to be a human being in the world.

The writer begins by comparing our situation in life to that of a captured bird. We are victims of our own weakness, as well as the crafty wiles of the "fowler" (v. 3). We are so gullible. The snares out there are legion. From get-rich-quick schemes, to amazing diets, to the lure of drugs and alcohol, to the temptations of illicit sex — there are traps everywhere, and we, like mindless birds, walk right into them.

But the "fowlers" who set the traps know us pretty well. They know just how to package their traps, to make them seem enticing. They know just how to market their snares to convince us we can't live without them. How ironic and sad it is to discover that what was sold to us as necessary to make life meaningful becomes a trap that makes life miserable. (Anyone making monthly payments on a multi-function exercise machine knows exactly what I am talking about!)

There is a subtle subtext to all this: not from the psalmist, but from the depths of our own being. It's bad enough to live in the trap we find for ourselves, but we compound the problem by despising our bird-brained existence. There is a tendency, fueled by a judgmental religious and political culture, to condemn ourselves relentlessly for the stupid things we do. We are just dumb birds and deserve whatever trap we fall into.

That's our mistake. The psalmist does not take us there. Our birdlike vulnerability is simply part of the human situation. It is something to be aware of and learn from, it is not a matter for self-loathing. In fact, it is as a bird that the psalmist offers us the gracious help of God. "Under his wings you will find refuge" (v. 4).

We are little birds with big problems. Every predator on the block has a trap waiting for us. Because we are weak and vulnerable, and sometimes not too smart, we fall into those traps.

But God is a big bird, smart and cunning. God is able to thwart the fowler's snare by sharing wisdom and experience with us. God helps us overcome some of our stupidity. And for our weakness, for those aspects of our bird-brained existence that we cannot school away, God offers us refuge.

There is a certain theological elegance in all this. We speak freely, and correctly, of being created in God's image. That idea points to lofty possibilities for our existence as humans. But according to the psalmist, sometimes God takes on our image, becomes like us. When we act like birds, for instance, God becomes a bird and dwells among us, and we behold God's glory as we find shelter beneath wings of grace.

—J. E.

Proper 22/Pentecost 20/Ordinary Time 27

Lamentations 3:19-26

The little-known book of Lamentations was likely composed in the ashes of Jerusalem, following the Babylonian invasion which carried the leaders of the Jewish community off into exile. It speaks to the concerns of the Jerusalem community for their long-term survival under occupation by a foreign power. While the book's title sounds grim, and its setting is dark, the book is fundamentally life-affirming. It is a testimony to the steadfast love of God that may be discovered through renewed faith, even in troubled times.

Although the book is traditionally attributed to Jeremiah and is possibly contemporaneous with him, there is no particular reason to claim him as the author. Still, the tradition of calling it "The Lamentations of Jeremiah" is a strong one in both Judaism and Christianity, despite the lack of textual evidence to that effect. It is entirely possible that the book is an anthology of poetry by different authors.

Lamentations 3:19-26 is part of a larger poem that struggles frankly with the possibility that the Lord is an adversary. In 3:1-18, the author figuratively shakes his fist at the heavens, questioning why God could allow such terrible suffering to come to the people: "[The Lord] is a bear lying in wait for me, a lion in hiding; he led me off my way and tore me to pieces; he has made me desolate" (vv. 10-11).

In today's passage, however, we see the beginning of the transition from despair to hope. The key transition is verses 19-21, in which we can see the poet move from "wormwood and gall" to an abiding awareness of God's faithfulness. Then, in the remaining verses of this selection, we see the poet offer up a defiant song of praise: "The steadfast love of the Lord never ceases, his mercies never come to an end; they are new every morning; great is your faithfulness" (vv. 22-23).

This is, of course, the basis for the well-loved hymn, "Great Is Thy Faithfulness," which is an excellent choice to go along with a sermon on this passage.

Verdan Smailovic, a classical cellist, was famous for playing in the great concert halls of Europe, as well as in the small towns and villages of his native Yugoslavia. "Music is not just for the rich and privileged," he used to say, justifying his decision to play these smaller venues. "Music is for everyone."

Smailovic was the famous lone cellist who sat in the rubble of Sarajevo in formal attire and played his instrument, after his opera theater had been destroyed and many of his neighbors had been killed by mortar rounds. A television reporter asked him if he were crazy for playing his cello while Sarajevo was being shelled. Smailovic replied: "You ask me, 'Am I crazy for playing the cello?' 'Why do you not ask if they are crazy for shelling Sarajevo?' "

Smailovic would have found a kindred spirit in the author of Lamentations, chapter 3.

— C. W.

Psalm 137

This psalm's opening verses are among the most recognizable for understanding the experience of a worship community in exile. The evocative, "How can we sing the songs of Zion in a foreign land?" (v. 4) has become biblical shorthand for this experience. In a single poetic stroke the psalmist is able to convey not only the tragedy of social displacement, but also the agony of spiritual despair.

The psalmist's insight into this dilemma goes beyond mere context. Separation from the temple was certainly an issue. The songs don't ring as true, the prayers as meaningful, and the benedictions as helpful outside the proper setting for worship. But there is much more at risk.

The psalmist understands that the words themselves are important, that they carry meaning and are essential to maintaining identity. If members of the community of faith ever give up the particularity of their language, they will have no meaningful way to talk about their faith. Even more critical, if the community of faith adopts the language of the culture that holds it captive, the people will not only lose their own faith, but will become participants by default in a new faith.

Christianity in America certainly faces similar challenges. As we become more and more like our culture, we lose a distinctively biblical and Christian identity. These changes happen subtly and often without much fanfare. While in graduate school, I attended a multi-disciplinary seminar that included professors and students from several different schools of study. There were lawyers, doctors, scientists, classicists, historians, psychologists, and graduate religion students.

In the course of the seminar, a local church contacted me about becoming their pastor. Using the language of my tradition (Baptist) I mentioned to my peers that I was being considered for a "call." Many of them found this a strange way to talk about employment and began to have fun with it at my expense. It became a running joke for several days, as different students in the seminar mimicked my language that seemed provincial to them. I have caught myself later, and on some occasions since, using the language of the secular marketplace to talk about being "hired" by a church.

The particularity of our language is essential to communicating to each other the theological meaning of what we do and who we are. To use the language of "call," instead of the more commonplace "hired," reminds us that in the clergy/church relationship, there is a presumption that God is involved in the process. While the church may use standard business practices to evaluate candidates, we still cling to the idea that somehow God works in the mix to bring together clergy and congregation.

There are other issues and challenges from culture that are even more insidious than the language of hiring. It makes a difference whether we meet in an "auditorium" or a "sanctuary." Which word best captures the biblical meaning of "pastor": CEO or educator or counselor or activist? Is it possible anymore to meaningfully invoke images such as prophet or shepherd?

It's difficult to sing the songs of Zion in a foreign land — but necessary. "If I forget you, O Jerusalem, let my right hand wither" (v. 5). Jesus understood this very well when he reminded his followers that they were to be "in the world but not of the world." In the world we work and contribute to the peace of the city, but by not being of the world we speak and live a language of faith that creates our character and carries our hope.

— J. E.

Proper 23/Pentecost 21/Ordinary Time 28

Psalm 66:1-12
(See Easter 6, Cycle A for an alternative approach to vv. 8-20.)

All successful sports programs include a vigorous practice regimen. These practice sessions have a dual purpose. First, there is physical conditioning. Players must have the strength and endurance to play through the whole game. Without conditioning, they may falter in the fourth quarter or the last inning. The other purpose of practice is to teach players how to react. Practice sessions simulate any number of responses from the other team, or situations on the field. The players must learn to think and act in a certain way. They must know their position and responsibility, but also what others on the team are doing and where they will be in different situations. Players must know, before the ball is snapped or the pitch hit, exactly what they will do, what their role is. Practice sessions rehearse these scenarios over and over again until they become second nature.

In a sense, that is what the psalmist is doing. For him, worship is a practice session — practicing the presence of God. In the safety of the sanctuary, surrounded by a company of like-minded believers, the psalmist invokes praise and thanksgiving. In the setting of worship it is easy to say: "Sing the glory of his name; give to him glorious praise." The psalmist believes that whatever the situation on the field, praise is the proper response.

The conditioning he provides is theological memory. The psalmist knows, and the worshipers must learn, that it will not always be easy or safe to sing God's praises. Obstacles of many sorts may arise. Unexpected exiles or injuries or wars or social collapse may strike at the heart of our ability to express praise. When these events come, the psalmist wants his people ready. He wants their minds and their memories sharp.

"Come and see what God has done: he is awesome in his deeds among mortals" (v. 5). Week after week, the worship leader guides the community to remember God's "awesome deeds." The people are reminded that their forbears suffered under the cruel hand of Pharaoh's oppression, but God brought God's people out on dry land.

This is not merely an exercise in wishful thinking. It is an act of faith. The psalmist's community is either already in the midst of a difficult situation or it is headed for one. "For you, O God, have tested us; you have tried us as silver is tried" (v. 10). If he can prepare them to think theologically about their situation, if they can remember the pathways of worship and praise, then when the trouble comes, or as it continues, the people of the community of faith can remain faithful.

"Remember," the worship leader intones. "Remember, and praise while it is easy, so that when your day of trouble comes you will continue to remember and will be able to praise."

— J. E.

Proper 24/Pentecost 22/Ordinary Time 29

Psalm 119:97-104

Psalm 119 is well-known as the longest chapter in the Bible. The poem is actually an extended, and extensive, meditation on the meaning of the law. Given the sterile connotations often associated with "law" and "legalism," it's hard sometimes to appreciate the lyrical beauty of these reflections. One thing is for certain, the writer of this psalm does not view the law as either sterile or void of vitality.

We help ourselves somewhat if we remember that "law" in this psalm, and its corresponding "your word," have reference to Torah — the Law of Moses. Torah is more than just legislative matters, case law, injunctions, and statutes, though it includes all of that. Torah is best understood as "instruction." This is what the psalmist celebrates throughout his long poem. Torah is life-giving. Torah, when internalized, creates a meaningful life. Torah frees us from foolishness by instilling wisdom. Torah does not do its work through legislative coercion. Torah does its work by changing the essential character of those who reflect on its meaning.

This principle is amply illustrated in the section of the psalm we consider here. The psalmist does not hold back his emotions: "O how I love your law" (v. 97). This is a passionate relationship with truth — and with the hope of personal, as well as community, maturity.

The psalmist employs relational and sensory images to communicate the power of the law to transform us. The law makes us wiser than both our enemies and our teachers. The law has the power to advance our learning in spite of our age. The law is like a safety harness that keeps us from being pulled into evil. Yet the law is sweet, like honey on the tongue.

There is an important point to understand in all this — though not so much in what the psalmist says about the law, though his words are important and instructive. Equally important is his model of commitment to the law. The example the psalmist offers us, of how to love the law and pursue truth, is an excellent model for spiritual formation and Christian education.

We will not make much headway in any endeavor without commitment. The artist who masters the piano or some other musical instrument cannot do so without regular attention to the instrument. The athlete who seeks to compete at some high level cannot afford to miss a day of training and conditioning. The writer who would compose a masterpiece must sit with the words every day if the work is ever to be finished.

Similar comparisons could be made to other endeavors. If a married couple expects their relationship to survive and thrive over a number of years, they must be intentional about communication, conflict management, and nurturing affection. Parents who want to see their children grow and mature into fully functioning adults must commit the time needed to train and guide them.

The psalmist shows us the wisdom of the passionate pursuit. Whether it is God's truth or a chance to perform at Carnegie Hall, it is disciplined and intentional attention to the task that brings about the desired result. In the case of the law, the result is wisdom and the doorway to a meaningful relationship with God.

—J. E.

Proper 25/Pentecost 23/Ordinary Time 30

Psalm 65
(See Thanksgiving Day, Cycle A, for an alternative approach.)
In Psalm 65, the psalmist brings together two different aspects of God's activity and uniquely connects them. This unusual

pairing of ideas may shed important light on one of the most important aspects of our relationship with God.

The psalm begins with a call to recognize that God is worthy of our praise. The psalmist immediately lists a series of activities that are intended to let us know just how praiseworthy God is. God is praised for answering our prayers; for the forgiveness of transgressions; and for providing a place to worship.

The psalmist then launches into an eloquent song celebrating God's awesome deeds and amazing power, especially as it is revealed in creation. God's strength is evident in the roaring seas and in the great mountains. God's loving strength is also evident in the recurring pattern of life seen on the earth.

The unusual pairing of ideas lies at the transition in this psalm. Just as the psalmist is leading us to praise God's grace and forgiveness, he is also reminding us that these attributes are evidence of God's strength: "By awesome deeds you answer us with deliverance" (v. 5). Just as God is strong enough to rein in the seas or create the mighty mountains, so also God is strong enough to provide redemption, forgiveness, and hope for us.

There are two insights for us to carry away from this interesting pairing. First, if great strength is needed to forgive us and save us from our misdeeds, then the power of disobedience must be great in the world. It makes sense when we think about it. If God has indeed given us a privileged place in the scheme of creation, and if we in our freedom have genuine power to choose and to create, it stands to reason that we also have enormous power to destroy.

Does this mean that human beings could ultimately thwart God's will for creation? Probably not, though we can certainly undermine God's plan for us individually. Because of the privileged place given us in the scheme of creation, when we do throw a wrench in the works, God must exert great power to overcome our iniquities. Salvation, redemption, and forgiveness do not come easily. Of course, we should have already known that from the cross.

The second insight has more to do with our own practice of forgiveness, particularly as it relates to interpersonal relationships.

There is perhaps an unstated sense that the act of forgiveness is an act of weakness. If forgiveness in relationships is understood as "letting someone off," or "letting something go," it's easy to see how those views might be interpreted as "weakness."

But we learn from this psalm that forgiveness is hard, and is only possible for the spiritually strong. The key with God, of course, is God's desire to see us succeed. God is heavily invested in the relationship and is willing to do the hard work of forgiveness.

The same will be true for us. If we are invested in relationships, if our desire is to see family or community thrive, if we understand the importance of reconciliation and forgiveness in relationships, then we, too, will do the hard work necessary to make sure it happens.

— J. E.

Proper 26/Pentecost 24/Ordinary Time 31

Psalm 119:137-144

The psalmist exuberantly expresses his sense of joy and love for God's Law. We may have trouble understanding this emotion simply because of the way the word "law" functions in our culture. Mentioning the law may evoke images of courtrooms, judges, lawyers, and law libraries. We may get a picture of the legislative process or an image of law enforcement.

While some of this can be accurately associated with God's Law, those elements are not the primary characteristic. As we read the psalmist, we get the feeling that the law he is connected to is a vital force. It is alive and "life-giving."

In the verses 137-144, the psalmist turns his attention to the force behind the law — the character of God. "You are righteous, O Lord, and your judgments are right" (v. 137). It is the force of God's own character that gives the law its vitality. It is as if God has put the very essence of God's own self in the law. This element of the presence of God is what gives the law its life-giving property.

Of course, the psalmist states the matter much more strongly than that: "Your decrees are righteous forever; give me understanding that I may live" (v. 144). For the psalmist, the Word of God is not only life-giving, but is essential to life itself. Without the law, without these words, we do not and cannot live.

We are immediately struck by the similarity of this line of thinking with what Jesus said during the temptation. When the devil tempts Jesus to turn stones into bread, Jesus replies that humankind does not live by bread alone but by every word that proceeds from the mouth of God (Matthew 4:4; Luke 4:4).

The psalmist would add a hearty "Amen" to that sentiment. The wisdom offered in God's Law, and the access to God's character that the law provides, are as necessary to survival as is the food we eat. Without food, our bodies wither and die: but without God's Word, the deeper purpose of our existence comes to an end. We may continue to breathe and walk around, existing on some biological level, but we will not be alive in the deepest sense of the word. Although the psalmist does not use the following words, I do not think he would disagree with the meaning: It is God's Law and God's truth that makes us truly human.

—J. E.

All Saints

Psalm 149
(See Proper 18/Pentecost 16/Ordinary Time 23, Cycle A, for an alternative approach.)
In the first verse of this psalm, the writer calls on his audience to praise the Lord and to sing a new song to the Lord "in the assembly of the faithful." In the closing verse, the writer returns to this theme as he writes, "This is glory for all his faithful ones." It is this image of the faithful assembly, gathered for praise and then being glorified for their praise, that draws this psalm into service for All Saints.

Liturgical churches are wise to keep this day and observe its meaning with as much enthusiasm as this psalm suggests — not just as a memorial to those who have gone before, though that is certainly fitting. The idea of All Saints needs to be retained as a reminder of the calling of the faith community here and now. We are part of an unbroken succession of believers whose singular, unifying characteristic is our praise and adoration of God. It is the one thing that links all believers together, past and present.

That linkage is more important now than it ever has been. The immediacy of the electronic age has given us more information than we can possibly assimilate — but at the same time, made it more difficult for us to maintain traditions and pass along a heritage.

This is particularly true in regard to worship. The present flux in worship styles has created a highly fluid situation. For many people, there is only the present moment of worship, only the now. The idea that they are somehow connected to a history of worship and service, that there have been and are others with whom we share a legacy, is not often voiced.

This does not mean we live in the past or get stuck in another worship moment fifty or one hundred years ago. However, there is a certain advantage to understanding that what we do in church has a history. There is also an advantage in remembering that there have been others who have been this way before us.

So, let us sing our praises in the presence of God, and remember the faithful who have sung and are singing with us throughout the ages. Let us celebrate the part we play in the great chorus of witnesses who seek to live out a certain truth, and experience God in our songs. This is not only our privilege, but it is also our glory — to praise God with God's people forever.

— J. E.

Proper 27/Pentecost 25/Ordinary Time 32

Psalm 145:1-5, 17-21

Psalm 145 is known not so much in its entirety, but piecemeal, by those who are familiar with Christian worship texts. Words like "Great is the Lord, and greatly to be praised" (v. 3); "The eyes of all look to you, and you give them their food in due season" (v. 15) and "The Lord is near to all who call on him, to all who call on him in truth" have often called us to worship. The words, "The Lord is gracious and merciful, slow to anger and abounding in steadfast love" (v. 8) have often called us to confession, or assured us of God's pardon. Psalm 145 is a veritable repository of worship texts.

It would be entirely understandable if a sermon on this psalm zeroed in on one of these familiar texts, and left the rest of it alone. Yet Psalm 145 also has integrity of its own, as a complete work. It is the only psalm identified by superscript as both a praise-song (*tehillah*) and a psalm of David. It has long had a special place in Jewish liturgical tradition. James Luther Mays quotes the following Talmudic saying, which gives Psalm 145 pride of place in Jewish devotion: "Every one who repeats the *Tehillah* of David thrice a day may be sure that he is a child of the world to come" (*Psalms*, in the *Interpretation* series [Louisville: John Knox Press, 1994], p. 437).

As for its position in the psalter, Psalm 145 is the preface to the concluding section of five hymns of praise, all of which begin and end with the word "Hallelujah!" Its theme is praise, pure and simple. A sermon that seeks to interpret the psalm as a unified whole will undoubtedly have praise and worship as its theme.

A Sunday school teacher once asked her students to discuss how they felt about coming to church. As is often the case, the teacher's question was met with several wisecracks and spurious answers, but then one little girl — who was new to the class and had not until then found the courage to speak — raised her hand. Her answer was profound, and caused her less-serious classmates to sit and reflect in awed silence. She said that, for her, going to church was "like walking into the heart of God."

Long ago, in *Between God and Man*, (Harper, 1959), renowned Jewish biblical scholar Abraham Joseph Heschel penned these words, about the wonder that is worship:

> *The awareness of the grandeur and the sublime is all but gone from modern man. We teach our children how to measure, how to weigh. We fail to teach them how to revere, how to sense wonder and awe. The sense for the sublime, the sign of the inward greatness of the soul is now a rare gift. Yet without it, the world becomes flat and the soul a vacuum ... The sublime is that which we see and are unable to convey. IT is the silent allusion of things to a meaning greater than themselves. IT is that which our words, our forms, our categories can never reach. The sublime is but a way in which things react to the presence of God. It stands in relation to something beyond itself that the eye can never see. The sublime is not simply there. It is not a thing. IT is a happening, an act of God, a marvel. There are no sublime facts; there are only divine acts.*

— C. W.

Psalm 98
(See Christmas Day, Cycle A, and B; also, Easter 6, Cycle B.)

Proper 28/Pentecost 26/Ordinary Time 33

Isaiah 12
(For an alternative approach to vv. 2-6, see Advent 3, Cycle C.)

This psalm embedded in the writing of Isaiah is a beautiful meditation on the journey we take as human beings: beginning from failure and moving on to forgiveness, to gratitude, to praise.

In our failure we encounter the anger and disappointment of God. We have expectations for ourselves, expectations that are rooted in what we believe God expects of us. When we fail to live up to those expectations — either by omission or commission —

guilt is the result. If our actions or inactions have consequences, those consequences become for us the very embodiment of the wrath of God.

Then forgiveness comes. We find that God's anger "has turned away." In the act of contrition and whatever accompanying penance we may impose on ourselves, we encounter a gracious God whose interests are not in our destruction but in our salvation. As we encounter this forgiveness, we discover that guilt gives way to confidence. We feel our relationship with God mending. The anxiety that had once gripped us in our failure now gives way to hope, with the acceptance God bestows on us. We are free, and are released from our sin.

To this there is but one response — gratitude. We know that God was under no compulsion to forgive us. Forgiveness comes as a free and undeserved gift. There is no way to pay for it or pay it back. We can only be grateful. Out of that gratitude we experience a sense of joy. Isaiah writes that it is with this joy that we draw from the well of salvation. In other words, there is a reservoir of grace that will flow over us and refresh us for as long as we drink from its depths.

That's when the praise begins. "Sing praises to the Lord," Isaiah declares, "because he has done gloriously." That glory reaches as far as the skies and as deep as the depths of the earth. The glory of God reflects God's great creative power, the power to shape the heavens, but it also celebrates God's power to forgive lowly sinners. Because of God's grace, and because we are set free from our failure by that grace, we are able to lift our voices with the voices of the universe in singing praise to God.

Of course we know that the whole cycle is likely to begin again. As hard as it is to imagine, it is nonetheless true. We often move from failure to forgiveness to gratitude to praise, and then back to failure. Thankfully, God is long-suffering and kind. God will keep the way open for us to find our way back, again and again, to the well of salvation.

—J. E.

Christ The King/Proper 29

Luke 1:68-79
(See Advent 2, Cycle C, for an alternative approach.)

The words of Zechariah concerning the arrival of the Messiah, and the role Zechariah's son will play in announcing that arrival, are among the most beautiful and evocative in the Bible. They are also especially significant as we seek to gain an understanding and appreciation of the meaning of Christ as King.

We have several handicaps in modern American culture when it comes to understanding the meaning of Christ as King — the first one being right there. Christ as King literally, in its Hebrew background, means King as King. The nuances of the meaning of the Greek word, *Christos*, and how that word connects to the Hebrew notion of "Messiah" — both words meaning "anointed" — are all but lost on us. When we hear the word, "king," there are typically two associations we make.

The first is actually the lack of an association. Our contact with a king is so far removed from our national experience as to be totally irrelevant. Simply put, we have no idea what it means to have a king, to expect a king, to honor a king, and so on. When we do try to conjure up some associations, we almost always resort to stereotypes presented to us by popular media.

Additionally — and here we share a struggle with all people throughout history — it is difficult for us to think of a political leader of any sort, king or president, and not think of that role almost exclusively in terms of coercive power. Even in Zechariah's song there is a tacit assumption that the king can do whatever he wants. Yet the power we associate with the idea of king is power for the powerful. In other words, the king in our world acts on behalf of the privileged, not on behalf of the needy.

We must listen carefully to songs of kingship offered in the New Testament, and in particular this song in Luke, and seek to understand power in a different way and for different people.

Twice in this passage, Zechariah celebrates the hope that the king, when he comes, will free people from bondage. "Our enemies," he writes, "will be vanquished." The people who wait for this king are not privileged people; these are oppressed people. The king they hope for is not so much regal as he is compassionate. He will be adored, not for his pomp and circumstance, but for his commitment to justice.

This is the king Zechariah saw, that his son would help introduce to the world. This was the king he saw who would bring hope like the light of a new day. This is the king we now celebrate as Christ our King — even though we don't know much what that means. We know we have hope because of him, and to him we owe our loyalty and our praise.

—J. E.

Thanksgiving Day

Psalm 100
(See Proper 29/Christ the King, Cycle A.)

Scriptural Index

Exodus
15:1b-11, 20-21	Proper 19, B	109

1 Samuel
2:1-10	Proper 28, B	208

Psalm
1	Easter 7, B	173
	Proper 20, B	196
	Epiphany 6, C	225
2	The Transfiguration Of Our Lord, A	51
4	Easter 3, B	167
5:1-8	Proper 6, C	254
8	The Holy Trinity, A	82
	The Holy Trinity, C	252
9:9-20	Proper 7, B	180
13	Proper 8, A	87
14	Proper 12, B	188
	Proper 19, C	271
15	Epiphany 4, A	42
16	Easter 2, A	71
17:1-7, 15	Proper 13, A	97
19	Proper 22, A	114
	Lent 3, B	156
	Proper 19, B	196
	Epiphany 3, C	224
20	Proper 6, B	179
22	Good Friday, A	68
	Good Friday, B	164
	Good Friday, C	240
22:1-15	Proper 23, B	201
22:23-31	Lent 2, B	155
22:25-31	Easter 5, B	169

23	Lent 4, A	59
	Easter 4, A	74
	Easter 4, B	168
	Easter 4, C	245
24	Proper 10, B	185
	All Saints, B	206
25:1-10	Lent 1, B	154
	Advent 1, C	215
26	Proper 22, B	199
27	Lent 2, C	233
27:1, 4-9	Epiphany 3, A	41
29	Epiphany 1, A	38
	Epiphany 1, B	140
	Epiphany 1, C	222
	The Holy Trinity, B	175
30	Epiphany 6, B	147
	Easter 3, C	243
	Proper 9, C	258
31:1-5, 15-16	Easter 5, A	75
31:1-5, 19-24	Epiphany 9, A	49
31:9-16	Liturgy Of The Passion, A	65
	Liturgy Of The Passion, B	161
	Liturgy Of The Passion, C	238
32	Lent 1, A	55
	Lent 4, C	236
33:1-12	Proper 5, A	85
34:1-8 (19-22)	Proper 25, B	204
34:1-10, 22	All Saints, A	120
36:5-10	Epiphany 2, C	222
37:1-11, 39-40	Epiphany 7, C	227
40:1-11	Epiphany 2, A	40
41	Epiphany 7, B	148
42	Proper 7, C	255
43	Proper 7, C	255
45:1-2, 6-9	Proper 17, B	193
45:10-17	Proper 9, A	88
46	Proper 4, A	83

47	The Ascension Of Our Lord, A	77
	The Ascension Of Our Lord, B	171
	The Ascension Of Our Lord, C	250
48	Proper 9, B	184
50:1-6	The Transfiguration Of Our Lord, B	152
50:1-8, 22-23	Proper 14, C	265
51:1-12	Proper 13, B	189
	Lent 5, B	158
51:1-17	Ash Wednesday, A	53
	Ash Wednesday, B	154
	Ash Wednesday, C	231
52	Proper 11, C	261
62:5-12	Epiphany 3, B	143
63:1-8	Lent 3, C	234
65	Thanksgiving Day, A	125
	Proper 25, C	282
66:1-12	Proper 23, C	279
66:8-20	Easter 6, A	76
67	Easter 6, C	248
68:1-10, 32-35	Easter 7, A	79
71:1-6	Epiphany 4, C	224
	Proper 16, C	268
72:1-7, 10-14	The Epiphany Of Our Lord, A	37
	The Epiphany Of Our Lord, B	139
	The Epiphany Of Our Lord, C	222
72:1-7, 18-19	Advent 2, A	24
77:1-2, 11-20	Proper 8, C	257
78:1-4, 12-16	Proper 21, A	113
78:1-7	Proper 27, A	120
79:1-9	Proper 20, C	273
80:1-2, 8-19	Proper 15, C	266
80:1-7	Advent 4, C	218
80:1-7, 17-19	Advent 4, A	28
	Advent 1, B	129
81:1-10	Epiphany 9, B	151
81:1, 10-16	Proper 17, C	269
82	Proper 10, C	260

84	Proper 16, B	192
85	Proper 12, C	263
85:1-2, 8-13	Advent 2, B	130
86:1-10, 16-17	Proper 7, A	86
89:1-4, 19-26	Advent 4, B	133
89:20-37	Proper 11, B	187
90:1-6, 13-17	Proper 25, A	117
91:1-2, 9-16	Lent 1, C	231
91:1-6, 14-16	Proper 21, C	275
92:1-4 (12-15)	Epiphany 8, C	228
93	The Ascension Of Our Lord, A	78
	The Ascension Of Our Lord, B	172
	The Ascension Of Our Lord, C	250
95	Lent 3, A	58
96	Christmas Eve, A	30
	Christmas Eve, B	134
	Christmas Eve, C	218
	Proper 4, C	253
96:1-9	Epiphany 9, C	229
97	Christmas Day, A	32
	Christmas Day, B	135
	Christmas Day, C	220
	Easter 7, C	250
98	Christmas Day, A	33
	Christmas Day, B	135
	Christmas Day, C	220
	Easter 6, B	170
	Proper 27, C	288
99	Proper 24, A	116
	The Transfiguration Of Our Lord, A	52
	The Transfiguration Of Our Lord, C	230
100	Christ The King, A	123
	Thanksgiving Day, C	291
103:1-13, 22	Epiphany 8, B	150
104:1-9, 24, 35c	Proper 24, B	202

104:24-34, 35b	The Day Of Pentecost, A	80
	The Day Of Pentecost, B	173
	The Day Of Pentecost, C	251
105:1-6, 16-22, 45b	Proper 14, A	99
105:1-6, 23-26, 45c	Proper 17, A	104
105:1-6, 37-45	Proper 20, A	111
105:1-11, 45b	Proper 12, A	95
106:1-6, 19-23	Proper 23, A	115
107:1-3, 17-22	Lent 4, B	157
107:1-7, 33-37	Proper 26, A	118
107:1-9, 43	Proper 13, C	264
111	Epiphany 4, B	145
	Proper 15, B	191
112:1-9 (10)	Epiphany 5, A	44
114	Proper 19, A	107
116:1-2, 12-19	Maundy Thursday, A	66
	Maundy Thursday, B	163
	Maundy Thursday, C	240
	Proper 6, A	86
116:1-4, 12-19	Easter 3, A	73
118:1-2, 12-29	Liturgy Of The Palms, A	63
	Liturgy Of The Palms, B	161
	Liturgy Of The Palms, C	238
118:1-2, 14-24	The Resurrection Of Our Lord, A	70
	The Resurrection Of Our Lord, B	165
	The Resurrection Of Our Lord, C	240
118:14-29	Easter 2, C	242
119:1-8	Epiphany 6, A	45
119:9-16	Lent 5, B	159
119:33-40	Epiphany 7, A	47
119:97-104	Proper 24, C	281
119:105-112	Proper 10, A	92
119:137-144	Proper 26, C	284
121	Lent 2, A	57
122	Advent 1, A	23
123	Proper 28, A	122
124	Proper 16, A	103
	Proper 21, B	198

125	Proper 18, B	195
126	Advent 3, B	131
	Thanksgiving Day, B	211
	Lent 5, C	237
127	Proper 27, B	207
128	Proper 12, A	96
130	Lent 5, A	62
	Proper 8, B	182
	Proper 14, B	191
131	Epiphany 8, A	48
132:1-12 (13-18)	Christ The King, B	210
133	Proper 15, A	101
	Easter 2, B	167
	Proper 7, B	182
137	Proper 22, C	278
138	Proper 5, B	177
	Epiphany 5, C	225
139:1-12, 23-24	Proper 11, A	94
139:1-6, 13-18	Epiphany 2, B	142
	Proper 4, B	176
	Proper 18, C	271
145:1-5, 17-21	Proper 27, C	287
146	Proper 26, B	205
	Proper 5, C	253
146:5-10	Advent 3, A	25
147:1-11, 20c	Epiphany 5, B	146
147:12-20	Christmas 2, A	36
	Christmas 2, B	138
	Christmas 2, C	222
148	Christmas 1, A	34
	Christmas 1, B	137
	Christmas 1, C	220
	Easter 5, C	247
149	Proper 18, A	106
	All Saints, C	285
150	Easter 2, C	242

Isaiah
12	Proper 28, C	288
12:2-6	Advent 3, C	218

Song Of Solomon
2:8-13	Proper 9, A	90

Lamentations
3:19-26	Proper 22, C	276

Luke
1:47-55	Advent 3, A	26
	Advent 3, B	133
	Advent 4, B	133
	Advent 4, C	218
1:68-79	Advent 2, C	216
	Christ The King, C	290

U.S./Canadian Lectionary Comparison

The following index shows the correlation between the Sundays and special days of the church year as they are titled or labeled in the Revised Common Lectionary published by the Consultation On Common Texts and used in the United States (the reference used for this book) and the Sundays and special days of the church year as they are titled or labeled in the Revised Common Lectionary used in Canada.

Revised Common Lectionary	Canadian Revised Common Lectionary
Advent 1	Advent 1
Advent 2	Advent 2
Advent 3	Advent 3
Advent 4	Advent 4
Christmas Eve	Christmas Eve
The Nativity Of Our Lord/ Christmas Day	The Nativity Of Our Lord
Christmas 1	Christmas 1
January 1/Holy Name Of Jesus	January 1/The Name Of Jesus
Christmas 2	Christmas 2
The Epiphany Of Our Lord	The Epiphany Of Our Lord
The Baptism Of Our Lord/ Epiphany 1	The Baptism Of Our Lord/ Proper 1
Epiphany 2/Ordinary Time 2	Epiphany 2/Proper 2
Epiphany 3/Ordinary Time 3	Epiphany 3/Proper 3
Epiphany 4/Ordinary Time 4	Epiphany 4/Proper 4
Epiphany 5/Ordinary Time 5	Epiphany 5/Proper 5
Epiphany 6/Ordinary Time 6	Epiphany 6/Proper 6
Epiphany 7/Ordinary Time 7	Epiphany 7/Proper 7
Epiphany 8/Ordinary Time 8	Epiphany 8/Proper 8
The Transfiguration Of Our Lord/ Last Sunday After The Epiphany	The Transfiguration Of Our Lord/ Last Sunday After Epiphany
Ash Wednesday	Ash Wednesday
Lent 1	Lent 1
Lent 2	Lent 2
Lent 3	Lent 3
Lent 4	Lent 4
Lent 5	Lent 5
Sunday Of The Passion/Palm Sunday	Passion/Palm Sunday
Maundy Thursday	Holy/Maundy Thursday
Good Friday	Good Friday

The Resurrection Of Our Lord/ Easter Day	The Resurrection Of Our Lord
Easter 2	Easter 2
Easter 3	Easter 3
Easter 4	Easter 4
Easter 5	Easter 5
Easter 6	Easter 6
The Ascension Of Our Lord	The Ascension Of Our Lord
Easter 7	Easter 7
The Day Of Pentecost	The Day Of Pentecost
The Holy Trinity	The Holy Trinity
Proper 4/Pentecost 2/O T 9*	Proper 9
Proper 5/Pent 3/O T 10	Proper 10
Proper 6/Pent 4/O T 11	Proper 11
Proper 7/Pent 5/O T 12	Proper 12
Proper 8/Pent 6/O T 13	Proper 13
Proper 9/Pent 7/O T 14	Proper 14
Proper 10/Pent 8/O T 15	Proper 15
Proper 11/Pent 9/O T 16	Proper 16
Proper 12/Pent 10/O T 17	Proper 17
Proper 13/Pent 11/O T 18	Proper 18
Proper 14/Pent 12/O T 19	Proper 19
Proper 15/Pent 13/O T 20	Proper 20
Proper 16/Pent 14/O T 21	Proper 21
Proper 17/Pent 15/O T 22	Proper 22
Proper 18/Pent 16/O T 23	Proper 23
Proper 19/Pent 17/O T 24	Proper 24
Proper 20/Pent 18/O T 25	Proper 25
Proper 21/Pent 19/O T 26	Proper 26
Proper 22/Pent 20/O T 27	Proper 27
Proper 23/Pent 21/O T 28	Proper 28
Proper 24/Pent 22/O T 29	Proper 29
Proper 25/Pent 23/O T 30	Proper 30
Proper 26/Pent 24/O T 31	Proper 31
Proper 27/Pent 25/O T 32	Proper 32
Proper 28/Pent 26/O T 33	Proper 33
Christ The King (Proper 29/O T 34)	Proper 34/Christ The King/ Reign Of Christ
Reformation Day (October 31)	Reformation Day (October 31)
All Saints (November 1 or 1st Sunday in November)	All Saints' Day (November 1)
Thanksgiving Day (4th Thursday of November)	Thanksgiving Day (2nd Monday of October)

*O T = Ordinary Time

www.ingramcontent.com/pod-product-compliance
Lightning Source LLC
Chambersburg PA
CBHW070937230426
43666CB00011B/2471